Enterprise Rails

Other resources from O'Reilly

oreilly.com   *oreilly.com* is more than a complete catalog of O'Reilly books. You'll also find links to news, events, articles, weblogs, sample chapters, and code examples.

oreillynet.com is the essential portal for developers interested in open and emerging technologies, including new platforms, programming languages, and operating systems.

Conferences   O'Reilly brings diverse innovators together to nurture the ideas that spark revolutionary industries. We specialize in documenting the latest tools and systems, translating the innovator's knowledge into useful skills for those in the trenches. Visit *conferences.oreilly.com* for our upcoming events.

Safari Bookshelf (*safari.oreilly.com*) is the premier online reference library for programmers and IT professionals. Conduct searches across more than 1,000 books. Subscribers can zero in on answers to time-critical questions in a matter of seconds. Read the books on your Bookshelf from cover to cover or simply flip to the page you need. Try it today for free.

Enterprise Rails

Dan Chak

O'REILLY®

Beijing · Cambridge · Farnham · Köln · Sebastopol · Taipei · Tokyo

Enterprise Rails
by Dan Chak

Published by O'Reilly Media, Inc., 1005 Gravenstein Highway North, Sebastopol, CA 95472.

O'Reilly books may be purchased for educational, business, or sales promotional use. Online editions are also available for most titles (*http://safari.oreilly.com*). For more information, contact our corporate/institutional sales department: (800) 998-9938 or *corporate@oreilly.com*.

Editor: Mike Loukides

Production Editor: Loranah Dimant

Copyeditor: Colleen Gorman

Proofreader: Loranah Dimant

Indexer: Joe Wizda

Cover Designer: Karen Montgomery

Interior Designer: David Futato

Illustrator: Robert Romano

Printing History:

October 2008:   First Edition.

ISBN: 978-0-596-51520-1

[M]

1223662105

Table of Contents

Preface

It would be quite unusual for a person not trained as a surgeon to walk into a hospital operating room, ask a nurse for a scalpel, and start cutting. However, anyone—even those without computer science degrees—can walk into a bookstore, pick up a programming book, and start programming that afternoon. To build a website, you once needed to be adept in a number of languages and technologies: SQL, HTML, JavaScript, and of course, the language *du jour* for the application itself. But with Ruby on Rails, the bar seems to have dropped almost through the floor. You can learn only Rails, and the development of the database, HTML, and JavaScript layers are waved away by the Rails magic.

It's an excellent sales pitch for Rails, but is it true?

As much as we might like it to be, the sad truth is that if your goal is to design high-performance scalable websites, there is still much to be learned beyond the syntax of a programming language. Nothing comes for free. Of course, this argument for the need for thorough training in software engineering principles applies to all languages equally. But does using Ruby on Rails rather than some other application language and framework significantly reduce the topics you need to master to be a great application developer?

Sadly, the answer is still no. Throughout the history of web development, the constants have been SQL, HTML, and JavaScript. It's the language *du jour* that keeps changing, well, seemingly daily. Is it possible that a Johnny-come-lately like Ruby on Rails can redefine the landscape so definitively that the rest of the stack becomes obsolete?

Rails *is* redefining the landscape of web development. Ruby is a wonderful programming language, and the Rails framework does dramatically increase productivity. However, databases, legacy systems, and third parties who don't share our love of Rails are a fact of life. Even though Rails does, at times, seem downright magical, it does not make the rest of the stack obsolete.

The Tale of Twitter

Java™, with its long (and constantly improving) track record, is now—along with its Microsoft twin .NET—the de facto enterprise language. But there was a time when you could brew a pot of coffee while the Java runtime environment (JRE) booted, and enjoy each sip of your cup of joe while the hits flipped hither and thither.

So much research has gone into the JRE that it is now blazingly fast. Having shed its perception as a slow language, a rewrite to Java is often the first recommendation new management or venture capitalists might suggest when introduced to your project. Imagine if Java had been perceived the way Ruby on Rails sometimes is today. It would have been amazing if one poorly designed Java application had convinced all technology decision-makers that Java itself was a bad platform for developing applications. In fact, much of the emphasis on Java's speed was likely a result of early failures that were as much due to scaling or design problems as they were speed-related. Now, with Java's speed on par with or faster than that of C++, it's the developer who becomes immediately suspect when an application underperforms, rather than Java itself or the framework being used.

Twitter has become the whipping boy for Rails's perceived scalability problems. Twitter is a new twist on the everyday blogging platform. Unlike a standard blog, posts to Twitter, or "tweets," are limited in length. They can be written online in a web browser, but are more commonly written via SMS text message, or from a variety of third-party applets. Subscribers, or "followers," of your Twitter blog can read your tweets in the traditional way online or via RSS, but more commonly subscribers receive your posts in realtime via SMS messages to their phone. In essence, Twitter is a messaging service, brokering many-to-many communication. Although individuals predominantly use it to keep up-to-date with what their friends are up to, Twitter "streams" have also been used to spread messages quickly to conference participants, or to share other types of topic-based messaging with interested parties.

Like many companies before it, Twitter encountered problems when its success exceeded its expectations. A successful viral marketing company, its site's user base quickly jumped into the millions, but the site couldn't handle them. The result was slow page load times and, at times, outages.

This type of problem is one of scaling: you're doing perfectly fine until the demand for your site suddenly increases. Scaling issues suggest that you've achieved some level of success (what a silver lining!), but it's the type of problem you'd like to avoid, lest you become the whipping boy, or worse, lose all of your users to a competitor.

But Ruby on Rails was not the culprit in Twitter's scaling problems—a fact Twitter engineers reiterated on many occasions. It was the *architecture* that was at fault, and architecture has to do with how you structure data and applications and how they communicate, not what language the applications are written in.

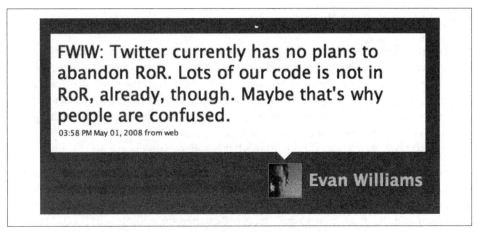

FWIW: Twitter currently has no plans to abandon RoR. Lots of our code is not in RoR, already, though. Maybe that's why people are confused.

03:58 PM May 01, 2008 from web

Evan Williams

Figure P-1. Twitter is sticking with Rails, but rethinking architecture

Because Twitter was the largest, most public Rails site around, its stumbles were watched carefully, and the steps Twitter took to alleviate its scalability issues were thoroughly documented online. In one instance, the database was becoming a bottleneck. In response, Twitter added a 16 GB caching layer using Memcache to allow them to scale horizontally. Still, many queries involving complex joins were too slow. In response, the Twitter team started storing denormalized versions of the data for faster access. In a another instance, Twitter found its use of DRb, a mechanism for *remote method invocation* (RMI), had created a fragile single point of failure. It replaced DRb with Starling, a distributed messaging queue that gave it looser coupling of message producers and consumers, and better fault tolerance. After these and other architectural improvements, Blaine Cook, Twitter's lead architect, said:

> For us, it's really about scaling horizontally—to that end, Rails and Ruby haven't been stumbling blocks, compared to any other language or framework. The performance boosts associated with a "faster" language would give us a 10–20% improvement, but thans to architectural changes that Ruby and Rails happily accommodated, Twitter is 10,000% faster than it was in January.

It is of no small significance that Twitter's engineers chose to absolve Rails of being at fault for their problems; instead of offloading the blame to an external factor, they chose to take responsibility for their own design decisions. In fact, this was a wise choice. Twitter's engineers knew that reimplementing the same architecture in a different language would have led to the same result of site outages and site sluggishness. But online rumor mills were abuzz with hints that Twitter was planning to dump Ruby and Rails as a platform. Twitter's cofounder, Evan Williams, posted a tweet (shown in Figure P-1) to assure everyone that Twitter had "no plans to abandon RoR."

Speed Versus Scalability

It is true that Ruby, as a language, does execute software programs more slowly than some other programming languages. However, this is a red herring in the discussion of scaling websites, as speed and scalability are not equivalent. If the stuff of websites was real-time processing of complex data, then Ruby's speed could be problematic. However, most websites don't do much more per request than look up some information and display it, or otherwise accept some information and store it. The time required to process this type of task is fast no matter what language you choose.

On the other hand, once you start building up simultaneous requests, these requests will compete with each other, and requests will begin to appear slow to end users. In an ideal situation, you would simply add more hardware to restore your site to optimal performance levels. In fact, in an architecture designed for scaling, you should be able to add hardware in a linear fashion to handle any number of users imaginable.

This is where speed and scalability get confused. A language may be slow or fast, but it's your architecture that is scalable or not. This pertains not just to your code itself—the algorithms and how you string together your syntax—but also on the edges of your applications, how they fit together, and the expectations and demands placed on different parts of the system. Are any spots likely to become bottlenecks or single points of failure? Can each piece improve its own scalability with the addition of hardware, and if not, can that piece be removed from the critical path of rendering web pages? If your architecture is not designed for scaling, you may not be able to simply add hardware to scale up for additional users. And while a faster language may buy you some more time, no language can avoid the scalability issues of a poorly designed architecture forever.

Unfortunately, architectural problems are so fundamental to how an application is written that it is nearly impossible to rescue a bad design once it has been implemented. Band-aid solutions may work for a while, but scalability problems are usually widespread and entrenched. It's like plugging holes in a leaking dam; eventually the dam will give beneath the pressure of the water, regardless of how many patches have been applied. The only way to be confident your scaling efforts will work is to design for scale from the beginning.

So why wouldn't developers plan for scaling from the beginning? One reason is that they don't know how. Most books in the bookstore, intended for as wide an audience as possible, frequently don't get past syntax. In this book, design is a major and repeated theme. Another reason is that they believe too much up-front design will slow them down. This *may* be true, but it certainly becomes less and less so as you get the hang of it. The final reason is that many leaders in the Rails community itself have advocated not worrying about scaling until you really, really, really need to. They say it's an unnecessary waste of time up front and that Rails scales easily because it's a share-nothing architecture. This, of course, is baloney. In the early days, this was good propaganda to get Rails onto developers' desktops, but today it is simply hurting Rails's image as an option for enterprise deployment. As Twitter proved, waiting until you really, really, really need to worry about scaling is too late.

Of course, you don't always have the choice of starting your project from scratch. You may be reading this book when you're well into a project and are looking for tips, or perhaps even later in the game; you might be trying to save a poorly designed project that's already straining under the pressure of load. To help readers in these scenarios, many chapters contain a section called "Refactor Steps," intended to give you step-by-step instructions on how to transition an existing design to the one described in the chapter.

What to Expect in This Book

If you are new to Rails, the first book to read is *Agile Web Development with Rails* by Dave Thomas et al. (Pragmatic Bookshelf). The book you have in your hands, by contrast, is not a how-to guide for writing your first Rails application. This should be the second book you read.

This book deals in larger concepts, the formulas for how pieces fit together. It is not a compendium of the Rails API or a reference of the Ruby programming language. Books on these topics exist, and they are good to keep on your bookshelf, but they contain descriptions of tools rather than a formula for putting those tools together to get your job done.

This book gives you the tools to develop applications for the enterprise world for websites with global scale. Scaling comes in two forms. The first is the scaling we traditionally think of in terms of handling thousands, hundreds of thousands, or even millions of users, typified by Twitter and other large scale websites like Google, Amazon, or ebay. The second type of scaling is a more practical, human-focused concern. As your business needs change or expand, and as the types of developers in your organization and their quantities increase, will each developer still have the ability to contribute to the product in a meaningful way? Can new features be added easily and in parallel without conflict, or is the application difficult to modify by multiple developers at once? Will you be able to harness the hard work of the past in building the future, or will each new bold direction require a rewrite of the entire application?

Scaling of both varieties is facilitated through careful design of your application's software architecture, rather than through the choice of language or platform. It's a common misconception that scaling problems will be solved by the materialization of a faster Ruby interpreter, or by learning a magical set of Ruby incantations that aren't described in the beginner books. Certainly, there are good and bad ways to describe any algorithm, but these are problems solved by those with comprehensive computer science training, not by the speed of the interpreter. Choosing a bad implementation for an algorithm will have similarly poor results in Ruby as in Java or Perl or otherwise.

The purpose of the Ruby interpreter and the Rails framework is to give you a tableau on which to develop your masterpiece. That's where this book comes in. This book is about the principles involved in architecting serious web applications. The principles are universal, regardless of which technology you are using in the application tier. Of course, as you may have guessed, Ruby and Ruby on Rails will be used to describe all of these principles.

As it happens, Ruby is a terrific language, with many advanced features not found in today's compiled languages. Not only is Ruby feature-rich, but it is also succinct to the point of marvel. What often takes dozens of lines of code in Java can often be written in just a few lines in Ruby. Rails, too, is a best-of-breed platform for developing web applications with little overhead. The commonly touted benchmark is that Ruby on Rails development proceeds at a clip of 10 times the rate of Java development. Big names like yellowpages.com (*http://yellowpages.com*) have invested a lot of time and effort (and money) into rebuilding their entire sites on Ruby on Rails for the long-term benefits they will reap down the road in having a simpler and more efficient (by metric of code volume) framework.

However, there is a problem with this benchmark, and with the ethos of many in the Rails community as it exists today. Because so much effort has been put toward showing how simple it is to develop with Rails, and how much more productive you can be than with Java or other alternatives, little effort has been put toward showing Rails developers how to build applications that can truly stand up to the challenges that their Java cousins have had to prove themselves worthy against.

This doesn't mean that a Rails application cannot stand up to the challenges imposed by constant traffic and large scale. Of course Rails can. However, there has been a dearth of public examples, and by the same token, there has not been much public discourse within the Rails community about *how* to design Rails applications to scale to the same levels that have been achieved by Java applications.

The secret is that the principles are the same. They were the same even before Java was de facto. The difference is that in Rails, with Ruby, the principles are so much easier to achieve once you know what you are doing. Because Ruby is so succinct, describing how to achieve the goals of good software architecture for the web is almost invisible when written in Ruby code.

Whether or not the revered "Gang of Four" *Designs Patterns* by Erich Gamma et al. (Addison-Wesley) needed to be explicitly retooled and retold for a Ruby audience has received its share of debate; achieving patterns is trivial in Ruby even though they required intricate structing of code in Java and C+. Indeed, the *singleton pattern* is achieved in Ruby by saying `include Singleton`. The *factory pattern* is so simply reproduced it barely warrants a name.

Most of the effort of architecting in Ruby is not found in tens of thousands of lines of application code. Instead, it's in how you use Ruby and Rails to tie together all the other parts of your application stack: the database, your servers and clients, other services, and users of your application.

In this book, we begin by putting Rails in the correct context. The purpose of the original Rails book, *Agile Web Development with Rails* by Dave Thomas et al. (Pragmatic Bookshelf), was to sell Rails to the world, so the viewpoint is somewhat myopic. From its perspective, Rails may as well be the only element in the stack. The database is obligatory, so magical *migrations* are created to hand wave it away and ensure you never need to learn a scrap of DDL; anything else is pejoratively labeled as "legacy" and ignored. In the real world, databases and legacy systems tend to outlive everything else, hence the seemingly inescapable term "legacy" itself, so it's worth paying them their due.

Topics

This book introduces "architecture" for enterprise web applications, from the ground up. What are the topics of web architecture, and why aren't they found in most books on Rails? In truth, the success or failure of a web application has only partially to do with what is classically called the application layer. This may come as a surprise to those who have cut their development teeth on Rails, because the Rails view is that the application layer is all there is. It turns out that it's the edges *around* the application that can make the biggest difference: databases, caches, and in a service-oriented architecture (SOA), the constellation of back-end services and front-end websites that make up the entire application.

First, below your application is the database. A schema stays with you for a very long time, so how you structure your data determines whether you can guarantee the integrity of your data, and whether your queries will be fast or slow. How those queries are written makes a big difference too, meaning you need to understand SQL even if you are using an object-relational-mapper like ActiveRecord. To write an application that is fast, you need to know into which queries a set of ActiveRecord statements will translate so that you can issue your queries in an intelligent way. "It works" usually is not enough for an enterprise application; as a developer you need to know how it works, how it *should* work, and why each way is as it is.

If you plan to avoid the hassles of optimizing a database schema and writing optimized queries by caching query results or rendered pages, be prepared for difficult times ahead if you want speed and consistency at the same time. It's easy to make a cache that returns old, stale, invalid data. Correctly implementing a cache that is up-to-date in real-time is no simple task. What goes in the cache should be chosen carefully, as well as in what format. And the most difficult challenge still remains: when and how to invalidate or rebuild elements in the cache. Many people naively treat caching as a trivial problem, but depending on a cache that is out of sync with reality can be far worse than a slow site. Relying on stale data can lead you to make incorrect decisions, sell products you don't have, double-book a flight, or not sell products you *do* have because the cache doesn't know about them.

Once you have mastered these areas, suddenly the problems are raised an order of magnitude. It's the rare website that is powered by a single monolithic application with a single database. To scale, not only to handle ever more users, but also to handle application and organizational complexity, SOA is almost always a necessary architectural evolution. In SOA, many applications are responsible for different slices of the overall problem. How do you choose how to split up a monolithic application, and further, how to glue the pieces back together to give a site's visitors a unified experience?

In this book, we'll cover these topics in detail. Of course, the application layer itself is extremely important, so we'll start there, with the proper way to think about and structure your application. We'll see how and when to separate code into logical elements, called *modules*. Then we'll extract code into plugins to be shared by multiple applications. In many books, these topics are treated as advanced topics; in this book, they come first so you will actually have an opportunity to use them before you get entrenched in a design.

After looking within, we'll look downward to the database layer. We'll see how to build a solid foundation for our application with proper data modeling. First, we'll learn about referential integrity and database constraints, culminating in writing trigger-based stored procedures to ensure complex relationships are satisfied. Then, we'll discuss rigorous levels of database normalization, including third normal form and domain key/normal form, which will help us ensure our data's integrity.

We'll introduce the concept of *domain tables*, and how these special tables can be incorporated naturally in Rails. We'll see how to base Rails models on database views. After that, we'll get our first taste of caching by materializing a database view, increasing database performance by orders of magnitude.

Next, we'll look to the sides as we explore service-oriented architecture. An oft-misunderstood concept, we'll spend a good deal of time concentrating on theory. Then we'll build multiple RPC-based back-end services to be consumed by a thin front-end client. We'll build a REST web service, too, but we'll see how to build any type of REST service, not just the subset supported by ActiveResource.

Finally, we'll revisit caching, treating it like the sleeping monster it really can be, giving you the tools to ensure with certainty that the caches you create can be depended upon to be accurate.

Throughout the book, a heavy emphasis will be placed on testing, both unit tests within an application and integration tests when we connect multiple applications together. In fact, we never create a single view or traditional controller, instead, we exercise the model classes we write with our tests.

How This Book Is Organized

In Chapter 1, we start out by taking a tour of an ideal enterprise systems layout, highlighting all of the elements that aren't Rails, as well as noting the various places where Rails can fit in.

The rest of this book can be divided principally into three major sections. The first deals with the Rails framework itself. The next few chapters examine Rails itself. While Rails gives you a Model-View-Controller (MVC) framework to start your projects, there is much to be desired in terms of structuring and maintaining large applications. Chapters 2 and 3 fill these gaps. First, Chapter 2 dives into plugins, and how they can be used to improve application clarity, while also encouraging you to write reusable code. Chapter 3 introduces modules: what they are, and how and when to use them.

The next major section of the book, Chapters 4 through 12, deals with the database. The database layer has not really been given its due in the Rails community, and Chapter 4 begins by providing an overview of why it is such a critical part of your application. In Chapter 5, we start building a data model for the example application we'll work with throughout this book: a sales website for movie tickets.

Although the schema we'll design would be sufficient for most Rails books, we'll see quickly that it was a naive design. In Chapter 6, we refactor the schema to be in third normal form (3NF). In Chapter 7, we'll pick out a special type of table called a domain table, and we'll incorporate these tables naturally into a Rails application. In Chapter 8, we'll expose some more problems with our schema, then tighten it one step further by moving from third normal form to *domain key normal form*. In Chapter 9, we'll get even more advanced with our introduction of stored procedures and triggers. We'll use them to enforce relationships that built-in database constraints cannot handle, giving you the power to completely lock down your database schema.

Chapters 10 through 12 introduce some new database-related features to Rails developers. In Chapter 10, you'll see how to base an ActiveRecord model on a database view. This is useful for automatic filtering, or for filtering on data that's not easily available at the application layer. In Chapter 11, we'll show how to build support for *multiple table inheritance* in Rails. Rails supports single table inheritance, but it is not always the right tool for the job. In Chapter 12, we'll get our first taste of caching when we materialize the view we created in Chapter 10, giving our view a huge boost in performance.

Chapters 13 through 18 deal with service-oriented architectures and different techniques for connecting systems together. In Chapter 13, we start by defining SOA, as well as going over the scenarios when it is the right choice to solve a problem. Chapter 14 covers considerations that go into designing a service-oriented architecture, including guidelines for designing an API. In Chapter 15, we build our first SOA service. In Chapter 16, we build upon our accomplishments in Chapter 15, connecting two back-end services together and testing them with the same interface a thin front-end client would use. Chapter 17 is a critical exploration of REST, helpful for placing it in its proper context for web services, but not necessarily for service-oriented architectures. In Chapter 18, we build a RESTful web-service.

Chapter 19 is a culmination of many of the previous chapters. There, we implement a fully correct service-layer cache to enhance application performance. We also go over other places where caching can be a dependable way to improve performance.

Who Is This Book For?

The purpose of this book is to provide the background you need to build your bridge: a large-scale, enterprise website. It is assumed that you've already read the manuals of the tools you need to get the job done, e.g., books on the syntax of Ruby and of Rails. This book fills in the background that transforms you from a layman who has tools into an expert ready to make the most of those tools.

This book is geared toward three general types, which we'll call the Student, the Glass Ceiling, and the Travelers.

For the Student, this book is full of the theory behind engineering large-scale enterprise web applications, so if you are embarking upon a class on software engineering for the Web, this book is for you. This may even be your textbook, and if so, Mazel Tov! You will learn a lot here.

Our Glass Ceiling audience are those who have read half a dozen manuals about their tools and toolkits, but still find they don't have the background to jump to the next level of web application design. These are the so-called newbies. The tools are beginning to make sense, but how to use them together effectively may still seem murky. If you are in this group, this book is for you, too. Soon all the pieces will be dovetailing nicely.

The final group that may benefit from this book are the Travelers. Travelers may have a lot of experience with other frameworks, but they are wondering how to make it all go smoothly with Ruby on Rails. For this audience, this book is a great refresher in all the basic theory behind solid web application design, followed by a hearty dose of how to integrate all that theory into Rails.

Conventions Used in This Book

This book uses the following typographic conventions:

Constant width
> Used for program listings. Also used within paragraphs to refer to program elements such as namespaces, classes, and method names.

Italic
> Used for example URLs, names of directories and files, options, and occasionally for emphasis.

This icon indicates a tip, suggestion, or general note.

This icon indicates a warning or caution.

Using Code Examples

This book is here to help you get your job done. In general, you may use the code in this book in your programs and documentation. You do not need to contact us for permission unless you're reproducing a significant portion of the code. For example, writing a program that uses several chunks of code from this book does not require permission. Selling or distributing a CD-ROM of examples from O'Reilly books *does* require permission. Answering a question by citing this book and quoting example code does not require permission. Incorporating a significant amount of example code from this book into your product's documentation *does* require permission.

We appreciate, but do not require, attribution. An attribution usually includes the title, author, publisher, and ISBN. For example: "*Enterprise Rails*, by Dan Chak. Copyright 2009 Dan Chak, 978-0-596-51520-1."

If you feel your use of code examples falls outside fair use or the permission given above, feel free to contact us at *permissions@oreilly.com*.

Safari® Books Online

When you see a Safari® Books Online icon on the cover of your favorite technology book, that means the book is available online through the O'Reilly Network Safari Bookshelf.

Safari offers a solution that's better than e-books. It's a virtual library that lets you easily search thousands of top tech books, cut and paste code samples, download chapters, and find quick answers when you need the most accurate, current information. Try it for free at *http://safari.oreilly.com*.

Comments and Questions

We at O'Reilly have tested and verified the information in this book to the best of our ability, but mistakes and oversights do occur. Please let us know about errors you may find, as well as your suggestions for future editions, by writing to:

O'Reilly Media, Inc.
1005 Gravenstein Highway North
Sebastopol, CA 95472
800-998-9938 (in the U.S. or Canada)
707-829-0515 (international or local)
707-829-0104 (fax)

To ask technical questions or comment on the book, send email to:

bookquestions@oreilly.com

We have a website for this book where examples, errata, and any plans for future editions are listed. You can access this site at:

http://www.oreilly.com/catalog/9780596515201/

The author has also set up his own site for the book at:

http://enterpriserails.chak.org/

For more information about this book and others, see the O'Reilly website:

http://www.oreilly.com

Acknowledgments

Thank you to the members of my team at CourseAdvisor who put these ideas into practice in our projects, large and small. You proved that Rails really does scale, both for traffic and for teamwork. In order of appearance: Courtney Wade, Alistair Israel, Aries Andrada, Kristof Redei, Nikki Ramirez, Reid Lynch, Sergey Rozum, Arthur Pyrogovski. Vladimir Bober, and Dimitry Lukyanenko. Thanks also to Derek Yimoyines for being an early reader of this material and for providing valuable feedback.

Also thank you to my technical reviewers (in alphabetical order) whose critical insights were most valuable: Hal Abelson, Ben Adida, Jeff Davis, Matt Debergalis, and Brad Ediger.

## CHAPTER 1

The Big Picture

What Is Enterprise?

You may have heard that big Internet sites like Amazon, eBay, or Google have thousands—sometimes tens of thousands, or more—of servers powering their websites. If you're reading this book, you've probably already built at least one web application of your own, and it probably had only a handful of machines behind it, perhaps even just one application server and one database. In fact, maybe you had shared hosting and only had a fraction of a full server at your disposal.

If you had a great idea for an online business and were given 1,000 servers, what would you do with them? How would you make the most of them? What operational goals would you define for reliability and speed, and how would you leverage all of that hardware to achieve those goals?

Before diving into the pieces of an enterprise system, or discussing how to build one, a good starting point is to simply define *enterprise*.

Unfortunately, that is not an easy task. There is no particular set of tools that, if used, will make your architecture qualify as enterprise, even if the word "enterprise" is in the product names of the tools you use. The big companies mentioned earlier have built many of their own tools to support their software stack, but they are definitely still "enterprise." Similarly, there is no single configuration of pieces that together spell enterprise. If you looked at the configuration of Google's servers and compared their it to Amazon's, the two would look quite different. But they are both enterprises nonetheless—it just happens that the two enterprises have different goals, and therefore need different architectures to reach those goals.

In some sense, a site is enterprise when it feels like it is. All of the Internet behemoths once started out with a single application server and single database, just like you. It's anyone's best guess when they crossed the blurry line into "enterprise."

That said, there are certainly some criteria that, when satisfied, do make a site feel like it's enterprise. These criteria are topics of this book, and will be referred to again and again:

- It's fast. You can define a service level agreement (SLA) for how long it takes each component to do its job, which in turn allows you to define an SLA for end-to-end load times of any given web page.

- It's always available. You can define an SLA for your minimum uptimes for all critical components and aim for "four nines"—99.99% uptime.

- It scales linearly. You can scale to hundreds of thousands or even millions of users by adding additional hardware.

- It's fault-tolerant. If noncritical components go down, the majority of functionality stays intact, and your users don't know the difference.

There are other criteria that make your site feel like it's enterprise, too, although they are mainly operational concerns, and aren't covered in depth this book:

- All source code is in a source control repository.

- All new code goes through a QA cycle before it is deployed.

- There is a deployment procedure, and failed deployments can be rolled back.

- Errors are logged in a central location, and the appropriate personnel are notified in real-time.

- Logfiles and databases are backed up in a central location.

- Statistics about the website's operation can be collected and analyzed to determine which areas need attention.

Implicit in the preceding list is a number of job functions and departments other than software development. Reading between the lines, you find:

- A database administrator (DBA) who sets up failover databases and ensures back-ups are available. A DBA can also tune database configuration parameters and control the physical mapping of data to disks to improve performance. Many also consult on schema design to ensure optimal performance and data integrity.

- A quality assurance engineer (QA) who tests release candidates before they are put into production and tracks issues to be fixed by developers.

- An operations or release engineer who manages the releases, creates deployment plans, and rolls out your new software in the wee hours of the night.

- An information technology engineer (IT) who maintains internal machines that house backups, logfiles, etc.

Having these people in your organization will push your systems architecture toward "enterprise." Similarly, designing your system to be enterprise creates the need for all of these individuals. In some sense, when your company itself feels like an enterprise, your software is probably getting to be enterprise, too. When the two are out of step, you will know it because either half of the engineers will have nothing to do or everyone will be stepping on each other's toes.

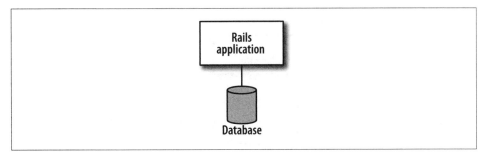

Figure 1-1. A basic website configuration

Growing Slowly

Every website begins its life with a single developer and a single line of code. Figure 1-1 shows a simple configuration of a Rails application connected to a database. You will likely spend quite a bit of time developing your application on this setup before it's ready for its first user.

When it's time to launch, there some issues that ought to be considered. Figure 1-2 shows the same configuration, but with redundancy at the application level, and failover at the database level.

There are two copies of the application so that in the event one machine fails, there is still another that can handle incoming traffic. Similarly, in the event of a hardware failure on the database machine, a copy that is a transaction or two behind can be brought online quickly.

Even if you are barely using any of the resources on either the application or database machine, redundancy and failover are a very good idea. At this point, neither of these considerations is aimed at managing load—that comes later. Rather, both are intended to ensure the availability of your web application. Reprovisioning a machine, configuring it, and loading all your software and data from backups can cause quite a bit of downtime. During that time, your customers will can find your competitors' sites, and they are likely to form negative opinions about your site's reliability as well.

With this configuration, and perhaps even a good deployment strategy, there is plenty of work within the application and data layers that can be done before you need to add any additional complexity to your system in the form of encapsulated services or asynchronous processes. Depending on the feature set of your web application, this may even be as far as you need to go. You are already satisfying a number of the criteria that define the elusive concept of "enterprise."

There is, within an enterprise, the need to scale horizontally as well. Only so many engineers can work in one codebase before no one can work at all. Even if there is only one chef in the kitchen, there is still only so much space for the sous-chefs.

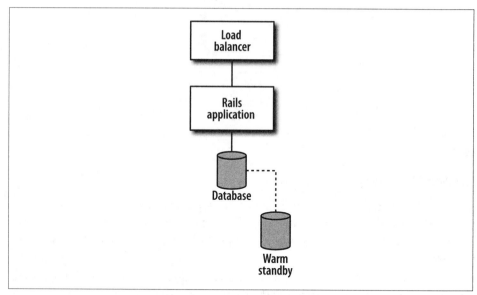

Figure 1-2. A basic website configuration with failover and redundancy

A common way to deal with this human scaling problem is to break up a large application into smaller pieces, or services, each responsible for a specific function within
the enterprise. It's no surprise that the software splits often follow organization boundaries so that individual teams can take on full ownership of their pieces of the overall
system.

Each service has its own full stack that mirrors the stack of the traditional website from
Figure 1-2. The difference is that a service is responsible for a small fraction of the duties
that make up the entire website, usually one specific, specialized group of related functionality. It's possible—and sometimes preferable—to abstract all database access behind services. The front-end website then becomes a consumer of these services and
has no need for a database of its own, as shown in Figure 1-3.

When you add services into the mix, it's hard to argue your system is not enterprise.

There are a number of other components commonly found in an enterprise setup.
Figure 1-4 shows a generic enterprise configuration. Powering the front-end website
are a number of services. There are also a collection of asynchronous processes that
receive information from services via a messaging queue. In addition to the front-end
website, there is a web services layer aimed at providing external clients with a subset
of the functionality available inside the firewall. There is also redundancy and failover
in all critical places. Finally, each service database feeds a data warehouse, which powers site reporting and decision support.

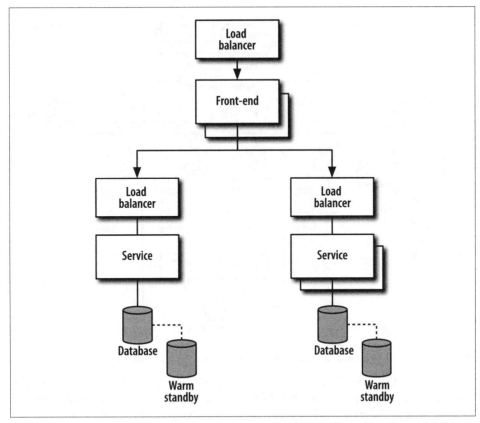

Figure 1-3. A front-end website backed by services, which in turn are backed by relational databases

Note, of course, that simply replicating this configuration is not enough. Each piece of the system is an independent, isolated, and encapsulated system in its own right and deserves thorough and thoughtful design. What goes where and how to implement each individual unit is as much an art as it is a science.

Understanding All the Pieces

This section gives a brief introduction to each piece of the enterprise system.

Persistence Layer

The *persistence layer* is where you store your business's data. As the name implies, data here sticks around for a long time; it persists until you explicitly change or remove it. Most frequently, the persistence layer is a Relational Database Management System (RDBMS).

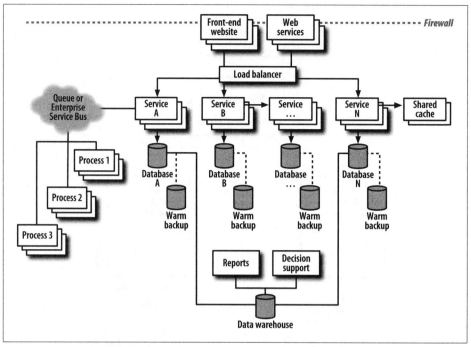

Figure 1-4. A generic enterprise architecture with redundancy and failover

Because protecting your data is critical, the persistence layer should provide certain guarantees, collectively referred to as ACID: atomicity, consistency, isolation, and durability. Each of these properties plays a different role in maintaining the integrity of your data:

Atomicity

The ability to group a number of operations together into a single transaction: either they all succeed, or they all fail. The RDBMS should ensure that a failure midway through the transaction does not leave the data in an intermediary, invalid state. For example, a bank account transfer requires debiting funds from one account and crediting funds in another. If one of the operations fails, the other should be rolled back as well; otherwise, one account may be debited without making the corresponding credit in the other account.

Consider the following instructions:

```
account1.debit(50)
# power failure happens here
account2.credit(50)
```

If the database fails between the two statements, where we have a comment to the same effect, the user of the ATM system will likely see an error on-screen and expect no transaction took place. When the database comes back up, though, the bank customer would be short $50 in account one, and be none the richer in account two. Atomicity provides the ability to group statements together into single, atomic units. In Rails, this is accomplished by invoking the method `transaction` on a model class. The `transaction` method accepts a block to be executed as a single, atomic unit:

```
Account.transaction do
  account1.debit(50)
  # power failure happens here
  account2.credit(50)
end
```

Now, if the power goes out where the comment suggests, the database will ignore the first statement when it boots back up. For all intents and purposes, the first statement in the transaction never occurred.

Consistency

The guarantee that constraints you define for your data are satisfied before and after each transaction. Different RDBMS systems may have different allowances for inconsistency *within* a transaction. For example, a complex set of bank transfers may, if executed in the wrong order, allow an account to drop to a balance below zero. However, if by the end of all the transfers, all balances are positive, the consistency check that all balances are positive has been guaranteed.

Isolation

The guarantee that while a transaction is in process, no other transaction can access its intermediary—and possibly inconsistent—data. For example, a bank deposit requires checking an account's existing balance, adding the deposit amount to this balance, and then updating the account record with the new balance. If you are transferring $100 from one account to another, with one statement to debit $100 from the first account, and another statement to add $100 to the second account, isolation prevents your total balance from ever appearing to be $100 less between the two statements. Figure 1-5 illustrates this. Without the transaction in thread 1, the output time 3 would have been `0 + 100`.

Durability

The guarantee that once your database accepts data and declares your transaction successful, the data you inserted or modified will persist in the database until you explicitly remove or modify it again. Similarly, data you deleted will be gone forever. There is no code example to demonstrate durability. It is a property of how the RDBMS interacts with the operating system and hardware. Short of a disk failure that *actually* destroys data, if the database returns control to you after a statement, you can assume the effects of the statement are permanently stored on disk, and a reset of the database or some other activity that clears system memory will not affect this assumption.

Note that many databases do allow you to relax the durability restriction to increase speed at the expense of reliability, but doing so is not generally recommended, unless your data is not very important to you.

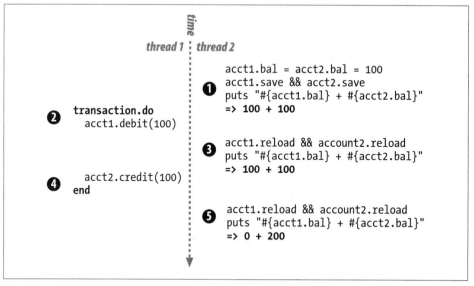

Figure 1-5. Transactions isolate multiple queries into a single atomic unit

Of course, having a database that is ACID-compliant is not enough to guarantee your data's integrity. Armed with this set of guarantees, it is now up to you, the database designer, to properly set up the database schema to do so. In Chapters 4 through 9, we will build up a complex schema, and then provably guarantee our data's integrity.

Application Layer

The application layer represents everything that operates between the data layer and the outside world. This layer is responsible for interpreting user requests, acting on them, and returning results, usually in the form of web pages. When you start your first Rails project by invoking `rails {projectname}`, what you have created is the application layer.

Depending on what your application *is*, the application layer can have different relationships with the data layer. If, for example, the purpose of your website is to provide Flash games for visitors to play, the application layer—and most developer effort—will focus on the games users play. However, the application layer may also facilitate user login, as well as storage and retrieval of high scores in the database.

More commonly, though, websites present information to users and allow them to act upon it in some way; for example, online news sites that display articles or movie ticket vendor sites that provide movie synopses and show times in theatres nationwide. In these cases, the application layer is the interface into the data stored in database.

In its simplest form, a single Rails application comprises the whole of the application layer. When a user requests a web page, an instance of the full application handles the request. The entry point into the code base is determined by the requested URL, which translates into a controller class and action method pair. Code executes, usually retrieving data from the database, culminating in the rendering of a web page. At this point, the handling of the request is complete. This is the simplest of architectures (it was shown in Figure 1-1).

A front-end and services

The configuration above can take you quite far, but it can only take you *so* far.

As your company grows, the complexity of your business needs may become too large to be managed well within a single application. The complexity can come either in the user interface, or in the back-end logic that powers it.

If you operate a blog site that is wildly successful, you may want a variety of different user interfaces and feature sets based on the target audience. For example, the young-adult site may have a feature set geared toward building discussion within a social network, while the adult-targeted site might be devoid of the social aspect altogether, and instead include spell-checking and other tools to make the content appear more polished. Or you might even spin off a completely different application that uses the same underlying content structure, but with a completely different business model. For example, a website for submitting writing assignments, where students are able to read and comment on other students' work, could easily share the same underlying data structures as the blog sites. Figure 1-6 illustrates.

The first front-end may be the teen-targeted site, the second the adult-targeted site, and the third the homework-submission site. All three contain only the user-interface and the workflow logic. They communicate over the network with a single content management service, which is responsible for storing and retrieving the actual content from the database and providing the correct content to each site.

The opposite type of complexity is perhaps even more common. As your website grows in leaps and bounds, with each new feature requiring as much code as the originally launched website in its entirety, it often becomes beneficial to split up the application into smaller, more manageable pieces. Each major piece of functionality and the corresponding portions of the data layer are carved out into its own service, which publishes a specific API for its specialized feature set. The front-end, then, consumes these service APIs, and weaves a user interface around them. Based on the level of complexity and the need to manage it, services can even consume the APIs of other services as well.

In this configuration, shown in Figure 1-7, the front-end is a very manageable amount of code, unconcerned with the complex implementations of the services it consumes

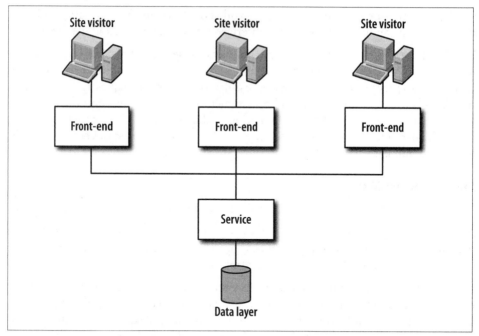

Figure 1-6. An application layer split into a single service and many front-ends

behind the scenes. Each service is also a manageable piece of code as well, unconcerned with the inner workings of other services or even the front-end itself.

Web-services layer

Services, as in service-oriented architecture, and web services are distinct, but oft-confused concepts. The former variety live within your firewall (described later in this chapter) and are the building blocks of your larger application. The latter, web services, straddle the firewall and provide third parties access to your services. One way to think of this distinction is that the services have been placed "on the public Web." Functionally, a service and a web service may be equivalent. Or, the web service may impose usage restrictions, require authentication or encryption, and so on. Figure 1-8 shows a web service backed by the same two services as the front-end HTML-based web application. Users equipped with a web browser visit the front-end HTML site, while third-party developers can integrate their own applications with the web service.

This was the briefest introduction to SOA and web services possible. In Chapter 13, we'll look much more closely at what a service is, as well as how one fits into a service-oriented architecture. We'll also examine a variety of circumstances to see when moving to SOA makes sense—organizationally or technically. In Chapter 14, we'll go over best practices for creating your own services and service APIs, and in Chapters 15 and 16, we'll build a service-oriented application using XML-RPC. Chapter 17 will provide an

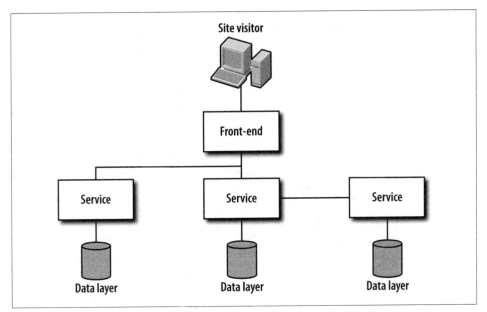

Figure 1-7. An application layer split into a single a single front-end, and many back-end services

introduction to building web services RESTfully. In Chapter 18, we'll build a RESTful web service.

Caching Layer

All of your data lives in databases in its most up-to-date, accurate form. However, there are two shortcomings to retrieving a piece of data from the database every time you need it.

First, it's hard to scale databases linearly with traffic. What does this mean? Imagine your database system and application can comfortably support 10 concurrent users' requests, as in Figure 1-9.

Now imagine the number of requests doubles. If your application adheres to the share-nothing principal encouraged in Dave Thomas's *Agile Web Development with Rails* (Pragmatic Bookshelf), you can easily add another application server and load balance the traffic. However, you cannot simply add another database, because the database itself is still a shared resource. In Figure 1-10, the database is no better off than it would have been with 20 connections to the same application server. The database still must deal with 20 requests per second.

The second shortcoming with requesting data from the database each time you need it is due to the fact that the format of information in the database does not always exactly match the format of data your application needs; sometimes a transformation

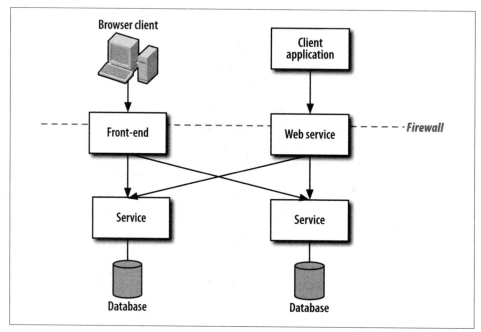

Figure 1-8. A web service backed by service applications

or two is required to get data from a fully normalized format into objects your application can work with directly.

This doesn't mean there's a problem with your database design. The format you chose for the database might very well be the format you need to preserve your data's integrity, which is extremely important. Unfortunately, it may be costly to transform the data from the format in the database to the format your application wants it in each time you need it. This is where *caching layers* comes in.

There are many different types of, and uses for, caches. Some, such as disk caches and query plan caches, require little or no effort on your part before you can take advantage of them. Others you need to implement yourself. These fall into two categories: *pre-built* and *real-time*.

For data that changes infrequently or is published on a schedule, a pre-built cache is simple to create and can reduce database load dramatically. Every night, or on whatever schedule you define, all of the data to be cached is read from the database, transformed into a format that is immediately consumable by your application, and written into a scalable, redundant caching system. This can be a Memcache cluster or a Berkley Database (BDB) file that is pushed directly onto the web servers for fastest access (Figure 1-11).

Real-time caches fall into three main categories. The first and simplest real-time cache is a *physical model cache*. In its simplest incarnation, this is simply an in-memory copy

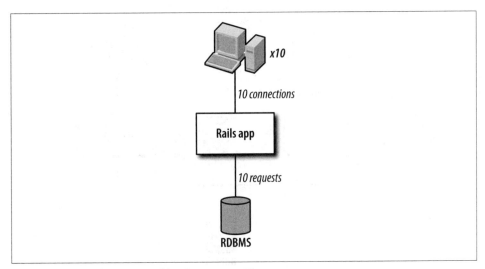

Figure 1-9. An application capable of supporting 10 user requests

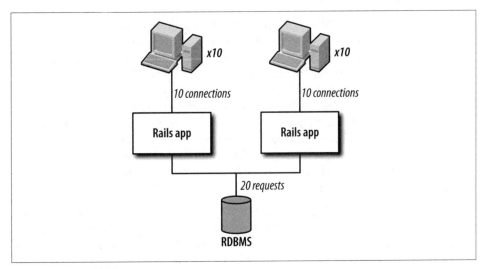

Figure 1-10. Double the requests

of the results of select queries, which are cleared whenever the data is updated or deleted. When you need a piece of data, you check the cache first before making a database request. If the data isn't in the cache, you get it from the database, and then store the value in the cache for next time. There is a Rails plugin for simple model caching called `cached_model`, but often you will have to implement caching logic yourself to get the most out of it.

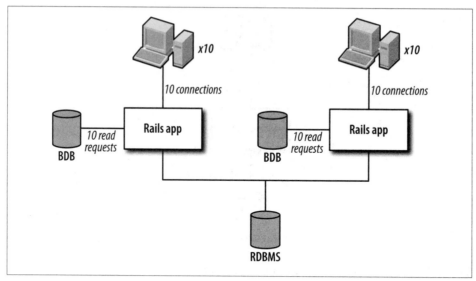

Figure 1-11. BDB file caching system

The next type of real-time cache is a *logical model cache*. While you may get quite a bit of mileage out of a physical model cache, if your application objects are complex, it may still take quite a bit of processing to construct your objects from the smaller constituent pieces, whether those smaller pieces are in a physical model cache or not. Caching your logical models post-processed from physical models can give your application a huge performance boost. However, knowing when to expire logical model caches can become tricky, as they are often made up of large numbers of records originating from several different database tables. A real-time logical model cache is essentially the same as a pre-built cache, but with the added complexity of expiry. For maximum benefit, a physical model cache should sit underneath and feed the logical model cache rebuilding process.

Note that both physical and logical model caches must be shared in some way between all application servers. Because the data in the cache can be invalidated due to actions on any individual application server, there either needs to be a single shared cache, or otherwise the individual caches on each application server need to notify each other of the expiry somehow. The most common way this is implemented in Rails is via Memcache, with the configuration shown in Figure 1-12.

The final type of real-time cache is a local, *user-level cache*. In most load-balanced setups, it's possible to have "sticky sessions," which guarantee that a visitor to your site will have all of her requests handled by the same server. With this in mind and some understanding of user behavior, you can preload information that's likely to be useful to the visitor's next request and store it in a local in-memory cache on the web server where it will be needed. This can be information about the user herself, such as

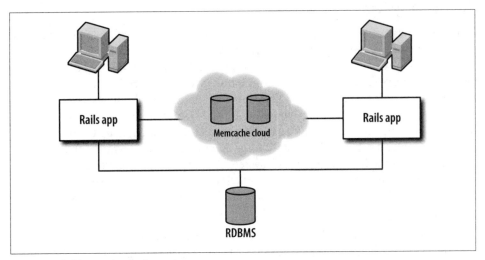

Figure 1-12. Memcache configuration

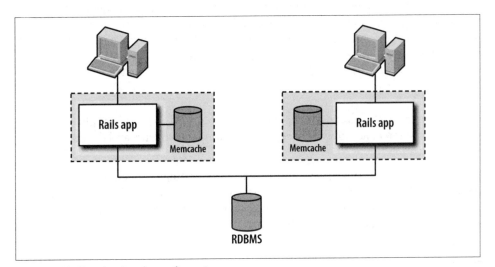

Figure 1-13. User-level cache configuration

her name and any required authentication information. If the last request was a search, it could be the next few pages of search results. Figure 1-13 shows a user-level cache, local to each application server, backed by Memcache.

Depending on the nature of your application, as well as where your bottlenecks are, you may find you need one type of cache, or you may find you need all of them.

Messaging System

A messaging system, such as an Enterprise Service Bus (ESB), allows independent pieces of your system to operate asynchronously. An event may occur on your front-end website, or perhaps even in the service layer, requiring actions to be taken that do not affect the results to be presented to the user during his current request. For example, placing an order on a website requires storing a record of the transaction in the database and processing credit card validation while the user is still online. But it also may require additional actions, such as emailing a confirmation note or queuing up the order in the fulfillment center's systems. These additional actions take time, so rather than making the user wait for the processing in each system to complete, your application can send a single message into the ESB: "User X purchased Y for $Z." Any external process that needs this information can listen for the message and operate accordingly when it sees a message it's interested in.

Using a messaging system like this, which allows many subscribers to listen for any given message, enables you to add additional layers of processing to data without having to update your main application. This cuts down on the amount of systems that need to be retested when you add additional functionality. It also cuts down on the number of issues the application responsible for user flow needs to be aware of. That application can concentrate on its specific function—user flow—and other parts of your application can take over and manage other tasks asynchronously.

Web Server

The web server has a relatively simple role in the context of a Rails application. The purpose of the server is simply to accept connections from clients and pass them along to the application.

The one subtle point to keep in mind is that users visiting your site are not the only clients of your application who will interact with the web server. When you break up your application into separate services with separate front-ends, each piece is a full Rails application stack, including the web server.

Firewall

The firewall is the barrier of trust. More than protecting against malicious hacking attempts, the firewall should be an integral part of large systems design. Within the firewall, you can simplify application logic by assuming access comes from a trusted source. Except for the most sensitive applications (e.g., controlled government systems that must protect access to secret information), you can eliminate authentication between different pieces of your application.

On the other hand, any piece of the system that accepts requests from outside of the firewall (your application layer, front-end, or web services) may need to authenticate the client to ensure that client has the correct level of access to make the request.

## CHAPTER 2

Organizing with Plugins

In most Rails books, this chapter comes last. It takes a lot of complicated examples to show why you need to organize your code at all. Examples at the beginning of books are simple enough that organizational strategies aren't necessary. By the end of a book, if you get that far, it's often too late for this sort of wisdom to be practical. Most readers, myself included, are actively programming while reading a new book for useful tips and insights and want to get to the meat of things right from the start. Unfortunately, the result of this pattern is that many Rails projects end up poorly organized. By the time you get to the chapter on code organization, you may already have a functioning application with millions of users (I hope this is your problem).

In this book, I'm going to break with tradition and present some high-level principles of code organization before we even write any code. Because of this "backward" presentation, some of what follows may seem unnecessary, burdensome, or even purposeless. Rest assured, the ideas that follow have none of these properties. They come from three years of incremental development of a 100% pure Rails website that, as of this writing, receives approximately two million unique visitors per month.

From this experience, I can tell you honestly that at some point, the amount of code you have will begin to strangle you. You may have started with a dozen classes, but a couple years down the road you have hundreds. You start with a simple request-response architecture, but before you know it, you're running a dozen asynchronous processes to manage that website alongside regular user requests; you're sending emails, resizing images, or talking to third-party services.

For any new application that I might start today, I would follow these guidelines uncompromisingly. When followed from the start, organizational principles add no burden. It's trying to organize a live site's code jumble where the heavy burden lies. In fact, working in a well-organized project is like strolling down a manicured path in an enchanted forest. The opposite is true of a poorly organized code base; it's like running through a jungle. You never know what might pop out at you—oh look, you just tripped over a rock and a tiger ate you!

Complex organizational refactorings can be exceedingly difficult late in the game. It's easiest if you start down the right path from the beginning, but of course, it's hindsight, not foresight, that's 20/20. At this stage, your applications may not be complex enough that lack of organization is a critical issue. If that's the case, feel free to skim this chapter and then come back to it as you read on. All of the examples in the book will adhere to the principles laid forth here, so at least a cursory understanding is definitely in your best interest.

Benefits

Plugins sound like something you get from third parties, or optional add-on features. While there are a great many plugins available from third parties that you can add to your application, writing your own plugins is central to your development process. It's true that writing and releasing plugins to the public at large will make you famous and powerful (well, maybe not), but getting in the habit of writing plugins has many benefits even if you have no plans to distribute them. The following is a short list of the benefits:

- Plugins provide a convenient mechanism to separate architectural enhancements from business logic. Intertwining these two can be a quick route to bugs.
- Plugins can be tested independently from the rest of your application, giving you greater confidence in the overall robustness of your code.
- It's trivial to test plugins against new versions of Rails. Similarly, limiting application code to business logic makes applications themselves easier to upgrade when new Rails versions are released.
- Plugins can be easily shared between multiple applications. In a service-oriented architecture, where different apps serve different business purposes, code sharing is a big win.
- If your first business plan fails and you need to scrap your application code, you can take your plugins with you to your next big idea.
- Releasing plugins *may* make you famous and powerful.

There are two common themes here, and one overriding principle. The first theme is the separation of business logic from code aimed at architectural enhancement. This has great implications for code quality, maintainability, and testing. Think of your application as layers. There's the Ruby language itself. On top of that is the Rails framework. Instead of dumping a behemoth, unorganized "code layer" on top of the framework, you can gain a lot by splitting that layer in two: architecture enhancements (plugins) and business logic.

The second theme relates to isolating functionality into manageable chunks. Doing so lets you test, upgrade, or deploy bits of code without needing to think about all the other pieces. That can save you a lot of time and hassle when you need to further extend

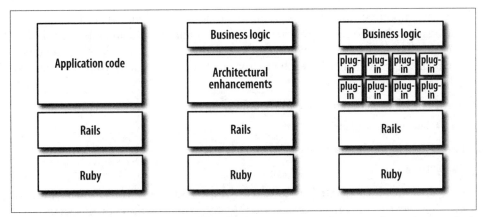

Figure 2-1. Make your applications manageable by separating application code into business logic and separate plugins for each architectural enhancement

or reengineer some crucial chunk of architecture. It's also a lifesaver when that big upgrade day comes.

The overriding principle here is *organization*. The more organized you are from day one, the better your results will be. There are a number of ways to organize code in Rails. Using plugins is just one strategy, but it is an extremely powerful one. Figure 2-1 illustrates.

Writing Your Own Plugins

To create a plugin, type this from your application's root directory:

```
./script/generate plugin {plugin-name}
```

The code generator creates a directory under *vendor/plugins* with the name you specified in the command. You should see the output shown in Example 2-1. The minimum set of files you need to modify is shown in bold.

Example 2-1. Output from generating stub files

```
ChakBookPro:example chak$ ./script/generate plugin my_plugin
      create  vendor/plugins/my_plugin/lib
      create  vendor/plugins/my_plugin/tasks
      create  vendor/plugins/my_plugin/test
      create  vendor/plugins/my_plugin/README
      create  vendor/plugins/my_plugin/MIT-LICENSE
      create  vendor/plugins/my_plugin/Rakefile
      create  vendor/plugins/my_plugin/init.rb
      create  vendor/plugins/my_plugin/install.rb
      create  vendor/plugins/my_plugin/uninstall.rb
      create  vendor/plugins/my_plugin/lib/my_plugin.rb
      create  vendor/plugins/my_plugin/tasks/my_plugin_tasks.rake
      create  vendor/plugins/my_plugin/test/my_plugin_test.rb
```

The most important files for 99% of the plugins you will write are in bold. Unfortunately, the two most important files, *init.rb* and the plugin code itself, in *lib/my_plugin.rb* (substitute your own plugin's name here), are empty. There is no guidance whatsoever on which to base plugins, the most important part of your architectural strategy.

In *init.rb*, the code generator gave us the following:

```
# Include hook code here
```

In *lib/my_plugin.rb*, the start we get is similarly useless:

```
# MyPlugin
```

In fact, all of the files generated are essentially empty. But don't worry; writing plugins is easy. The next section gives you some templates to make writing them a snap.

Core Enhancements

Core enhancements are modifications you make to the layers below you, either Ruby classes or parts of the Rails framework. Ruby has great flexibility in that classes are not static once they are defined. You can reopen them at any point and stuff in more functionality or modify functionality that already exists.

Keep in mind that power comes with a price: modifying the core can be dangerous. It's not a good idea to change behavior of core classes to do unexpected things. Bad modifications to the core can come back to bite you, and bite you hard. With that in mind, here's how you do it.

Initialization template

When your Rails application starts up, the *init.rb* file of every plugin is loaded. It's single purpose is to load the rest of your plugin. Therefore, all you really need is one line that will load the actual plugin code:

```
require 'my_plugin.rb'
```

Of course, you should replace *my_plugin.rb* with the filename that was generated for you.

Core plugin template

What do you put in the *my_plugin.rb* file? Since this is a core enhancement, the assumption is that we are going to reopen a class and make changes there. Therefore, you need to know what you're opening. If we were enhancing the Hash class, our file would look like this:

```
class Hash
  # our enhancements go here
end
```

It's that simple. It's almost *too* simple, so let's look at a concrete example.

Suppose we wanted to modify the Hash class so that it could be manipulated with more object-like syntax. The normal way to access a hash is like so:

```
>> h = Hash.new
=> {}
>> h['foo'] = 'bar'
=> "bar"
>> h['foo']
=> "bar"
>> h['baz!']
=> nil
```

Imagine instead we wanted the following syntax to work, too:

```
>> h = Hash.new
=> {}
>> h.foo = 'bar'
=> "bar"
>> h.foo
=> "bar"
>> h.baz!
=> nil
```

In effect, we want the values stored within the hash to be accessible just as an object's properties are accessed, with dot notation. We could do this by defining the method_miss ing method within the Hash class. When you call a method that is undefined on an object, method_missing is called with two parameters. The first is a symbol for the method you attempted to call. The second is an array of parameters that you tried to pass.

Our plugin file, *my_plugin.rb* (actually, we're going to call the plugin hash_extension, which would result in a main plugin file called *hash_extension.rb*), would look like Example 2-2.

Example 2-2. A core enhancement plugin that lets you access hashes like objects: lib/hash_extension.rb

```
class Hash
  def method_missing(method, *params)
    method_string = method.to_s
    if method_string.last == "="
      self[method_string[0..-2]] = params.first
    else
      self[method_string]
    end
  end
end
```

First, we convert the symbol to a string. Then we check to see if the last character of the string is an equals sign. Are we trying to do an assignment? If so, we invoke the normal hash assignment syntax using the string, minus the trailing =, as the key. Otherwise, we return whatever value is in the hash keyed on the method name we used.

Testing

The stub test file will be created under your plugin directory in *test/my_plugin_test.rb* and will contain the code shown in Example 2-3.

Example 2-3. Auto-generated test stub for a plugin: test/my_plugin_test.rb

```
require 'test/unit'

class MyPluginTest < Test::Unit::TestCase
  # Replace this with your real tests.
  def test_this_plugin
    flunk
  end
end
```

As the comment says, you replace the dummy test with your own tests. A test file for our hash extension plugin is shown in Example 2-4.

Example 2-4. Unit test for the hash_extension plugin: test/hash_extension.rb

```
require 'test/unit'
require File.expand_path(
  File.join(File.dirname(__FILE__), '../../../../config/environment')
)

class HashExtensionTest < Test::Unit::TestCase
  def setup
    @h = Hash.new
  end

  def test_missing_value
    assert_nil @h.baz!
  end

  def test_assignment
    @h.foo = 'bar'
    assert_equal @h.foo, 'bar'
  end
end
```

Note the second through fourth lines in this example. We instruct the test code to load the *environment.rb* file, which was missing from the generated test code. This line boots up the Rails environment for us, and loads our plugin (and any plugins on which it might depend). This change allows us to run our test directly from the command line with the following command:

```
ruby vendor/plugins/hash_extension/test/hash_extension_test.rb
```

The output should look like this:

```
Loaded suite vendor/plugins/hash_extension/test/hash_extension_test
Started
..
Finished in 0.000609 seconds.

2 tests, 2 assertions, 0 failures, 0 errors
```

You can also run your tests with the built in rake command:

```
rake test:plugins
```

The problem with this command is that it runs tests for *all* of your plugins, which may not be what you want.

Using a core plugin

Using a core plugin is easy. You actually don't have to do anything at all within your application for the code to take effect. The *init.rb* file is automatically loaded when the application starts, and the core functionality modification is applied straightaway. The plugin just being there is all that's necessary.

Why Extend Hash?

A criticism often leveraged against Ruby on Rails is that it's slow. It's true that the Ruby language is slower at some things than other languages used in web development contexts. That just means that you as a developer need to be aware of where Ruby and Rails can eat up valuable processor cycles. Then you can avoid those hot-spots by choosing less processor-hungry alternatives to some of the great Rails sugar when it doesn't provide justifiable benefits.

Once cause of slowness I've found is in converting the results of a SQL query into ActiveRecord objects. A row from an SQL query result set is just a set of key-value pairs; in other words, a hash. ActiveRecord objects are great in that they come bundled up with methods that let you traverse object relationships, and they also contain methods you've written into the classes to facilitate custom behavior. But along with all the sugar that ActiveRecord provides comes a heavy overhead of creating the object itself.

Very often, especially when you're selecting records to display a web page, all you need are the key-value pairs. A hash would suffice, and it turns out getting your results out of the database as hashes is much faster—more than 50% faster than requesting ActiveRecord objects.

Whereas a regular query that retrieves ActiveRecord objects looks like this:

```
MyObject.find(:all)
```

a query that returns hashes looks like this:

```
MyObject.connection.select_all("select * from my_objects")
```

True, you resort to SQL here, but in slow pages where you need to eke out that last bit of render-time performance, the trade-off can be worth it. In a test of retrieving 40

---

thousand objects on a MacBook Pro 2.33 Ghz Intel Core 2 Duo, the ActiveRecord approach took seven seconds of Ruby time, while the hash method took three.

The other caveat worth noting when replacing ActiveRecord queries with hash queries is that objects and hashes are accessed differently. You access objects with dot notation: `my_object.foo` versus `my_object['foo']`. But that's exactly the problem taken care of by our core hash extension! Using this extension, you can cherry-pick slow ActiveRecord queries that aren't using all the "extras" given to you by the ActiveRecord object itself, and swap out the query to boost performance.

Custom Extensions

Whereas core extensions are intended to modify classes that already exist, custom extensions allow you to modify the behavior of classes that have yet to be written. It's best to think of this type of extension in two separate ways, based on levels of complexity and on how you intend to use it.

The first level is essentially nothing more than making a plugin out of a mixin. A mixin is a module containing methods that gets "mixed in" to a class with the `include` keyword. All of the methods in the module become available to the class. These might be utility functions or an interface to a remote system.

The second level builds on the first. The plugin still contains a mixin module, but this mixin defines declarative class methods that further modify a class's behavior when they are called. An example of this sort of plugin is the well-known `acts_as_list`, which gives an ActiveRecord class list-like properties. When the `acts_as_list` plugin is added to your Rails application, it is mixed in to ActiveRecord, giving your classes the ability to call the method `acts_as_list`. Upon doing so, that calling class is bestowed with a number of add-ons and modifications that give it its list-like behavior.

We'll cover the more complicated case here. We'll create a mixin that defines a declarative method `acts_as_animal`, which when applied to a class, creates a `noise` method within the class. When we call it, it will print out the appropriate noise. The plugin will also define a generic animal method that acts identically for any class that `acts_as_animal`: that is, to poop. The first step is to run:

```
./script/generate plugin acts_as_animal
```

Initialization template

The initialization template follows the same pattern as our core extension plugin:

```
require 'acts_as_animal'
```

Extension plugin template

The template for our mixin is shown in Example 2-5.

Example 2-5. Template for an "acts_as" style plugin, which extends the behavior of an existing class

```ruby
module MyModule
  module ClassMethods
    # class methods and instance method generators go here
    def acts_as_my_module(params)
      class_eval do <<-DELIM
        def some_method
          # remember, string substitution
          # is OK here.  e.g., #{params[:foo]}
        end
      DELIM
    end
  end

  module InstanceMethods
    # generic instance methods go here
  end

  def self.included(base)
    base.extend ClassMethods
    base.class_eval do
      include InstanceMethods
    end
  end
end
```

There are three main sections. The first section defines class methods we want to add to classes that are extended by this module. These can be generic class methods, or declarative-style generator methods that are defined based on some parameters passed in.

Well-known generator methods are the `acts_as` variety, which add additional instance methods to the class. The preceding is a boilerplate for defining these sorts of methods. The trick is to invoke `class_eval` inside a class method. Inside this `class_eval` block, you can define dynamic methods that are based on the parameters passed to the `acts_as` method. Inside the method, we pass a string to `class_eval` so that we can perform string substitution.

Note that in order to avoid having to escape string delimiters, we use a special, multi-line string syntax. Text between `<<-DELIM ... DELIM` is treated as a plain old string. In this case, our string is Ruby code intended to be evaluated by `class_eval`.

The second section defines the module `InstanceMethods`. There we place any generic instance methods that we want to add to a class that decides to act like our module.

You don't need to modify the last section at all. Its purpose is to include the other two sections—one for class methods and one for instance methods—in the correct way. The method `self.included(base)` is hook code that runs when the module is actually included by another class.

The first thing we do is extend that class with the class methods we defined. Then, using `class_eval`, we include the instance methods module as if we had written that statement within the class itself.

The extension plugin template expanded for our animal example is shown in Example 2-6.

Example 2-6. An acts_as_animal extension plugin based on the template in Example 2-5

```
module Animal

  def self.included(base)
    base.extend ClassMethods
    base.class_eval do
      include InstanceMethods
    end
  end

  module ClassMethods
    def acts_as_animal(params)
      class_eval <<-STUFF
        def noise
          '#{params[:noise]}!'
        end
      STUFF
    end
  end

  module InstanceMethods
    def generic_animal_thing
      'poop'
    end
  end
end
```

First, in the `InstanceMethods` module, we define a method `generic_animal_thing`, which when called, should return `'poop'`.

Then, in the class level code, we define the method `acts_as_animal`, which is at the heart of our plugin. This method invokes `class_eval` again, to create a custom method in the class from which it is invoked.

Using a custom extension

Unlike core extensions, which are automatically loaded, to use a custom extension, you must first include it somewhere using the `include` keyword. Depending on what you are trying to extend, you might do this in a model class, a controller, or even *environment.rb*. The syntax is simple:

```
include Animal
```

The class methods defined will be available in the class that had scope where you placed this line. The instance methods will be available in all instances of that class.

Of course, you can also combine the two types of plugins covered here, core and custom, to add custom generator extensions to core functionality like ActiveRecord. This is how `acts_as_list` and other well known ActiveRecord behavior modifications work. To do so, just reopen the class and issue the `include` statement.

Testing

To test a custom extension module independently of application code, you must do two things. First, include the module again. Second, define a class in your test that will actually do the "acting as." In Example 2-7, we define a `Pig` class and create an instance variable of that type in the `setup` method. We then test that the pig can make a noise and do the generic animal thing, that is, poop.

Example 2-7. Unit tests for the acts_as_animal custom extension plugin

```
require 'test/unit'
require File.expand_path(
  File.join(File.dirname(__FILE__), '../../../../config/environment')
)

include Animal

class Pig
  acts_as_animal :noise => 'oink'
end

class ActsAsAnimalTest < Test::Unit::TestCase
  def setup
    @p = Pig.new
  end

  def test_makes_proper_noise
    assert_equal @p.noise, 'oink!'
  end

  def test_generic_animal_thing
    assert_equal @p.generic_animal_thing, 'poop'
  end
end
```

We run the tests with:

```
ruby vendor/plugins/acts_as_animal/test/acts_as_animal_test.rb
```

And they both pass:

```
Loaded suite vendor/plugins/acts_as_animal/test/acts_as_animal_test
Started
..
Finished in 0.000307 seconds.

2 tests, 2 assertions, 0 failures, 0 errors
```

Deployment

Creating the plugin is the first step toward componentization of code and achieving the goals set forth at the beginning of this chapter. However, if you don't have a way to share plugins between applications, and you resort to copying the plugin directory from one project to the next, you aren't getting the full benefit of a shared library.

There are many methods to share plugins across applications. One is to package the plugin as a gem, and install it on the systems where you want to use the plugin. If you're using subversion, another good method requiring very little setup is to use subversion's "externals" property. This technique is covered below.

svn:externals

If you are using subversion to manage your source code, you can put your plugins in some standard location in your repository and then create an `svn:externals` reference in your application's *vendor/plugins* directory that references the plugins' location.

For example, suppose we checked our `hash_extension` plugin directory into subversion under the path *plugins/acts_as_hash*.

In any application that we want to have access to the plugin, we modify the `svn:externals` property of the *vendor/plugins* directory. We do this like so:

```
cd vendor/plugins
svn propedit svn:externals .
```

This will bring up the editor defined in your `EDITOR` environment variable. The contents of the editor session will contain any externals properties already set; in this case, probably none. The format is:

```
directoryname [-rev] svnpath
```

So for our `hash_extension` plugin, it might look like this:

```
hash_extension svn://rubyforge.org/var/svn/hash_extension/trunk
```

After saving and quitting, the following two commands will check out the files and set up the link in the repository:

```
svn update
svn commit
```

## CHAPTER 3

Organizing with Modules

Like most projects, the first Rails website I worked on started with just a handful of tables and a handful of classes. In those early days, we couldn't imagine the features or reports we would need in our third year, which is where we are at the time of this writing. We only knew what we knew about the business at the current moment.

When you just have a handful of tables to deal with, there doesn't seem to be much reason to impose an organizational strategy. At that time, Rails was at version 0.13, and there weren't many big Rails sites around whose teams could offer their expert advice on Day One organization either. Such advice can often only be dispensed in hindsight, and back then—and even frequently today—most new Rails users were new to Ruby as well.

So we plodded along, developing our site, and along with it our own 20/20 hindsight. Today, our hindsight is really good, but the organization of our original core application is not so good. As of this writing, the *models* directory of that core application contains 188 classes.

Such a pile of classes is overwhelming for new employees and even some veterans. It can be quite a challenge to remember where everything is, or what effects a change in one class might have on the other 187 classes. The advice from the original developer of a "big Rails site," in hindsight, is to organize into modules from Day One.

Even in the initial development of our application, at around class number 40, we sensed something wasn't right and that some kind of namespacing and organization was necessary. But even with 40 classes, the instinct to move forward as opposed to laterally was strong, and it seemed that there wasn't ever time to refactor. If 40 classes represents inertia, then 188 is simply far too late to start organizing. An early investment of time to set up some organization will pay big dividends when your site has grown an order of magnitude or two in complexity.

Files and Directories

When you first create your Rails application, a number of directories are created. Example 3-1 highlights the four we are concerned with in this chapter, namely the *controllers*, *helpers*, and *models* directories under the *app* directory.

All but the simplest projects will eventually need to be broken up into modules to minimize the number of classes a developer needs to be concerned with at any given time, but the skeleton created by the `rails` command doesn't set us up to start working within modules from Day One.

Example 3-1. Abbreviated output from the rails command to create a new project

```
bash-3.2$ rails example_app
      create
      create  app/controllers
      create  app/helpers
      create  app/models
      create  app/views/layouts
      ...
```

Luckily, even without knowing a single thing about our application, we can start organizing our *model*, *controller*, and *helper* files into three categories that will pave the way for a well-organized application down the road: *physical*, *logical and service*, and *utility*. Not every one of the top-level directories will need each of these subdirectories, and you may find some will need others as well, but these three are a good start. Below we'll see what each directory is for and where it belongs.

The first category, physical, corresponds to the models, controllers, and helpers and views normally associated with a Rails application. These are the models that descend from `ActiveRecord::Base` and correspond directly to physical database tables.

The next category, the pair of logical and service, comes into play when your application is large or complex enough that it is ready to evolve to an SOA. At this point, you will define an API for clients that should remain relatively fixed. To prevent your service API from changing every time you tweak your database design, an abstraction layer that's not tied directly to database tables is necessary. Under the *models* directory, add a directory *logical*, where the logical or domain model classes will go. Under *control lers*, create a directory called *service*, which we'll use later in this book when we break our application into a service-oriented architecture. Although you won't have anything to put in these directories right now, create them anyway. The mere presence of this hierarchy will remind you that something does go here, and that it's of a different sort than what we put in the *physical* directories.

The third category is for utility scripts intended to be run with *script/runner*. These are background processes that send out emails or do various other tasks. Usually they run on a schedule or are run by hand. These classes don't have helpers, and the controller is cron or you, the operator.

You may find that your application has additional categories. You will also no doubt find the need, within each category, to further subdivide in order to maintain your own sanity. The main point to understand is that if you don't lay out a framework for managing different *types* of classes from the start, you will end up with a mess that is hard to tame late in the game.

Therefore, it's strongly recommended that right at the beginning you expand the initial set of directories created for you under *app*. Even if you don't use all of the directories right away, having them serves as a reminder that files should be organized up front. In the early days of your application, you will fill only the directories related to your physical models, but having them preorganized into their own directories makes it much easier to add other types of classes later.

A proposed generic directory hierarchy that can be used as a starting point is shown in Example 3-2. Additions from the basic set are in bold. You can pick whatever names you like for these. The rest of this chapter is devoted to organization *within* a given top-level module. The focus will primarily be on the physical models, since that's the first part of the application to be written. We'll also see how interactions from one module to another are possible. To do so, we'll present a standard way to write a utility model that interacts with physical models.

Example 3-2. Directory structure organized from Day One

```
app/controllers
app/controllers/physical
app/controllers/service
app/helpers
app/helpers/physical
app/models
app/models/physical
app/models/logical
app/views/layouts
app/views/physical
```

Module Boundaries for Namespacing

Namespaces are a feature of many computer programming languages, and they have great benefits for large projects, especially those with multiple programmers working simultaneously. At the simplest level, a namespace is a way to group related classes together, and at the same time separate those classes from other, unrelated classes.

A project that uses namespaces has three big wins over a project that doesn't:

- One developer can work on a feature within the confines of one namespace, while another developer works on a different feature within the confines of its own namespace. They don't risk stepping on each other's toes.
- If it makes sense for the overall project, two classes can have the same name, as long as they are in different namespaces. For example, a `Clothing::Boot` can exist

alongside an `Automobile::Boot` (as in the trunk of the car) without any problem. The namespace provides the context, and there are no naming collisions.

- Namespaces can provide an abstraction barrier between large, disparate sets of code. If documentation is published describing what's "public" in the namespace, everything else within it can be changed safely as long as classes in other namespaces restrict themselves to using the published API.

 Namespaces do for classes what classes do for data and methods.

In Ruby, namespaces are implemented with modules. Around every class in the module, or around a set of classes, you specify the start and end of the module:

```
module MyModule
  class Foo
  end
end
```

There can now be another class called `Foo` in another module:

```
module YourModule
  class Foo
  end
end
```

From within each module, to access the `Foo` class, just say `Foo`. From another module, you prefix the class name with the module name: `::MyModule::Foo`.

ActiveRecord Associations Between Modules

As shown earlier, to place a class within a module, you simply open and close the module around the class. Within a module, you define relationships between Active-Record classes no differently than you would when there are no modules at all.

However, because modules provide namespacing and scoping, when crossing a module boundary, you need to tell ActiveRecord where to look for the class being referenced. In this book, we will build a movie ticket application that contains information about movies and also ticket sales. Ticket sales depend on the movies that exist, but not vice versa. Thus, let's take a very simple set of classes (they won't be the final classes we arrive at later) to illustrate how you define an order in one module to depend on a movie in another. Example 3-3 shows these two classes and the additional ActiveRecord code needed to make it work in bold.

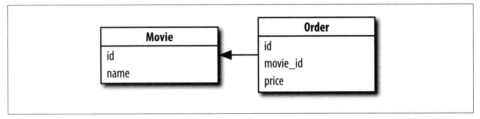

Figure 3-1. Two tables with a foreign key reference; is the relationship reciprocal?

Example 3-3. ActiveRecord relationships between modules

```
# models/physical/movies/movie.rb
module Physical
  module Movies
    class Movie < ActiveRecord::Base
    end
  end
end

# models/physical/orders/order.rb
module Physical
  module Orders
    class Order < ActiveRecord::Base
      belongs_to :movie,
                 :class_name => '::Physical::Movies::Movie'
    end
  end
end
```

Certainly, it would be more elegant if ActiveRecord's association methods could take a separate `:module` parameter so that the class name itself need not be repeated if it could be inferred from the name of the association itself, but at the present time ActiveRecord does not have this support. In a sense, only three years into the explosion of the Rails phenomenon, we are blazing the trail toward enterprise with each new day. Expect more features needed for large enterprise systems to emerge as more and more Rails sites grow to need them.

Reciprocal Relationships

In the previous example, our `Orders` class knows about `Movies`, but not vice versa.

Most Rails tutorials encourage you to create cross-dependencies where none exist. Indeed, if you examine Figure 3-1, you will see the table structure for the `Movies` and `Orders` classes.

ActiveRecord tutorials often encourage you to create the following classes to represent these tables:

```
class Movie
  has_many :orders
end
```

```
class Order
  has_one :movie
end
```

Suddenly, between two classes in the application layer, we have a cross-dependency that did not exist between the tables in the data layer. Defining the interrelationship provides convenient methods you may wish to use later, such as `movie.orders` and `order.movie`, but if you don't expect that you will ever need to access the relationship in both directions—in this case, `movie.orders` seems like a reporting rather than operational concept—it's better to leave out the reciprocal relationship definition. When a developer tries to access the relationship in reverse, he'll get an error, indicating the method does not exist, and that moment will provide an opportunity to examine the design. Either the access was inappropriate and the developer's goals could be achieved in another way, or the reverse relationship should be created.

None of this is to say that the vast majority of relationships between classes are or should be one-way relationships. In fact, the majority in your application probably will be reciprocal. There will be many more classes than there are modules. The art of design is to recognize the clusters of one-way relationships that *do* exist, because doing so opens up great possibilities down the road, both in terms of decreasing developer coordination overhead, as well as making the application more flexible and open to being split into separate services where and when appropriate.

Modules Presage Services

These ideas about reciprocal relationships may seem like making a bug fuss about something rather inconsequential. So why bother? In fact, being careful about class dependencies can help you identify borders for modules. And modules can provide guidance for an application split that comes along with a move to a service-oriented architecture.

For example, imagine if we added a third class, `Popcorn`, to represent our foray into selling snacks at the movie theatre. If we were defining reciprocal relationships de rigueur, without much thought to actual needs, we would have a reciprocal relationship between movies and orders, and another reciprocal relationship between popcorn and orders.

If we could recognize early on that movies and popcorn are completely unrelated, we could put them in separate modules from the start. This also necessitates that the `Orders` class be in its own separate module as well; certainly it doesn't belong in one of the `Movies` or `Popcorn` modules.

Figure 3-2 shows our three classes with interdependencies in Frame 1. With the names of the classes present, it's easy to gloss over the relationships because you know what the inherent relationships really are. Frame 2 shows the relationships again, but without class names. Would you imagine mapping `Movies`, `Popcorn`, and `Orders` onto this

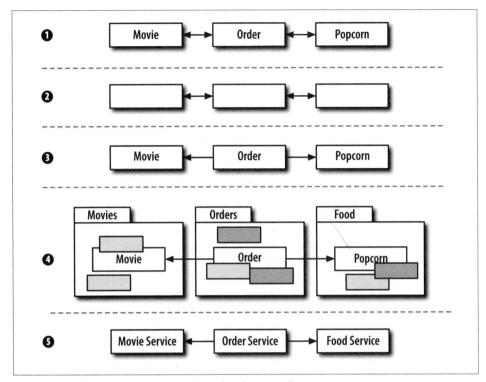

Figure 3-2. Adding reciprocal relationships that do not really exist

diagram? Frame 3 shows the classes, with only the relationship we want. An order can be for a movie or for popcorn.

Figure 3-2 then goes on to show the progression we might see in our software over time. The number of classes around each topic area increases. This is shown in Frame 4, where we've placed a module boundary around each set of classes. For example, the `Movies` module might also contain ratings, theatres, and showtimes. The `Orders` module might contain classes for credit cards and billing addresses. And the `Snacks` module could contain candy, soda, etc. From the start, you want to ensure that the defined relationships allow you to easily put boundaries around each set. Eventually, these boundaries can become physical ones—in a service-oriented architecture—rather than simply suggestions implied by module namespacing. Frame 5 shows the potential set of services and their interconnections. In effect, we're back full-circle to Frame 3. Abstractions allow us to keep complex relationships and processes simple to deal with.

Remember that good fences make good neighbors, and so too does modularization make for good software.

Ensuring Proper Load Order

Rails does a pretty good job of locating and loading classes when they are first accessed. As a convention over configuration issue, this means that everything will work fine unless you are pushing the envelope of convention too far.

There are two scenarios when the auto-loader can become confused. In the simplest case, it just doesn't know in which directory to find your files, and, in that case, you may see an error like the following one:

```
NameError: uninitialized constant Physical::Movie
```

For this type of error, you simply need to add the new path to the auto-loader's list of directories it searches. In *environment.rb*, in the `Rails::Initializer.run` section, add or modify the following statement to add your new load paths:

```
config.load_paths += %W(
    #{RAILS_ROOT}/app/models/logical
    #{RAILS_ROOT}/app/controllers/service
)
```

In the this example, the directories for logical models and service controllers were added.

The next type of auto-loader problem occurs when you define parts of your class in one file, and other parts of the class in another file. In Ruby, it's perfectly acceptable to reopen classes. You may have some basic class definition that should always be loaded, and then additional functionality that is loaded only under certain circumstances. Or, as we'll see in Chapter 15, you may need to split up your code for some other reason. When we break our app up into services, we'll break our logical model classes up into two components: one shared and one not. Once one piece of code is loaded, the auto-loader will refuse to load the other part. The errors you see when the auto-loader has not loaded all parts of your class will be specific to your classes; the class itself will be defined, but some method or piece of data inside the class will not be.

To deal with this type of issue, you actually need to explicitly load your class files, disregarding the auto-loader altogether. For us, this will come up for our *models/logical* directory. In general, to force loading of an entire directory, the code snippet in Example 3-4 can be placed in *application.rb*.

Example 3-4. Code to load an entire directory of files

```
Dir["#{RAILS_ROOT}/app/models/logical/*.rb"].each { |file|
  require_dependency "logical/#{file[file.rindex('/') + 1...-3]}"
}
```

Here, the directory *logical* was used, but it can be replaced with any directory for which you want to force loading. The code snippet works in the following way:

1. The directory listing of files ending in *.rb* is placed in an array to be iterated over.

2. For each item in the array, we construct the appropriate name to pass to the `require_dependency` method.

3. We construct the name by taking all characters after the last "/" character and up to the *.rb*. `rindex('/')` returns the index of the last slash, and `...-3` means "up to the third to last character." Put together, these become a range, which returns a substring of the filename. For example, *app/models/logical/foo.rb* becomes *foo*.

4. The filename is appended back onto the part of the path that is below one of the load paths, as defined earlier.

5. We then pass this to `require_dependency`, which loads a class from its expected location even if the class is already defined.

Exercises

1. Examine the classes in your problem space. Draw a dependency graph and find clusters of classes that can be broken up into modules.

2. For each module, determine the dependency type: cascading, independent, or container/contained.

Refactor Steps

Refactoring to modules can be a big process. If you haven't had modules in mind while developing your application, your list of classes may be messy. Two "big refactors" are detailed here. Step one is simply to get your physical classes (those derived from `Active Record::Base`) into a single module. Step two is to detangle "utility" functions intended to be run with *script/runner* into their own classes, which belong in the `Utility` module.

High-Level Module Refactor

1. Create the directories *physical*, *logical*, and *utility* under the *models* directory.

2. Move all of your classes that descend from `ActiveRecord::Base` (likely all of them) into the *models/physical* directory.

3. Wrap each class with the following:

```
module Physical
  # original code
end
```

4. Create the directories *physical* and *service* under the *controllers* directory.

5. Move all of your classes that descend from `ActionController::Base` (likely all of them) into the *controllers/physical* directory.

6. For each class, repeat step 3.

7. Adjust all routes in *routes.rb* to take the module name into account:

```
map.connect 'foo/:action/:id', :controller => 'physical/foo'
```

8. Make analogous changes in your test directory for unit and functional tests. Remember to repeat step 3 for each set of files.

Detangling Utility Methods

Utility methods are those that you never intend to be run while executing a user request. They are run exclusively via *script/runner*, either from the command line or through a *crontab* process. Often these methods will be mixed into your ActiveRecord models as class methods, but they don't belong there. Many beginning Rails programmers are surprised that you can create classes that don't descend from `ActiveRecord::Base` or `ActionController::Base`. You certainly can. Follow these steps to deconvolve utility methods from other classes:

1. Locate all of your *script/runner* processes. A good place to start looking is in your crontab settings.

2. For each method found, create a new file under the *models/utility* directory named after the process, e.g., *emailer.rb*.

3. Structure the file based on the following template:

```
module Physical
  module Utility
    class Emailer
      def self.run(params)
        # original code goes here
      end
    end
  end
end
```

4. Anywhere that the original code referenced the original class with `self`, replace it with the original class's name. In this case, it would likely be `Email`.

5. Wherever you run these scripts, alter the way the process is invoked. So:

```
./script/runner "Email.send_emails"
```

becomes:

```
./script/runner "Physical::Utility::Emailer.run"
```

## CHAPTER 4

Database As a Fortress

If you ask a bunch of CEOs what their company's greatest asset is, most will tell you it's their people. That certainly sounds nice. It may even be true for companies that don't deal with data. However, if a CEO who works for a company based around a website says people are her greatest asset, she is definitely lying. Great people got the company where it is today, but now that it's a success, the most important asset is the data that has accumulated. If Edwards, your super-star coder, gets hit by a bus, it will take you six to eight weeks to train Henderson or Stevens or Erikson to replace him. However, if you have a data meltdown—one that creeps in slowly, undetected at first, until all your precious data is turned to garbage—be prepared to start over from scratch. Not even your backups can help, because they're all corrupt, too.

The most important asset of a web-based company is its data. The most obvious type of data to protect is operational data. If you sell goods online, your site is useless if the product descriptions don't match the products. If you run a social networking site, who will come back if the network links get lost, crossed, or lead to user pages that no longer exist? What good is an online personal information management tool if your to-do list items disappear before you get to check them off yourself?

Historical data corruption is another common and insidious problem. Imagine if you could no longer report on how many units of a particular widget you sold month over month last year simply because you no longer sell that widget today. Was the item's database record deleted when the item was taken off the shelf, and now the historical data referencing it points to an empty record? Or what if data you think is important actually isn't? In your hosted blogs site, are you reporting statistics of total comments added site-wide, but half of the comments are for entries that have long since been deleted by the author? Operational data changes with the times, but historical data that references yesterday's operational data needs to be accessible and accurate today and tomorrow, too.

Most web frameworkbooks teach you how to add data to your database, but they don't teach you how to protect it. This book picks up where those books left off. This chapter is intended to help you frame the way you think about databases. Databases are a major part of your entire architecture, not just a place to store application data. The next four chapters show you how to design a solid data model incrementally and how to tightly integrate it with Rails.

Your Database Is an Application, Too

We tend to think of a web framework as the solution to all problems. Rails especially tends to abstract other pieces of web architecture away so that Rails itself seems to be the only piece of the puzzle. This is especially true of how Rails abstracts away the database. Rails now ships with SQLite as the default database, so you barely have to think about setting up a database at all. Next, the task of writing DDL has been buried behind *migrations*. DML, the bread and butter of SQL queries, are abstracted away behind ActiveRecord. Finally, the task of maintaining data integrity is left to ActiveRecord *validations*.

The problem with abstracting to this degree is that it requires that you make a few assumptions that are unlikely to be true.

"One Framework to Rule Them All"

There are many frameworks out there besides Rails. There's PHP/Cake, Drupal, Django, Struts, Perl/Mason, etc. The list goes on and on. If you're lucky, you're rewriting your legacy PHP or Java application in Rails right now. If so, one problem you now face while you're busy implementing the latest JavaScript interface magic is remembering all of those special cases and boundary conditions that led to bugs in your legacy PHP system. It took the previous engineers years to stamp out each pesky software bug, and you have to replicate all of this intricate logic again while also rewriting the interface from scratch so that the new site is 10 times snappier than the old one. Maybe you are painstakingly meticulous and everything turns out all right. But what happens in the next iteration when you switch to the yet newer, more whiz-bang framework? Hopefully your next framework is the next version of Rails, but you get the idea.

Software is constantly in flux, but the data you collect over the years is not. Wouldn't it be nice if you could ensure the integrity of your data without concern for the current software stack sitting on top?

"No One in My Company Will Ever Write a Bug"

The plain and simple truth is that software has bugs. Your application code will change much more frequently than your database schema. When you add new columns to a database table, it's very easy to forget to add all the appropriate ActiveRecord validations. It's also easy to comment out well-intentioned validations but then forget to uncomment them. Finally, there are lots of scenarios for which no ActiveRecord validations exist in the first place (referential integrity constraints being the prime example), so relying solely on ActiveRecord validations to maintain your data's integrity is simply a recipe for disaster. On the other hand, built-in mechanisms of an RDBMS can make protecting your data easy and worry-free. Accept that your application *will* have bugs, and leave it up to the data layer to be the final gatekeeper of what is allowed to enter database.

"This Rails Application Is the Only Application on Earth"

The next assumption is that the application you are writing is the *only* application that will ever access the data you are storing. Forget about wholesale framework switches here. As your application grows, you will add myriad scripts that run scheduled maintenance tasks to clean up or to summarize data. You will write quick-and-dirty tools that live outside of your website's main code base. You will even (probably more frequently than you expect) access the database directly through a database client and manipulate your data with raw SQL queries.

In all of these scenarios, you are likely to be bypassing your ActiveRecord validations. Therefore, it's necessary to rethink the main function of these validations. Since the scope of the validations is only the application in which they reside, they cannot possibly be relied upon to protect your data from other rogue programs, or even from a well-intentioned developer sitting in front of a SQL prompt. The validations *do* help generate an interface that gives the user helpful feedback before rejecting bad input. And that's the key: validations do not safeguard data. They can be bypassed, turned off, or easily deleted. Only at the data layer itself can this be accomplished.

Sit Atop the Shoulders of Giants

The field of database technology is large, mature, and there is ongoing academic research on storing, searching, and making sense of data stored in a database. The commercial Oracle database was first introduced in 1979. The first version of PostgreSQL, the best choice at the time of this writing for an open source RDBMS, appeared in 1989. An unparalleled amount of research and development has gone into these products, and best-of-breed choices in this area have not changed every few years they way they have for web scripting languages and frameworks.

If you treat the database simply as a place to dump your application's data for later retrieval, you are shortchanging yourself and your application. When used correctly, not only will your database safeguard your data from the effects of errant code, but it will also afford you aggregation, computation, and retrieval speed that you could never hope to reproduce with even the cleanest or most elegant application code.

It behooves a web application developer to learn not only the ins and outs of the web framework but also the RDBMS atop which that framework sits. Remember that your database, which contains your company's most precious asset—its data—is very likely to outlive the application you write on top of it.

Choosing the Right RDBMS

All examples in this book assume the use of PostgreSQL. For those using Oracle or another database that adheres closely to the SQL standard, the concepts are identical, although some of the syntax may vary slightly. Many features of the SQL standard are *not* implemented in MySQL, so unfortunately a number of the advanced topics are not possible to implement using MySQL as of version 5.0. For this reason, it's not recommended for a serious website, although MySQL is undeniably popular.

Why not MySQL? The Rails core team uses ySQL, and it is certainly more popular within the Rails community than PostgreSQL. This brings up two important questions. First, if MySQL isn't as good as PostgreSQL, why is it so popular? And if PostgreSQL isn't as popular as MySQL, why is it used for the examples in this book?

MySQL gained popularity for two important reasons. First, although it is open source and free, a company called MySQL AB got behind it to offer support to enterprise customers. When the shift from closed to open source software began, having this type of insurance was key to adoption of open source products. For whatever reason, in the early days, PostgreSQL did not have the same level of corporate support offerings as did MySQL—although today there is plenty of support from a variety of vendors.

The second reason for MySQL's ascension is that it always had much simpler point-and-click installers on Windows, whereas PostgreSQL remained, for a long time, the domain of Unix and Linux users. In the PostgreSQL community this made sense, because databases are hosted on *NIX servers—why would you need point-and-click Windows installers? It should be a lesson, then, that any barriers you erect to users using your software will be to your detriment. Of course, many developers and decision makers worked on Windows, and their inability to easily give PostgreSQL a test run often pushed them to MySQL.

So MySQL won the popularity contest—why don't we accept that in this book? It's for the same reason that *NIX is the *de facto* choice for servers, even as Windows dominates the desktop market. PostgreSQL is simply better at doing the job of being an RDBMS. In addition to implementing much more of the SQL standard, and more faithfully, PostgreSQL also has a much better query planner than MySQL. In addition, MySQL has a variety of strange vestiges from its early days, such as the number value zero being treated as equal to the absence of a value, NULL. MySQL is also case-insensitive by default. Idiosyncrasies like this seem small at the outset, but often come back later to haunt you.

Working with PostgreSQL instills a feeling of safety that MySQL does not. If you haven't made the switch yet, it's worth trying PostgreSQL out as you read this book.

A Note on Migrations

One of the strengths of the ActiveRecord Object Relational Mapping (ORM) library is that it provides an abstraction layer between the application developer and the database for the Data Manipulation Language (DML) components of SQL. With some exceptions, this abstraction provides a convenient interface to most inserts, updates, and deletes that your application will need to perform, and you won't have to worry about syntax peculiarities specific to a particular database product. In many situations, the abstraction is fully adequate, and for the exceptional cases, you can always execute arbitrary SQL to get the job done.

For anyone who has written a database-backed website without an ORM, it's probably not the absence of SQL, which is a supremely straightforward language, that makes ActiveRecord worthwhile. The real benefit of ActiveRecord is the automatic unmarshalling of results from SQL queries into Ruby objects, an otherwise tedious, manual task that can be painstaking and error-prone. The code in Example 4-1 to load a user record, which you would never write in a Ruby on Rails application, is an approximation of what life is like without an ORM.

Example 4-1. A dramatization of what accessing a database might look like without object-relational mapping tools

```
db_result = ActiveRecord::Base.select_one("
  select first_name, last_name, birthdate, favorite_food
    from users
   where id = #{id}
")
user = User.new
user.id = id
user.first_name = db_result[:first_name]
user.last_name = db_result[:last_name]
user.birthdate = db_result[:birthdate]
user.favorite_food = db_result[:favorite_food]
```

With ActiveRecord, the same is accomplished with a single statement:

```
user = User.find(id)
```

Abstracting DML provides a fantastic reduction in the amount of rote code that must be written (and rote code that seldom needs special cases, at that). However, one less successful consequence of the desire to fully abstract the database layer has been an attempt to abstract the Data Definition Language (DDL).

DDL statements are those that define tables and sequences, create indexes on tables, and define stored procedures. While DML statements occur throughout an application with every insert, update, or delete statement, DDL statements generally do not appear within applications at all. DDL statements, because they *define* the structure of your data layer, get executed only once, usually when your application isn't even running.

Therefore, the attempt to abstract DDL through migrations has not been the boon that abstracting DML has been. The first reason is the lack of benefit gained from using migrations rather than writing straight DDL. Whereas abstracting DML provides a huge savings in the amount of repetitive code that must be written to create objects, as shown earlier, migrations don't provide any such benefit.

The second reason to be wary of migrations is that as of this writing, they support only a small subset of the DDL language. Just as with DML, you can always mix in some custom DDL with your Ruby migration code, but in this case, the consequence is that you'll be writing much more code altogether, and the result will be much less succinct than if you had written it all with DDL statements.

Because migrations have had a number of shortcomings, they're continuously changing. Rails 2.1 solves the problem caused by multiple developers trying to write migrations at once; pre 2.1, migrations were named in a way that required lots of developer communication. While it's likely that migrations will continue to change, it's not guaranteed they will ever be a good replacement for DDL, which, as it happens, was designed specifically the purpose it serves: data definition.

Therefore, in this book, we forget about migrations and built and manipulate our schemas using plain old SQL DDL statements. Every developer should understand SQL DDL, and if your organization uses migrations, it shouldn't be hard to learn the state-of-the-art in migrations, and implement your DDL that way. The important thing is understanding what is supposed to be happening beneath the scenes, so you can still write DDL when you need to. Many operations that are easy with DDL are still—and some will always be—impossible with migrations. If you rely on migrations and skip the DDL that migrations don't support, you're shortchanging yourself.

Dispelling Myths

There is a camp of web developers who will tell you the topics in the following three chapters, all of which deal with different types of referential integrity, are unnecessary overhead. They will tell you that application level checks are sufficient to protect your data, and that database-level constraints are sure to make your application slow. It turns out that whenever I meet someone from this camp, it just so happens that they are die-hard MySQL users. Not surprising, because until recently, MySQL did not support referential integrity. MySQL, before version 5.0, was not a *relational* database management system, but rather simply a *database* management system. What these people are actually telling you is that RDBMSs are no better than DBMSs, and when the idea is framed that way, it becomes clear that this camp simply doesn't fully understand why *relational* databases exist in the first place.

When MySQL came on the scene, it had wild success because it was well-packaged and easy to install not only on Linux, but on Windows, too. MySQL and PHP swept the Internet community because they were so easy to set up, and you could be up and running and writing web pages in just a few hours.[*] As developers got used to their tools, they got used to the deficiencies in those tools, too. So the lacking of a feature

---

[*] Replace "MySQL and PHP" in this sentence with "Rails." In the Rails community, we must be careful not to fall into the same trap of defining as good all of those things that are in Rails and defining as bad all of those things that are not currently in Rails.

became a feature in and of itself. I have actually heard very highly paid consultants say, "MySQL doesn't support referential integrity because you don't need it!"

Since enterprise-level applications *do* need referential integrity, as well as many other features available in other more mature RDBMSs (e.g., views, transactions, triggers, isolation, etc.), MySQL has added support for it in version 5.0. Therefore, the argument that you don't need it because MySQL doesn't have it no longer holds water. MySQL now has it *because you need it.*

Another myth worth dispelling is that referential integrity is just training wheels that you should take off when your application is in production. This type of thinking could not be more backward. Referential integrity constraints certainly do help you find your application's bugs, but it's foolhardy to think you'll find them all before you decide it's time to throw users at the system. This warning holds doubly true when you start releasing updates once your application is already live. Testing every conceivable use-case, including full regression testing for each release, is next to impossible. On the other hand, your users—including Internet bots, both neutral and malicious—will make your application run the gauntlet. They will find use cases you never imagined. Production is not the place where you want to find referential integrity bugs. But worse, production is also not the place where you want referential integrity bugs to go unnoticed. Your database constraints and referential integrity checks are the last line of defense protecting your data before things go awry. If you want to keep your data intact, you want your constraints to be as complete as they can be.

Operations and Reporting

When you launch your website, it will be the primary (probably the only) consumer of your database. All of the queries your database handles will be related to making your app go. If everything goes well, you'll have lots of users and you'll start collecting and generating lots of data about those users and your website's operation in general.

Around this time, the business development team will start asking you questions. How many new users join your site each day? Each hour? Is there a geographic distribution to your user base? What features are heavily used and which go unused? How many repeat visitors did you have last week, and what was the revenue result of the costly marketing campaign?

The natural thing to do to answer these questions is to start building reports. You add a report that breaks down new visitors and repeat visitors by day and hour. You add a report that shows access by state—perhaps plotting hits on a U.S. and world map. You add a report that shows revenue events as they relate to different traffic sources—external links versus unreferred traffic versus links from your email campaign. You add more and more reports almost as quickly as your business users can request them. Your business users are delighted. They check the reports frequently to increase their pleasure at how well the website you wrote is functioning. That is, until suddenly, one day, performance plummets. All of the metrics in your reports take a nosedive. The business users, flustered, take to looking at the reports you've generated *all day*, hoping to make sense of what went wrong.

What went wrong is that your reports are killing your site. As your site's popularity and success increase, so does the amount of data your reports need to process. What seemed like a reasonably fast query—maybe 10 seconds to give user statistics for the last month by hour—now takes 30 seconds or maybe even a couple of minutes. And since your company became so successful, you hired more people who are looking at those reports. And since each report now takes minutes to generate, your business users fire off a *bunch* of simultaneous reports and then go get a cup of coffee. All of this has the effect of bogging down your site, and locking out the very users to whom you are trying to serve web pages to.

I call this the Heisenberg Uncertainty Principal of Website Reporting. If you try to report out of the same database in which you are collecting your data, the simple act of loading the reports creates abnormal load on your database. That in turn makes your web pages slow, which causes your users to leave your site frustrated, which causes you to load more reports to figure out what's going on, which frustrates yet more users, and so on. Whenever you look, you impact the system in a negative way.

The solution is simply to not run reporting queries on your production database. But that is easier said than done.

A common shortcut many people take around building a data warehouse is to create a slave copy of their database, and run heavy reporting queries there, out of the path of users. This is not a good idea. To understand why, it's important to be familiar with the difference between Online Transaction Processing (OLTP) and Online Analytical Processing (OLAP).

OLTP comprises the set of queries that store, update, and retrieve data. Examples would be creating blog entries, then displaying them to website visitors. OLTP queries are engineered to execute quickly, as there is generally a user waiting for the result of the query. Speed is realized through a highly normalized schema. Each row contains a small amount of data and pointers to related data in other tables. Virtually all websites are OLTP systems.

OLAP queries are geared toward garnering business intelligence out of large quantities of data. OLAP queries process millions upon millions of records generated by individual OLTP queries. A sample OLAP query might be one that answers the question, "How many customers who bought a sale item also bought a nonsale item, broken down by store location and week?" In addition to ad-hoc queries such as this one, nightly or quarterly generated reports are OLAP queries, too, and therefore real-time results are generally not a requirement of an OLAP system.

Because OLTP and OLAP queries are so different, it's not surprising that a database design that is well-suited for OLTP may not be well-suited for OLAP, and vice versa.

In fact, as the amount of data in a highly normalized system increases, coupled with increasing complexity of reporting queries, it's often the case that reporting queries start to take seemingly infinite time, or infinite memory, or both.

In OLAP, the goal is not to have quick inserts, updates, and deletes, but rather to filter, group, and aggregate huge amounts of data based on certain criteria. For this task, highly normalized schemas result in lots of costly joins on massive amounts of data. Denormalizing the schema to avoid most, or even all, of the joins can make OLAP queries complete in a reasonable amount of time.

So a highly normalized database is good for normal site operations, but a denormalized database is good for reporting. Can these two be reconciled? Unfortunately, no, they should not be reconciled within the same database. Denormalizing data in an operational database can quickly lead to bugs (so-called *insert, update,* and *delete anomalies*). And staying normalized causes reporting queries to be unreasonably slow, and downright dangerous if they are executed in the same database as are your OLTP operational queries.

The proper place to run reporting queries is in a *data warehouse*. A data warehouse is, in rough terms, a place where all of your historical data resides, and in a format that is optimized for complex reporting queries. OLAP systems rely on highly denormalized data, usually in a star or snowflake normalization pattern, which increases the speed of processing huge amounts of data by eliminating joins on many tables. Here, inconsistencies are not a concern because your star schema data is generated from your DKNF data, which you bend over backward to keep accurate.

Getting data out of your production database and into a data warehouse is not an easy task, though, and it's hard to convince anyone that you need to spend loads of time building a data warehouse before you have any meaningful data to report on. However, as soon as your website appears to be doing reasonably well with users, it's time to invest some resources in building a data warehouse. And do it before you build lots of one-off reports that will surely cause the Heisenberg Uncertainty Principle of Website Reporting to set in.

Therefore, while chaining a slave off your database to run reporting queries (an extremely common practice in the MySQL world) seems like low hanging fruit, it's really not the fruit you want. It's really kind of like rotten fruit. The fresh, delicious fruit you want for reporting is a data warehouse.

Unfortunately, building a data warehouse is beyond the scope of this book. There are many books on the topic, though. A good introduction is *The Data Warehouse Toolkit: The Complete Guide to Dimensional Modeling* by Ralph Kimball (Wiley), but a topic that *does* fall squarely in the scope of this book is ensuring that your website scales for *users*. And that is the topic of the next several chapters on schema design.

## CHAPTER 5

Building a Solid Data Model

Data modeling is an art form. Based on the previous chapter, we begin with the principle that the database is not simply a place where information is temporarily dumped but rather it is the fortress that houses and protects your company's critical information assets. You've got to design the data layer so that it does its job of protecting your data.

This is accomplished in part by ensuring your schema provides for complete referential integrity and has appropriate constraint checking. Further, the data layer's design should be one that makes future changes and additions easy. Designed incorrectly, seemingly small changes in business needs, if they require changes to the data layer, can often become Herculean efforts if the initial design is not flexible, or is crippled by inconsistencies revealed by the design change. Adhering to domain key/ normal form (DK/NF) ensures, among other things, that it is easy to add additional layers of complexity on top of your data model without the need to redesign the entire schema. As it happens, DKNF is also a necessity to get the most protection out of referential integrity checks.

Theatre Tickets

Over the course of this book, we will build a website for movie ticket sales. In this chapter, we construct a first pass at the data model. We will start simple with a very small set of tables and secure those tables with database constraints and referential integrity checks in the data layer and analogous checks at the application layer. In Chapter 6, we will expand upon our data model, and refactor it into third normal form (3NF) to remove redundancy, achieve greater data integrity, and to ensure flexibility for future needs. In Chapter 8, we will dive into DK/NF to achieve referential integrity for more complex relationships that emerge. We conclude with advanced considerations in Chapter 9, such as the use of stored procedures and triggers for constraint checking that exceeds the database's built-in capabilities.

After we have added all of this structure, layer by layer, we finally have a very solid data layer atop which we can confidently build an application.

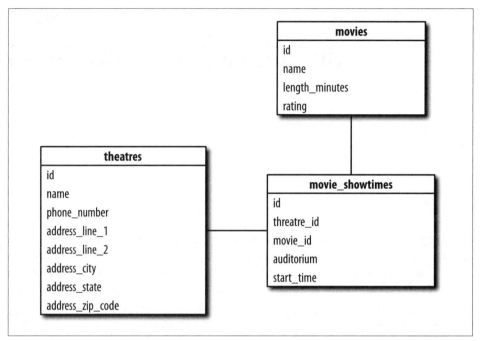

Figure 5-1. A simple schema for a movie ticket website

Starting Simple

The data model in Figure 5-1 shows a tiny subset of tables necessary for our ticket sales website.

At the heart of the schema is a table that stores basic information about movies, called `movies`. Movies have a name, a running length, and a rating. An entry in this table might be *Casablanca*, with a running time of 102 minutes, and a rating of *PG*.

There are also theatres, stored in the `theatres` table, which in addition to the theatre's name, contains the address and phone number of the theatre as well.

Movie showtimes are listed in the `movie_showtimes` table. Each movie showtime record stores the movie being shown, the theatre in which it plays, and its start time. Additionally, there is an auditorium field, which we can use to prevent double-booking a single auditorium. Example 5-1 shows the DDL for this schema.

Example 5-1. The DDL for our initial move showtimes schema

```
create sequence movies_id_seq;
create table movies (
  id integer,
  name varchar(256),
  length_minutes integer,
  rating varchar(8),
  primary key (id)
```

```
);

create sequence theatres_id_seq;
create table theatres (
  id integer,
  name varchar(256),
  address_line_1 varchar(256),
  address_line_2 varchar(256),
  address_city varchar(128),
  address_state varchar(2),
  address_zip_code varchar(9),
  phone_number varchar(10),
  primary key (id)
);

create sequence movie_showtimes_id_seq;
create table movie_showtimes (
  id integer,
  movie_id integer,
  theatre_id integer,
  auditorium varchar(16),
  start_time timestamp with time zone,
  primary key (id)
);
```

This is where most books that focus only on the framework generally stop; their next step would be to create model classes and a user interface and begin playing around with a budding site. That's strategy's fine for books that are essentially framework manuals, which don't have time to spend on issues that do not directly concern the framework.

This book does not stop here, however. First, because we know a lot more about our problem domain than we have shown here. For example, this is a ticket *sales* site, but we don't even have a place to store orders yet. Mapping out everything we know up front will reveal areas for refactoring, or other types of improvements that we can't see with just a subset of our overall data model. It doesn't make much sense to spend time and effort on application logic when we almost certainly will have to throw most or all of it away after the next tiny database revision.

The second reason we don't stop here is because this data model is tragically fragile. Indeed, this is a data model that represents a dumping ground for data, rather than a *fortress*. This is not only a problem from the perspective of our mantra: that an enterprise architecture cannot rely on the beneficence of the application layer to maintain order in the database layer; it is also a problem because our work in the application layer would be fraught with time wasted hunting for simple bugs that we would rather the data layer prevented us from creating in the first place. These problems would debilitate our site and our development process in short order.

It's a tenet held by the Rails community that development should start with a small kernel and proceed with many quick iterations, building organically upon that kernel until a perfect, living, breathing application has emerged. I don't not disagree with the tenets of agile development, but rather with the size of the starting kernel.

In fact, there *are* a number of problems with our simple data model already, and they should be managed before they cause us problems. These problems will be revealed in this chapter via negative unit tests. We will expect our invalid use of our models to cause errors, which our tests will check for. However, the tests will pass, making it plain that it would be foolhardy to place any faith in what we've got so far and additional work must be done to lock down the data layer before it makes sense to proceed.

Even after we have solved the problems described in this chapter, it is still too early to proceed. Although *this* simple data model will be locked down, as noted earlier, there are still many more things wrong with our schema, which will become evident when we start coding and find ourselves exploring obvious business needs that we could have foreseen easily. The next few chapters are devoted to eradicating these flaws, with an ultimate goal of making spotting problems and building solid, flexible data models second nature.

 To the point of kernel size, then, the following principle: at each step, we should add everything we know we need to the layer we are working on, and no more. It's at that point that we can rush off to tackle the layer above.

To get started, we must first define the classes against which we write our unit tests. At this point, there are no model-based validations because we are working on the data layer. We'll add model validations later in this chapter. We do, however, define the relationships at this point. See Example 5-2.

Example 5-2. Basic ActiveRecord model classes for the schema defined in Example 5-1

```
class Movie < ActiveRecord::Base
  has_many :movie_showtimes
end

class Threatre < ActiveRecord::Base
  has_many :movie_showtimes
end

class MovieShowtimes < ActiveRecord::Base
  belongs_to :movie
  belongs_to :theatre
end
```

Constraints

The first problem with our data model is that there is nothing constraining the values in any of the table columns except for our own good intentions and, frankly, that is not enough. Looking at the movies table, the rating column of the table could be anything, regardless of whether the value is a valid rating identifier; *asdf* would be acceptable. Any of the columns could be null or empty. The movie length could be zero or negative, which doesn't make sense for a movie. The schema as-is also supports duplicate entries, which we know we don't want.

Example 5-3 shows a set of unit tests that test for all of these conditions. They are negative tests that try to save invalid data to the databases.

Example 5-3. Unit tests for the Movie class defined in Example 5-2

```ruby
require File.dirname(__FILE__) + '/../test_helper'
require 'movie'

class MovieTestCase < Test::Unit::TestCase

protected

  def test_for_db_error(error_message, &block)
    begin
      yield
    rescue ActiveRecord::StatementInvalid
      database_threw_error = true
    rescue
      something_else_threw_error = true
    end
    assert !something_else_threw_error, "There is an error in our test code"
    assert database_threw_error && !something_else_threw_error, error_message
  end

public

  def test_db_no_name
    movie = Movie.new(:rating => 'PG', :length_minutes => '10')
    test_for_db_error("Database did not catch null name") do
      movie.save!
    end
  end

  def test_db_empty_name
    movie = Movie.new(:name => '', :rating => 'PG', :length_minutes => '10')
    test_for_db_error("Database did not catch empty name") do
      movie.save!
    end
  end

  def test_db_same_movie
    movie = Movie.new(:name => 'Casablanca', :rating => 'PG',
                      :length_minutes => '10')
    movie_dup = movie.clone
    test_for_db_error("Database did not catch duplicate movie") do
      movie.save!
      movie_dup.save!
    end
  end
```

```ruby
  def test_db_no_rating
    movie = Movie.new(:name => 'Casablanca', :length_minutes => '10')
    test_for_db_error("Database did not catch null rating") do
      movie.save!
    end
  end

  def test_db_invalid_rating
    movie = Movie.new(:name => 'Casablanca', :rating => 'Fred',
                      :length_minutes => '10')
    test_for_db_error("Database did not catch invalid rating") do
      movie.save!
    end
  end

  def test_db_no_length
    movie = Movie.new(:name => 'Casablanca', :rating => 'PG')
    test_for_db_error("Database did not catch null movie length") do
      movie.save!
    end
  end

  def test_db_zero_length
    movie = Movie.new(:name => 'Casablanca', :rating => 'PG',
                      :length_minutes => '0')
    test_for_db_error("Database did not catch zero length movie") do
      movie.save!
    end
  end

  def test_db_negative_length
    movie = Movie.new(:name => 'Casablanca', :rating => 'PG',
                      :length_minutes => '-10')
    test_for_db_error("Database did not catch negative movie length") do
      movie.save!
    end
  end

end
```

Note that these are all negative unit tests; the tests attempt to do something that should not work and verify that it was not allowed. Negative unit tests are just as important as positive tests, if not more so. Often, developers are drawn toward writing unit tests that test the obvious functionality of a class in the way they intend to use that class five minutes later. Although those tests are fine, and they *may* detect a code change that causes a bug down the road, negative tests that test the boundaries of valid data provide much more peace of mind. If code is written with a bug that might lead to data corruption, running negative unit tests ensures that the bug will cause no long-term damage.

To simplify writing the tests, and to conform to the tenet of Don't Repeat Yourself (DRY), a method test_for_db_error was created, which takes a block containing the offending negative test code. This method verifies that a database exception is thrown and not some other type of exception, such as a typo. If there is no exception thrown, the test fails because we were expecting our error to be caught by the data layer. To be even more DRY, we'll move this method to *test_helper.rb* before our next revision so that other test cases can utilize the method as well.

Below are the results of running these tests, highly condensed to show only the relevant information. As we expected, they all fail, indicating there is still work to be done in the data layer before we start getting any fancier in our application layer. See Example 5-4.

Example 5-4. Results from running the tests defined in Example 5-3

```
dan-chaks-computer-2:~/web/theatre-tickets chak$ ruby test/unit/movie_test_case.rb
Loaded suite test/unit/movie_test_case
Started
FFFFFFFF
Finished in 0.059249 seconds.

  1) Failure: test_db_empty_name(MovieTestCase)
Database did not catch empty name.
  2) Failure: test_db_invalid_rating(MovieTestCase)
Database did not catch invalid rating.
  3) Failure: test_db_negative_length(MovieTestCase)
Database did not catch negative movie length.
  4) Failure: test_db_no_length(MovieTestCase)
Database did not catch null movie length.
  5) Failure: test_db_no_name(MovieTestCase)
Database did not catch null name.
  6) Failure: test_db_no_rating(MovieTestCase)
Database did not catch null rating.
  7) Failure: test_db_same_movie(MovieTestCase)
Database did not catch duplicate movie.
  8) Failure: test_db_zero_length(MovieTestCase)
Database did not catch zero length movie.

8 tests, 16 assertions, 8 failures, 0 errors
```

Example 5-5 shows the `movies` table reworked to disallow invalid data.

Example 5-5. The movies table DDL from Example 5-1, extended to perform constraint checking

```
create sequence movies_id_seq;
create table movies (
  id integer not null
    default nextval('movies_id_seq'),
  name varchar(256) not null unique
    check (length(name) > 0),
  length_minutes integer not null
    check (length_minutes > 0),
  rating varchar(8) not null
    check (rating in ('Unrated', 'G', 'PG', 'PG-13', 'R', 'NC-17')),
  primary key (id)
);
```

First, all columns that should not be null (all of them in this case) are marked with not null.

Next, we've add check constraints to each column that takes freeform data. We check that the length of the name column is at least one character, the running length of the movie is at least one minute, and that the movie rating is one of six possible valid values: Unrated, G, PG, PG-13, R, or NC-17.

To ensure there are no duplicate movie entries, we also add the unique keyword to the name definition. Note that in Postgres, this creates an implicit index on the name column. The index is used to make the process of checking for uniqueness fast internally within the database, but it also will speed up any queries where we query movies by name. Indexing is covered in greater detail later in this chapter.

Finally, the id column has a default added. It's the same value that Rails would assign automatically to that column, but this helps if we ever have to add data from the psql prompt, or if we write advanced application code that bypasses ActiveRecord and uses raw SQL.

When we run our test cases against our updated schema, all of the tests pass, which is a good step forward. See Example 5-6.

Example 5-6. Results of running the unit tests defined in Example 5-3 after adding constraint checking to the movies table

```
dan-chaks-computer-2:~/web/theatre-tickets chak$ ruby test/unit/movie_test_case.rb
Loaded suite test/unit/movie_test_case
Started
........
Finished in 0.0751310000000001 seconds.

8 tests, 16 assertions, 0 failures, 0 errors
```

Unfortunately, we still have problems to work out. The goal of the tests was for a database exception to be thrown. However, we never want an exception to be thrown during normal operation. Exceptions are meant for exceptional situations only, and bad user input, for example, is not so exceptional. Our model class should detect when we are about to do something bad and prevent it. For example, when the error is related to user input, the application should prompt the user for better input.

What we would like, then, is for exactly the same code as we had in our previous set of tests to run, but rather than throw a database exception during a save call, the model class should simply refuse to save through to the database and return false.

In the following code, we've recast all of the database tests as model tests. In doing so, we've removed the wrapping of the code with test_for_db_error. These are still negative tests, but we want to assert that the records that would have been invalid did not get saved. Because save returns false and we want to ensure validations fails, we assert that !save is true.

Keep in mind that while the database tests themselves have been removed to save space, we would certainly want to keep them around in practice. See Example 5-7. These tests focus on the Model classes themselves complementing the tests of Example 5-3.

Example 5-7. Negative unit tests for the Movie class

```ruby
require File.dirname(__FILE__) + '/../test_helper'
require 'movie'

class MovieTestCase < Test::Unit::TestCase

  # model constraints tests

  def test_no_name
    movie = Movie.new(:rating => 'PG', :length_minutes => '10')
    assert movie.new_record?, "Model constraints did not catch null name"
  end

  def test_empty_name
    movie = Movie.new(:name => '', :rating => 'PG', :length_minutes => '10')
    assert !movie.save, "Model constraints did not catch empty name"
  end

  def test_same_movie
    movie = Movie.new(:name => 'Casablanca', :rating => 'PG',
                                :length_minutes => '10')
    movie_dup = movie.clone
    movie.save
    assert !movie_dup.save, "Model constraints did not catch duplicate movie"
  end

  def test_no_rating
    movie = Movie.new(:name => 'Casablanca', :length_minutes => '10')
    assert !movie.save, "Model constraints did not catch null rating"
  end

  def test_invalid_rating
    movie = Movie.new(:name => 'Casablanca', :rating => 'Fred',
                      :length_minutes => '10')
    assert !movie.save, "Model constraints did not catch invalid rating"
  end

  def test_no_length
    movie = Movie.new(:name => 'Casablanca', :rating => 'PG')
    assert !movie.save, "Model constraints did not catch null movie length"
  end

  def test_zero_length
    movie = Movie.new(:name => 'Casablanca', :rating => 'PG',
                      :length_minutes => '0')
    assert !movie.save, "Model constraints did not catch zero length movie"
  end

  def test_negative_length
    movie = Movie.new(:name => 'Casablanca', :rating => 'PG', :length_minutes =>
```

```
'-10')
    assert !movie.save, "Model constraints did not catch negative movie length"
  end

end
```

The output from running these new tests is shown below, again compressed for brevity. The eight database tests that test for exceptions continue to pass, but the model tests fail now because of those very exceptions. At this point, this is what we expect. The database is doing its job, but the model is not. See Example 5-8.

Example 5-8. The output of running the tests defined in Example 5-7

```
dan-chaks-computer-2:~/web/theatre-tickets chak$ ruby test/unit/movie_test_case.rb
Loaded suite test/unit/movie_test_case
Started
........EEEEEEEE
Finished in 0.050854 seconds.

  1) Error: test_empty_name(MovieTestCase):
ActiveRecord::StatementInvalid: PGError: ERROR:    new row for relation
"movies" violates check constraint "movies_name_check"

  2) Error: test_invalid_rating(MovieTestCase):
ActiveRecord::StatementInvalid: PGError: ERROR:    new row for relation
 "movies" violates check constraint "movies_rating_check"

  3) Error: test_negative_length(MovieTestCase):
ActiveRecord::StatementInvalid: PGError: ERROR:    new row for relation
 "movies" violates check constraint "movies_length_minutes_check"

  4) Error: test_no_length(MovieTestCase):
ActiveRecord::StatementInvalid: PGError: ERROR:    null value in column
 "length_minutes" violates not-null constraint

  5) Error: test_no_name(MovieTestCase):
ActiveRecord::StatementInvalid: PGError: ERROR:    null value in
 column "name" violates not-null constraint

  6) Error: test_no_rating(MovieTestCase):
ActiveRecord::StatementInvalid: PGError: ERROR:    null value in
column "rating" violates not-null constraint

  7) Error: test_same_movie(MovieTestCase):
ActiveRecord::StatementInvalid: PGError: ERROR:
duplicate key violates unique constraint "movies_name_key"

  8) Error: test_zero_length(MovieTestCase):
ActiveRecord::StatementInvalid: PGError: ERROR:
new row for relation "movies" violates check constraint "movies_length_minutes_check"

16 tests, 16 assertions, 0 failures, 8 errors
```

Note that the tests did not fail due to an assertion *failure*, but with a full-on *error*. That's because our data layer is now an active participant in enforcing our rules. Exceptions were thrown and consequently no records were saved. Without the constraints we added earlier, the tests would not have failed as a result of database exceptions but due to logic errors. Our assertions would have failed, but meanwhile invalid data would have snuck through to the data layer. Try it yourself: remove the database constraints and run the tests again. How does the output differ?

It's time now to add model validations that will prevent normal code flow from throwing database exceptions. Example 5-9 is our updated model class for the Movie class.

Example 5-9. The Movie class with model validations

```
class Movie < ActiveRecord::Base
  validates_presence_of :name, :rating, :length_minutes
  validates_uniqueness_of :name
  validates_length_of :name, :maximum => 256
  validates_numericality_of :length_minutes, :only_integer => true

  has_many :movie_showtimes

  VALID_RATINGS = ['Unrated', 'G', 'PG', 'PG-13', 'R', 'NC-17']

  def validate_length_minutes
    if length_minutes && length_minutes <= 0
      errors.add 'length_minutes',
        'must be greater than zero'
    end
  end

  def validate_rating_type
    if !VALID_RATINGS.include?(rating)
      errors.add 'rating',
        "must be #{VALID_RATINGS[0..-2].join(', ')} or #{VALID_RATINGS[-1]}"
    end
  end

  def validate
    validate_length_minutes
    validate_rating_type
  end
end
```

Each database constraint has an analogous model validation:

- Each not null constraint is translated into a validates_presence_of validation.
- Our unique constraint appears as a validates_uniqueness_of validation.
- The check constraint on the length of the name column is represented via a validates_length_of call. It's important to test upper-length boundaries on all freeform fields, as failing to do so would result in an exception thrown if a user enters an extremely long movie name.

- Similarly, for `length_minutes`, we verify that the input is of the correct type for the physical storage, with `validates_numericality_of` and the `:only_integer` flag set to true.

There are two tests accomplished easily in the data layer for which there aren't any analogous built-in Rails validators. For those—validating that the movie length is greater than zero and the rating is valid—we must write our own custom validators.

Armed with our new model validators, we run our unit tests again. Example 5-10 shows the results.

Example 5-10. The results of running the unit tests in Example 5-7 against the new model definition from Example 5-8

```
dan-chaks-computer-2:~/web/theatre-tickets chak$ ruby test/unit/movie_test_case.rb
Loaded suite test/unit/movie_test_case
Started
FFFFFFFF........
Finished in 1.194743 seconds.

  1) Failure: test_db_empty_name(MovieTestCase)
There is an error in our test code.
  2) Failure: test_db_invalid_rating(MovieTestCase)
There is an error in our test code.
  3) Failure: test_db_negative_length(MovieTestCase)
There is an error in our test code.
  4) Failure: test_db_no_length(MovieTestCase)
There is an error in our test code.
  5) Failure: test_db_no_name(MovieTestCase)
There is an error in our test code.
  6) Failure: test_db_no_rating(MovieTestCase)
There is an error in our test code.
  7) Failure: test_db_same_movie(MovieTestCase)
There is an error in our test code.
  8) Failure: test_db_zero_length(MovieTestCase)
There is an error in our test code.

16 tests, 16 assertions, 8 failures, 0 errors
```

All of the new unit tests pass, but now our old ones fail. This is because our database tests assume a database exception is thrown to validate the negative test. However, now our models correctly prevent the exception from ever being reached. We still want to test the data layer, though, and we still can. Rails provides a mechanism to skip validation on save. The `save` method, it happens, is a wrapper around calling the method `save_with_validation` with the parameter `true`. To make the tests run as we expect, we need to replace the `save` calls with calls to `save_with_validation` with the parameter `false`, like this:

```
def test_db_no_name
    movie = Movie.new(:rating => 'PG', :length_minutes => '10')
    test_for_db_error("Database did not catch null name") do
      movie.save_with_validation(false)
```

```
      end
    end
```

Here's the output of running the tests with this change:

```
dan-chaks-computer-2:~/web/theatre-tickets chak$ ruby test/unit/movie_test_case.rb
Loaded suite test/unit/movie_test_case
Started
...............
Finished in 0.445988 seconds.

16 tests, 24 assertions, 0 failures, 0 errors
```

Now all tests pass.

Mythbusting

It's time again to dispel some frequently propagated myths.

The first myth is that database constraints impose an undue burden on the database and slow down your application. It's worth pointing out, based on this controlled example, that the time consumed by checking database constraints in negligible. Adding database constraints contributed only 0.015 seconds to the overall test run.

The next myth is that model validations are all you need and database constraints are a waste of time. The repeated refrain is You Aren't Going to Need It (YAGNI). Unfortunately, the fact that the Rails API itself provides easy mechanisms to skip validation, as we did in our second iteration of database unit tests with save_with_valida tion(false), means you *are* going to need it. Perhaps as a disciplined developer you will pledge to avoid using the API this way. However, when your site becomes a success and you hire a dozen additional developers, will your own discipline be enough?

In addition to save_with_validation(false), there are also more innocuous sounding API methods that also skip validation, such as update_attribute. See the sidebar, next, where the API for this method and the related method update_attribute_with_valida tion_skipping is reproduced.

Rails API Methods That Lack Validation

Here are Rails API methods that skip validation:

update_attribute(name, value)
> Updates a single attribute and saves the record. This is especially useful for Boolean flags on existing records. Note: this method is overwritten by the Validation module that'll make sure that updates made with this method don't get subjected to validation checks. Hence, attributes can be updated even if the full object isn't valid. [sic]

update_attribute_with_validation_skipping(name, value)
> Updates a single attribute and saves the record without going through the normal validation procedure. This is especially useful for Boolean flags on existing records.

The regular `update_attribute` method in `Base` is replaced with this when the validations module is mixed in, which it is by default.

Although the documentation says skipping validation can be useful for toggling a Boolean value, there is nothing about these methods that ensures that's all you are doing. The reality of the situation is that the maintainers of the API had a need for a lightweight mechanism to make updates *they* were sure would be safe, but now Pandora's box has been opened, and along with it the ability to circumvent the safety of model validation on a whim.

Further, there are many types of constraints that are difficult or impossible to express or guarantee at the application level but are very simply expressed in the data layer. Our custom validators for movie length and rating are simple examples, and we will see more examples in the following chapters. As application-level validators become more and more complex, it becomes easier for bugs to creep in and prevent them from fulfilling their purpose. Data layer constraints, on the other hand, are generally very succinct, and in these cases, simple really does make a difference.

Finally, because model validations are often more verbose than the corresponding database constraints, it's easy to omit them, or to lose them during refactorings or rewrites of application code. Database constraints, on the other hand, do not need to be constantly declared and maintained in order to function. After they have been specified once, they *become* part of the data model and require a deliberate action to remove them. In the database, there is no such thing as `save_with_validation(false)`.

Referential Integrity

We now have a full set of constraints: physical at the data layer, and also logical at the application layer. However, we still have a major problem. Although we have references from the `movie_showtimes` table to the `theatres` and `movies` tables in the form of the `theatre_id` and `movie_id` columns, there is nothing in our data layer to guarantee that those references are valid, or even present, for that matter. Similarly, although we defined our `belongs_to` relationships in the `MovieShowtime` class, there is nothing guaranteeing those references are present from the model perspective, either. Our simple data model lacks referential integrity enforcement.

Now that we have gotten the hang of adding database and model tests, we'll proceed at a quicker pace in testing the `MovieShowtime` class. Example 5-11 shows our test cases. We define a `setup` method, which creates a `theatre` object and a `movie` object. Most of our other tests will be concerned with leaving one, the other, or both of these objects out of the attempts to save a new `MovieShowtime` object.

We normally would have tests for constraint checking for the presence and length of the `auditorium` field, and the presence of the `start_time` field. However, you've gotten the hang of that now from our experience with the movie test cases, so we'll leave those out to save space. See Example 5-11.

Example 5-11. Unit test cases for the MovieShowtimes class

```ruby
require File.dirname(__FILE__) + '/../test_helper'

class MovieShowtimeTestCase < Test::Unit::TestCase

  def setup
    @theatre = Theatre.create!(
        :name => 'Ruby Palace',
        :address_line_1 => '123 Broadway',
        :address_city => 'Cambridge',
        :address_state => 'MA',
        :address_zip_code => '02139',
        :phone_number => '5555555555')
    @movie = Movie.create!(
        :name => 'Casablanca',
        :rating => 'PG',
        :length_minutes => '10')
  end

  #
  # model tests - referential integrity
  #

  def test_add_showtime_no_movie
    st = MovieShowtime.new(:theatre => @theatre,
                           :auditorium => '1',
                           :start_time => Time.now.xmlschema)
    assert !st.save, "Model validation allowed save with no movie"
  end

  def test_add_showtime_no_theatre
    st = MovieShowtime.new(:movie => @movie,
                           :auditorium => '1',
                           :start_time => Time.now.xmlschema)
    assert !st.save, "Model validation allowed save with no theatre"
  end

  #
  # database tests - referential integrity
  #

  def test_db_add_showtime_no_movie
    test_for_db_error "Database allowed save with no movie." do
      st = MovieShowtime.new(:theatre => @theatre,
                             :auditorium => '1',
                             :start_time => Time.now.xmlschema)
      st.save_with_validation(false)
    end
  end

  def test_db_add_showtime_no_theatre
    test_for_db_error "Database allowed save with no theatre." do
      st = MovieShowtime.new(:movie => @movie,
                             :auditorium => '1',
                             :start_time => Time.now.xmlschema)
```

```
      st.save_with_validation(false)
    end
  end

  def test_db_add_showtime_invalid_references
    test_for_db_error "Database allowed save with invalid references." do
      st = MovieShowtime.new(:movie_id => 12,
                             :theatre_id => 99,
                             :auditorium => '1')
      st.save_with_validation(false)
    end
  end
end
```

As expected, because we have neither database constraints nor model validations, all of our tests fail. See Example 5-12.

Example 5-12. Results of running the unit tests from Example 5-11

```
dan-chaks-computer-2:~/web/theatre-tickets chak$ ruby
test/unit/movie_showtime_test_case.rb
Loaded suite test/unit/movie_showtime_test_case
Started
FFFFF
Finished in 0.112901 seconds.

  1) Failure: test_add_showtime_no_movie(MovieShowtimeTestCase)
Model validation allowed showtime save with no movie.
  2) Failure: test_add_showtime_no_theatre(MovieShowtimeTestCase)
Model validation allowed showtime save with no theatre.
  3) Failure: test_db_add_showtime_invalid_references(MovieShowtimeTestCase)
Database allowed save of movie_showtime with invalid references.
  4) Failure: test_db_add_showtime_no_movie(MovieShowtimeTestCase)
Database allowed save of movie_showtime with no movie.
  5) Failure: test_db_add_showtime_no_theatre(MovieShowtimeTestCase)
Database allowed save of movie_showtime with no theatre.
5 tests, 8 assertions, 5 failures, 0 errors
```

Example 5-13 shows our updated movie_showtime table, redesigned to catch these problems at the data layer and prevent invalid data from entering our database.

Example 5-13. movie_showtimes DDL updated with constraint checking

```
create table movie_showtimes (
  id integer not null
    default nextval('movie_showtimes_id_seq'),
  movie_id integer not null
    references movies(id),
  theatre_id integer not null
    references theatres(id),
  auditorium varchar(16) not null
    check (length(auditorium) > 0),
  start_time timestamp with time zone not null,
  primary key (id)
);
```

Here, because for each column we reference only one foreign column at a time, we use the simplest syntax for a foreign key reference:

```
column_name type references reftable(refcolumn)
```

We could also add the reference outside of the table definition. This gives us the added benefit of being able to name the foreign key reference and also specify compound key references:

```
alter table table_name add foreign key ( column_name [, ... ] )
   references reftable [ ( refcolumn [, ... ] ) ];
```

At the moment, we don't have any need for compound key references, but we will see them in Chapter 7.

Example 5-14 shows our updated model class definition, which also enforces the presence of the appropriate references.

Example 5-14. MovieShowtime class with model validation

```
class MovieShowtime < ActiveRecord::Base
  belongs_to :movie
  belongs_to :theatre

  validates_presence_of :movie, :theatre
  validates_presence_of :start_time, :auditorium
  validates_presence_of :auditorium

  validates_length_of :auditorium, :maximum => 16
end
```

Now all of our tests pass. Here are the results:

```
dan-chaks-computer-2:~/web/theatre-tickets chak$ ruby
test/unit/movie_showtime_test_case.rb
Loaded suite test/unit/movie_showtime_test_case
Started
...........
Finished in 0.117669 seconds.

5 tests, 8 assertions, 0 failures, 0 errors
```

One important point to note about our two sets of tests is that although our model tests checked for the *presence* of the foreign key references, they did not check the *validity* of those references. Take a closer look at our third test, test_db_add_showtimes_inva lid_references. We didn't create an analogous model test because there is no practical way to make the test pass. A scenario in which this type of bug might turn up would be if two editors were working with our site at the same time. One editor loads a page to create a movie showtime, and selects *Casablanca*. The other editor, meanwhile, deletes *Casablanca* from the movie database. When the first editor submits her showtime, passing the movie id for *Casablanca* to the back-end, the record is already gone and the save of the showtime would cause an error. The way around this possibility requires a hefty performance trade-off: load the record to be referenced first, and pass the object rather than the *id*, as in our other tests.

Another problem is that if we call the `destroy` method on a movie record referenced by the `movie_showtimes` table, ActiveRecord is happy to oblige, leaving the associated `movie_showtime` record in an invalid state. Luckily, our database foreign key references are already set up to prevent this from happening. Below are four new tests; the first two are database tests that attempt to destroy the `movie` and `theatre` objects after they have been referenced by a `MovieShowtime` object. These tests actually pass because we are testing that the data layer catches the bugs, and it does. The associated model tests fail, however. They throw database exceptions, as in the tests shown in Example 5-15. Note that without the database constraints, the tests still would not pass but due to an assertion failure.

Example 5-15. Database unit tests ensuring invalid destroys are not allowed

```
#
# database invalid destroy tests
#
def test_db_prevents_invalid_theatre_destroy
  st = MovieShowtime.create!(
    :theatre => @theatre,
    :movie => @movie,
    :auditorium => '1',
    :start_time => Time.now.xmlschema)
  test_for_db_error "Database allowed referenced theatre to be deleted" do
    @theatre.destroy_without_callbacks
  end
end

def test_db_prevents_invalid_movie_destroy
  st = MovieShowtime.create!(
    :theatre => @theatre,
    :movie => @movie,
    :auditorium => '1',
    :start_time => Time.now.xmlschema)
  test_for_db_error "Database allowed referenced movie to be deleted" do
    @movie.destroy_without_callbacks
  end
end


#
# model invalid destroy tests
#
def test_prevents_invalid_theatre_destroy
  st = MovieShowtime.create!(
    :theatre => @theatre,
    :movie => @movie,
    :auditorium => '1',
    :start_time => Time.now.xmlschema)
  @theatre.destroy
  dependent_showtimes_count =
```

```
    MovieShowtime.find_all_by_theatre_id(@theatre.id).size
  assert dependent_showtimes_count == 0,
    "Model allowed destruction of theatre with dependent objects"
end

def test_prevents_invalid_movie_destroy
  st = MovieShowtime.create!(
    :theatre => @theatre,
    :movie => @movie,
    :auditorium => '1',
    :start_time => Time.now.xmlschema)
  @movie.destroy
  dependent_showtimes_count =
    MovieShowtime.find_all_by_movie_id(@movie.id).size
  assert dependent_showtimes_count == 0,
    "Model allowed destruction of movie with dependent objects"
end
```

The results of running these tests can be found in Example 5-16.

Example 5-16. Results of running the unit tests in Example 5-15

```
dan-chaks-computer-2:~/web/theatre-tickets chak$ ruby
test/unit/movie_showtime_test_case.rb
Loaded suite test/unit/movie_showtime_test_case
Started
...........EE
Finished in 0.144437 seconds.

  1) Error: test_prevents_invalid_movie_destroy(MovieShowtimeTestCase):
ActiveRecord::StatementInvalid: PGError: ERROR:   update or
delete on table "movies" violates foreign key constraint
"movie_showtimes_movie_id_fkey"
on table "movie_showtimes"
  2) Error: test_prevents_invalid_theatre_destroy(MovieShowtimeTestCase):
ActiveRecord::StatementInvalid: PGError: ERROR:
update or delete on table "theatres" violates foreign key constraint
"movie_showtimes_theatre_id_fkey" on table "movie_showtimes"

14 tests, 19 assertions, 0 failures, 2 errors
dan-chaks-computer-2:~/web/theatre-tickets chak$
```

Here we find another situation in which model validations can leave us high and dry. Rails does provide a mechanism for dealing with these kind of interrelationships. Whenever we define a model relationship, such as belongs_to, we can define what should happen to dependent objects when the object in question is destroyed. The dependent objects can be defined to have the **destroy** method called on them first with:

```
has_many :movie_showtimes, :dependent => :destroy
```

This, in turn, calls **destroy** on any objects dependent on the original dependent object. Or, if it's known that the dependent objects themselves don't have dependencies, the model callbacks on the dependent objects can be skipped with:

```
has_many :movie_showtimes, :dependent => :delete
```

Because we have the option of skipping dependent objects' callbacks, it's important to note that if dependent objects later have bestowed upon them new dependent objects, we have to remember to commute any existing deletes into destroys.

Sometimes it really is an error to destroy data that has dependent objects, and the correct response to a deletion attempt is to fail, and fail fast.

Consider a medical records database. If you add a patient record and realize immediately that you misspelled the patient's name, or otherwise created the record with some set of invalid information, it is easiest to just start over. In fact, it might be all right to delete the record. However, once you've added dependent data, such as patient history or test results, deleting the patient record would not only be a mistake, it would also be grounds for a lawsuit. If there is a software bug that allows a delete statement to be issued when there is dependent data, a database constraint is the only surefire way to ensure that the deletion fails, as it should. In this case, we wouldn't declare a destroy or delete dependency because we wouldn't want that action to propogate; we *want* it to throw an exception.

Once we add declarations of what to do to dependent objects upon deletion to the movie and theatre classes, all tests pass again. See Example 5-17.

Example 5-17. The results of running the unit tests from Example 5-15 after adding model destroy dependency information

```
dan-chaks-computer-2:~/web/theatre-tickets chak$ ruby
test/unit/movie_showtime_test_case.rb
Loaded suite test/unit/movie_showtime_test_case
Started
...............
Finished in 0.146988 seconds.

14 tests, 21 assertions, 0 failures, 0 errors
```

Intro to Indexing

Our simple schema is almost complete. At this point, it is entirely locked down at the data layer and the model layer. Now, we *could* begin coding a front-end. However, if a site built atop this data model has any success whatsoever, it will quickly slow to a crawl as our tables become pregnant with data and will topple over the minute the site gets listed on Slashdot. This is due to lack of indexes. Without indexes, every query must scan the entirety of each table referenced in the query—not a problem when we have just a few entries in each table. However, if we load all movies ever made into our movies table, and all of the theatres in the U.S. into the theatres table, and then proceed to add movie showtimes, the speed (or lack thereof) would be unbearable.

Like all of data modeling, appropriate indexing is an art form. In our simple example, however, it's easy to identify a couple rules of thumb.

Rule #1: every foreign key reference should be indexed

Queries that ask questions such as, "What are all the movie showtimes for this movie?" or "What are all the movie showtimes in this theatre?" are sure to be frequent. In fact, these are exactly the queries generated when traversing Active-Record associations such as `theatre.movie_showtimes` or `movie.movie_showtimes`.

We create the indexes like this:

```
create index movie_showtimes_movie_id_idx on movie_showtimes(movie_id);
create index movie_showtimes_theatre_id_idx on movie_showtimes(theatre_id);
```

Rule #2: any column that will appear in any SQL where *clause should be indexed*

In our example, looking up theatres by zip code or showtimes by their start time are the most obvious queries and therefore deserve indexes:

```
create index theatres_zip_idx on theatres(address_zip_code);
create index movie_showtimes_start_time_idx on movie_showtimes(start_time);
```

The other obvious column we might want to search on is the movie name, but we don't need to create an explicit index for it. Recall that when we declared the movie name to be unique, Postgres created an implicit index for us.

Once you've created indexes, you don't have to do anything special in your application to use them. If when planning how to execute a query the database decides use of the index will improve performance, it will use it. If the index won't help a particular query, it will be ignored.

## CHAPTER 6

Refactoring to Third Normal Form

We ended the last chapter with a simple set of tables and models that is seemingly impervious to invalid data. Through careful unit testing of both the data layer and the models in the application layer, we guaranteed that all references between tables will be valid and that each individual column can contain only appropriate data.

It's tempting at this point to leave the realm of data modeling and begin writing a front-end for the theatre tickets website. We can imagine additional requirements for even the first version of our site, though, such as saving orders or knowing how many seats there are for sale in a given auditorium.

As secure as the physical layer we put together seems to be, the design itself is constricting. Features such as those just mentioned will be difficult to add in an elegant way. In this chapter, we will refactor the data model so that it is more open to future changes. First, the concept of *third normal form* (3NF) will be introduced. Applying 3NF will afford us the flexibility to add additional information to pieces of data that are *bound* currently, such as auditoriums and movie ratings. We will then add additional tables we know we will need relating to ticket orders; doing so presents more opportunities for refactoring.

Third Normal Form

In database theory, there are numerous normalization patterns, most of which are numbered ordinally: *non-first normal form* (NF^2), *first normal form* (1NF), *second normal form* (2NF), and so on. The study and formalization of normalization patterns has a set of overriding themes. The first is to guarantee the correctness of data across a series of insertions, updates, and deletes. The second is to facilitate the process of querying tables. There's also a positive by-product: the higher the level of normalization, the less repeated data there is in the data model. In addition to saving space, avoiding repeated data prevents data corruption because updating a value only requires changing it in single place, rather than meticulously updating it in many places. All of these properties of normalization tend to make our lives as programmers much easier.

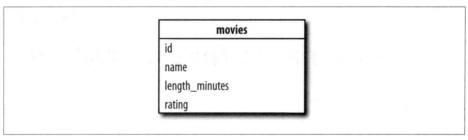

Figure 6-1. The movies table; 3NF not yet violated

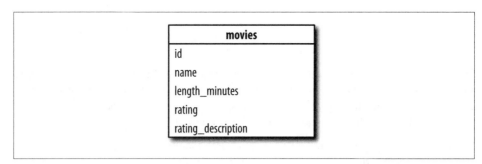

Figure 6-2. The movies table; 3NF is violated by the rating_description column

In this chapter, we will discuss third normal form, which is a sufficient target normalization to make our data model more open to future changes. The principle behind 3NF is that no columns in a table depend on any non-key columns.

Consider the `movies` table from the previous chapter, shown in Figure 6-1. The `id` column is the primary key. Technically, this table is 3NF because no columns depend on any other column that is not the primary key. However, if we decided to add additional information about the rating, we would be in trouble.

Figure 6-2 shows the `movies` table extended to hold a description of the rating. With this schema, as soon as we have more than one movie with the same rating, we begin to have duplicated data in the table. Not only are we wasting space, but we now run the risk of having two movies that are rated R, but have different rating descriptions. If the descriptions happened to be different, how would we know which one was correct?

The solution is to normalize the table on the rating column by creating a `ratings` table, and referencing that table with a `rating_id` column in the `movies` table, as shown in Figure 6-3. Now there is a single place where the movie description is stored, and we can see 3NF is satisfied.

In general, good candidates for normalization are columns that fit the following criteria:

- Not part of the primary key
- Not a foreign key reference into another table

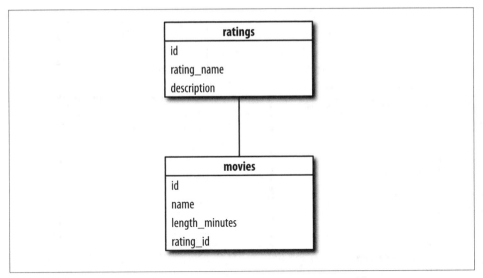

Figure 6-3. The movies table refactored to 3NF by referencing a ratings table

- Not intrinsic data, such as a name
- Not a measured value, such as the time or a temperature

We apply the same logic to the auditoriums table, which allows us to add a column to store the number of seats available in each auditorium. The resulting 3NF data model is shown in Figure 6-4.

Note that we didn't stop at adding an `auditorium_id` column to `movie_showtimes`. We also removed the `theatre_id` column. That's because `theatre_id` is actually functionally dependent on, or bound to, the `auditorium_id`. We can find the theatre for a showtime by first traversing the `auditorium_id` relationship to the auditorium table, and then traversing the `theatre_id` relationship to the `theatres` table.

If we had instead kept the `theatre_id` column to make the association simpler, as in Figure 6-5, it would be possible to have a `movie_showtimes` record that referred directly to some theatre *A*, but also referred indirectly, through its auditorium, to some other theatre *B*. This would be anomalous and disastrous, so at this stage, we don't give any more thought to keeping the `theatre_id` column around.

But it does seem strange to not be able to tell which theatre a movie plays in within first examining an auditorium record. In fact, it is strange. We'll come back to this problem in this chapter's exercises and again in Chapter 8.

In any case, now our schema is worlds more flexible. We can easily extend information about ratings or auditoriums, and we only need to worry about updating a single record to do so.

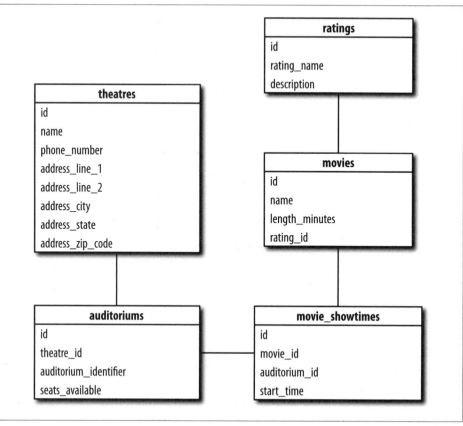

Figure 6-4. movie_showtimes table refactored to reference an auditoriums table and avoid 3NF violation

Here's the DDL for these new tables:

```
create sequence ratings_id_seq;
create table ratings (
  id integer not null
    default nextval('ratings_id_seq'),
  name varchar(16) not null unique
    check (length(name) > 0),
  description text,
  primary key (id)
);

create sequence auditoriums_id_seq;
create table auditoriums (
  id integer not null
    default nextval('auditoriums_id_seq'),
  theatre_id integer not null
    references theatres(id),
  auditorium_identifier varchar(64) not null
```

```
    check (length(auditorium_identifier) >= 1),
  seats_available integer not null,
  primary key (id),
  unique(theatre_id, auditorium_identifier)
);

create index auditoriums_theatre_id_idx on auditoriums(theatre_id);
```

Because we aren't done with all of our refactoring yet, we won't worry about models or tests here. Thinking about the unit tests necessary for these tables and what validations might be necessary are left as exercises for the reader.

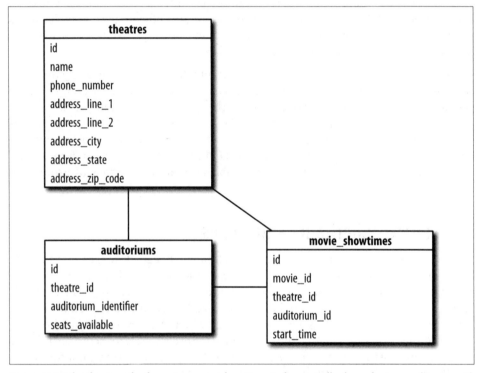

Figure 6-5. The theatre_id column in movie_showtimes is functionally dependent on auditorium_id, and must be removed

Timing Is Key

We could have created a separate ratings table from the start, when we defined our schema in the previous chapter, but we didn't know then that we might want to store extra information about ratings. Stemming violations of 3NF is something we'd like to do before the violation occurs. The trick is to notice bound data—the rating was literally *bound* to the movie—early in the design phase of the data layer. Once lots of code is written atop a data model, making changes can be painful. Worse, if your production application has collected lots of data and you can't start from scratch, the effort and time required to rearrange data within a live database can be prohibitive. Spotting columns that are likely to need full-fledged tables in the next iteration of feature sets is a skill that requires experience as well as intuition about the problem at hand.

Often, novice data modelers—even those who know about third normal form—skip these sorts of normalizations because the immediate benefits are not apparent. The short-term gain of not having to define a new table, model class, and unit tests seems irresistible. Skipping normalization for a quick gain is highly discouraged though. While it is absolutely true that it takes more effort up front to achieve a defensively normalized schema, the time required to normalize after the fact can easily take 10 times the effort of doing so right away. At that point, it's often tempting to pick a bad solution, such as adding a `seats_available` column to `movie_showtimes` rather than to an auditoriums table, where it belongs.

Once a schema goes down a sloppy path, it eventually—and sooner than you might think—becomes unusable. The application layer becomes riddled with bugs because the data layer is too permissive. For example, if the application layer must always update the `seats_available` column in `movie_showtimes`, code can creep in that sets it incorrectly: perhaps to zero or some random value. Or, possibly worse—those doing data entry might be expected to enter the value every time they add a new showtime. Suddenly the business is experiencing massive problems because the system oversold every show, or perhaps refused to sell any tickets at all.

Refactoring: Inheritance and Mixins

Since we know our website's purpose is to *sell* movie tickets, it makes sense to add tables to hold sales data before we begin coding up the front-end. Figure 6-6 shows our first stab at adding tables to store orders and ticket purchases. The `orders` table holds each transaction, including the purchaser's name, address, and credit card information. The `purchased_tickets` table is a line item table for each ticket purchased in the transaction. Rather than simply providing a column in the `orders` table to record the number of tickets purchased, we split up the tables, foreseeing the need to account for tickets at different prices, such as student or senior discounted tickets, matinees, and so on.

In adding these extra tables, we find a glaring violation of the Don't Repeat Yourself (DRY) principle. The violation of DRY occurs in the repetition of address data between the `theatres` table and our new `orders` table. If we kept the schema as is, with the data duplicated, we would also end up duplicating a lot of other code, including validation code and display logic for addresses.

Instead of duplicating this structure, we create a separate `addresses` table. If mimicking the previous examples, we would create `address_id` columns in the `theatres` and `orders` tables, and refer to individual addresses that are inserted in the `addresses` table.

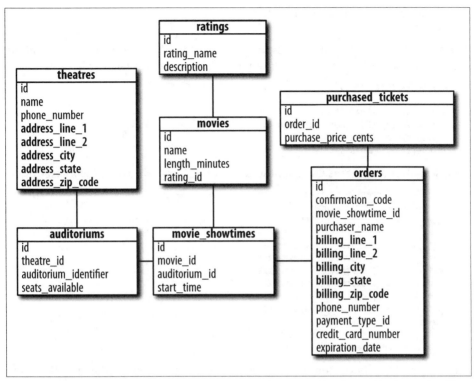

Figure 6-6. Theatre tickets data model with orders and purchased_tickets table, but with address schema repeated in two tables

We won't do that here, though. This data is not in violation of 3NF. It is dependent only on the primary key of the table it is in, not some other column in the table as in our other examples. The problem we are trying to solve is of repeated code, not repeated data. In code, we can solve this sort of problem with class inheritance (or in Ruby, with mixins). The same can be accomplished at the data layer with Postgres's table inheritance mechanism. We'll use this feature to solve our current problem. First, we create the addresses table, without a primary key—the tables that implement addresses functionality already have their own:

```
create table addresses (
  line_1 varchar(256) not null
    check (length(line_1) > 0),
  line_2 varchar(256),
  city varchar(128) not null
    check (length(city) > 0),
  state varchar(2) not null
    check (length(state) = 2),
  zip_code varchar(9) not null
    references zip_codes(zip),
  phone_number varchar(10) not null
```

```
      check (length(phone_number) = 10)
  );
```

The `addresses` table does not correspond directly to a Rails model class. Instead, its
columns are sucked into tables that need it using the `inherits` keyword:

```
create table theatres (
  id integer not null
    default nextval('theatres_id_seq'),
  name varchar(256) not null unique,
  primary key (id)
) inherits (addresses);
```

If we describe the `theatres` table, it now has all of the properties of the `addresses` table:

```
movies_development=# \d theatres
          Table "public.theatres"
     Column     |          Type
---------------+------------------------
 line_1        | character varying(256)
 line_2        | character varying(256)
 city          | character varying(128)
 state         | character varying(2)
 zip_code      | character varying(9)
 phone_number  | character varying(10)
 id            | integer
 name          | character varying(256)
Inherits: addresses
```

Because Postgres allows multiple inheritance, we want to allow for the same flexibility
within Rails. Ruby provides for multiple inheritance through the use of mixins, and
Rails takes this one step further with plugins. Below is our plugin for address support,
based on the template from Chapter 3. Example 6-1 shows the file *acts_as_ad
dress.rb*, in the plugin's *lib/* directory.

Example 6-1. acts_as_address.rb, from our acts_as_address plugin

```
module Addresses
  module ClassMethods
    def acts_as_address
      class_eval do <<-DELIM
        # define our validators and associations
        validates_presence_of :line_1, :city, :state, :zip_code, :phone_number
        validates_length_of :line_1, :maximum => 256
        validates_length_of :line_2, :maximum => 256
        validates_length_of :city, :maximum => 128
        validates_length_of :state, :maximum => 2
        belongs_to :zip_code, :foreign_key => :zip_code

        # define the find_within_miles proc for all models that contain addresses
        find_within_miles = Proc.new do |zip, miles|
          z = ZipCode.find_by_zip(zip)
          !z ? [] :
          self.class.find(:all,
                          :include => :zip_code,
                          :conditions => [
```

```
                    "miles_between_lat_long(?, ?,
                        zip_codes.latitude, zip_codes.longitude) < ?",
                    z.latitude, z.longitude, miles])
      end
      define_method :find_within_miles, find_within_miles
    DELIM
  end
end

def self.included(base)
  base.extend ClassMethods
  base.class_eval do
    include InstanceMethods
  end
end
end
```

Example 6-2 shows the *init.rb* file in the plugin's top-level directory.

Example 6-2. The init.rb file for our acts_as_address plugin

```
ActiveRecord::Base.class_eval do
  include Addresses
end
```

Now we can simply say, within the **theatre** and **order** classes:

```
acts_as_address
```

Our new schema diagram, shown in Figure 6-7, is much cleaner now that we have normalized the repetitive address information into its own table. Each table that inherits **addresses** is much easier to understand as well. In addition, our models that implement the **Addresses** module stay clean. In both the database and our application code, if we need to make changes to the way addresses work, we need only do it in one place.

Are there more opportunities for normalization here? Before reading on, examine the data model and brainstorm about the business. Put yourself in the shoes of the developer of this website. What are features you might want that would require dependent data?

Drawing from my own experience, I would say that there has never been a time where a zip code was entered in a database that the site in question would not have benefited from knowing additional information about the zip code. For example, in our application, what theatres within 25 miles of 02139 are playing the latest *Harry Potter*? Certainly, we can solve this by adding latitude and longitude columns to the **theatres** table, but we risk duplicating data (and therefore creating conflicting data) if we have multiple theatres in the same area. Further, if we ever want to validate user input, such as verifying that a city, state, zip code combination is valid, we will need an auxiliary table of zip code data.

Let's leave the refactoring of the zip code table for the next chapter.

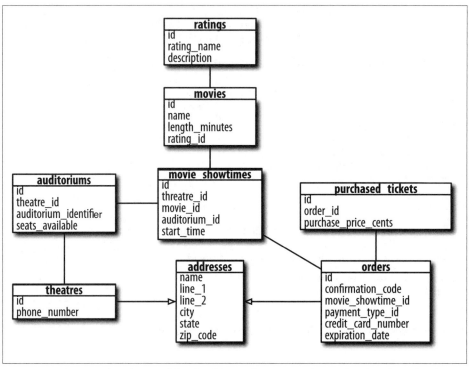

Figure 6-7. Theatre tickets data model with address information refactored at the schema level, using database inheritance

Exercises

1. Based on what you know about the problem domain, for each column in data from this chapter model, list the ranges of valid and invalid data.

2. Write unit tests for those boundary conditions. Where appropriate, add validations to make your unit tests pass.

3. Add the `theatre_id` column back to the `movie_showtimes` table. Prove to yourself that you can reproduce the anomalous situation described in this chapter. Is there any way you can use a database constraint to prevent the anomalies?

Refactor Steps

1. Find a table in which a column takes on one of a set of values, but those values are not foreign key references into another table, as in Figure 6-8.

2. Create a new table in which the rows represent the set of values from 1 and any other columns that were dependent on this value, rather than the original table's primary key (Figure 6-9).

We can create the table shown earlier with the following SQL statement (note that it is up to you to account for any data inconsistencies caused by improper normalization):

```
insert into colors(name, hex)
select distinct color, hex from my_table;
```

3. Create a column in the original table for the foreign key reference, then populate it. After doing so, delete the original columns (Figure 6-10).

```
alter table my_table add column color_id integer;
update my_table
   set color_id = (
     select id
       from colors
      where m.color = c.name
        and m.hex = c.hex
   );
alter table my_table drop column color;
alter table my_table drop column hex;
alter table my_table add constraint my_table_color_id_fkey
   (color_id) references colors(id);
alter table my_table alter color_set not null;
```

4. Create a model class for the new table. Add association references appropriately. The new model will have a has_many association to the original model class, and the original class will have a belongs_to relationship with the new model class.

id	name	color	hex
1	accord	red	0xff0000
2	prius	blue	0x0000ff
3	jeep	red	0xff0000

Figure 6-8. A table not in third normal form

id	color	hex
1	red	0xff0000
2	blue	0x0000ff

Figure 6-9. The color and dependent data from Figure 6-7 extracted to its own table

id	name	color_id
1	accord	1
2	prius	2
3	jeep	1

Figure 6-10. The table from Figure 6-8, with a foreign key reference to the table

Domain Data

Domain tables are a special type of table in data modeling. They contain knowledge known *a priori* about the application's domain, and the contents within these tables don't normally change through interaction with the application. In our data model, we already have an example of a domain table: the `ratings` table. Regardless of what our application looks like or how it changes over time, regardless of what data we intend to store about users, movies, or orders, the set of ratings and their meanings in the context of the domain of motions pictures is set.

Domain tables are particularly special because at first glance they can seem extraneous. Since they don't change frequently, you *could* encode the data they contain in application code rather than directly in the database. In fact, many beginners to data modeling leave out domain tables completely, preferring to store the concepts they encode in the code itself. However, promoting domain data to fully fledged relational tables and records provides numerous benefits.

First, domain tables play a key role in helping to maintain referential integrity. If multiple tables reference ratings, having them defined once in a single table ensures that all tables reference the same set. If multiple tables have a text column for the movie rating as our `movies` table did at the start of Chapter 5, it would be very easy for each table to store different sets of ratings, perhaps "PG-13" in one table, and "pg13" in another. It would be extremely difficult for our application to know these are the same thing. Even if we had check constraints on each table, we'd have to search for and update each check constraint if the motion picture association added a new rating. That process is also prone to error or omission, and it's certainly not very DRY.

The second benefit of domain tables is that they help maintain third normal form and keep our data model flexible; as with our example earlier, we were able to easily add a description for each rating without any need to change our software and without sacrificing 3NF. Just like with rating information, domain tables often "come from somewhere," meaning that the information can be researched ahead of time—if not on the Internet then by interviewing someone familiar with the business behind your application. It's a good idea to put everything you know in the domain table from the very beginning. What was initially a single column in a table sometimes turns out to be a large table full of rich data that can be leveraged in interesting ways as the application matures.

Perhaps the best thing about domain tables is how well they interface with Rails. A common convention to deal with the problem of mixing up literals like "PG-13" and "pg13" is to declare constants for the appropriate values. Of course, having a convention doesn't mean people will follow it. Data from domain tables can be treated like constants, which encourage good convention, but also enforce the use of the convention because referential integrity requires it.

Let's take the `ratings` table as an example. The first thing we do, since this is a domain table and is unlikely to change, is add `insert` statements to our schema definition for each rating type:

```
insert into ratings(name, description)
  values('G', 'General audiences');
insert into ratings(name, description)
  values('PG', 'Parental guidance suggested');
insert into ratings(name, description)
  values('PG-13', 'Parents strongly cautioned');
insert into ratings(name, description)
  values('R', 'Restricted');
insert into ratings(name, description)
  values('NC-17', 'No one under 17 admitted');
insert into ratings(name, description)
  values('Unrated', 'This movie has not been rated');
```

We can insert these records directly because we won't need an interface to manipulate domain data. Even though the table has an ActiveRecord model, the frequency with which it changes is likely to be much slower than the frequency with which our application goes through complete rewrites.

The next step is to create the constants that convention dictates you create anyway. In this case, however, rather than the value of constant being set to some arbitrary string value, such as "PG-13" for the constant `PG13`, we can set the value to the actual Active-Record object itself:

```
class Rating < ActiveRecord::Base
  validates_presence_of :name, :description
  validates_length_of :name, :maximum => 16

  G      = Rating.find_by_name('G')
  PG     = Rating.find_by_name('PG')
  PG13   = Rating.find_by_name('PG-13')
  R      = Rating.find_by_name('R')
  NC17   = Rating.find_by_name('NC-17')
  UNRATED = Rating.find_by_name('Unrated')

end
```

Now, to assign a rating to a movie, we can use the constant, such as `Rating::R` or `Rating::PG13`. Both of these constants correspond directly to the database record itself but have the additional flexibility of being a constant. Also, since we initialize these constants in the model class definition, the database query to get the record is performed only once—the first time the class is loaded:

```
>> Rating.find(:all).map{|r| r.name}
=> ["PG", "PG-13", "NC-17", "Unrated", "G", "R"]
>> Rating::R
=> #<Rating:0x34e6df0 @attributes={"name"=>"R", "id"=>"10",
"description"=>"Restricted"}>
>> Rating::PG13
=> #<Rating:0x34e7ac0 @attributes={"name"=>"PG-13", "id"=>"3",
"description"=>"Parents strongly cautioned"}>
>> Rating::G.description
=> "General audiences"
```

And of course, when we want to reference the rating, such as when creating new movies, we just use the constant. The ActiveRecord object is referenced just as expected, and the movie record saves normally:

```
>> m = Movie.new(:name => 'Rocky Horror Picture Show', :length_minutes => 100,
:rating => Rating::R)
=> #<Movie:0x34d41f0 @new_record=true, @attributes={"name"=>"Rocky Horror
Picture Show", "length_minutes"=>100, "rating_id"=>10}, @rating=#<Rating:0x34d832c
@attributes={"name"=>"R", "id"=>"10", "description"=>"Restricted"}>>
>> m.save
=> true
```

Dealing with Zip Codes

Zip codes, while they may not benefit from having constants defined within the Zip Code model, will nonetheless benefit from a table of all the valid zip codes (which certainly are known ahead of time), making validating zip codes a snap. If the zip exists in the table, it's valid. Similarly, if the zip does not exist, a database exception will be thrown before an application-level oversight lets faulty data through.

Generally for a zip code table, the zip code itself should be the primary key, contained in a varchar column to accommodate zip codes that begin with a zero. In our table, we've decided to name the primary key column zip to keep things clear. Even though Rails prefers the primary to be called id, we can use the declaration set_primary_key to inform Rails we've chosen a different name. This makes our table definition much more readable, and more importantly, self-documenting:

```
create table zip_codes (
  zip varchar(16) not null,
  city varchar(255) not null,
  state_abbreviation varchar(2) not null,
  county varchar(255) not null,
  latitude numeric not null,
  longitude numeric not null,
  primary key(zip)
);
```

Zip code data is available from a variety of sources online, and with some massaging, can be easily imported into your database. As we discussed earlier, one of the primary benefits of having a zip code domain table is the ability to do distance calculations to answer questions such as, "What theatres are playing *Casablanca* within 10 miles of my home?" Almost all zip code databases available online provide latitude and longitude coordinates for zip codes. To facilitate calculating the answer to our question quickly, we create a stored procedure, `miles_between_lat_long`, which provides a reasonably good approximation of distance with a minimal set of complex calculations (note that this equation is an approximation only; if your application requires high-precision distances, you will want to use a better—but likely slower—formula):

```
create or replace function miles_between_lat_long(
  lat1 numeric, long1 numeric, lat2 numeric, long2 numeric
) returns numeric
language 'plpgsql' as $$
declare
  x numeric = 69.1 * (lat2 - lat1);
  y numeric = 69.1 * (long2 - long1) * cos(lat1/57.3);
begin
    return sqrt(x * x + y * y);
end
$$;
```

We can then add a method, `zips_within_miles` to our `ZipCode` model, which returns all of the zip code objects within a given distance from the zip in question:

```
class ZipCode < ActiveRecord::Base
  set_primary_key 'zip'

  def zips_within_miles(miles)
    ZipCode.find(:all,
                 :conditions => ["miles_between_lat_long(?, ?,
                    zip_codes.latitude, zip_codes.longitude) < ?",
                    self.latitude, self.longitude, miles])
  end
end
```

The following example, using *script/console*, finds all of the cities within two miles of Cambridge, Massachusetts:

```
>> z = ZipCode.find('02139')=> #<ZipCode:0x3463cc0
@attributes={"city"=>"CAMBRIDGE",
"latitude"=>#<BigDecimal:3463d10,'0.42365079E2',12(12)>, "zip"=>"02139",
"county"=>"MIDDLESEX", "state_abbreviation"=>"MA",
"longitude"=>#<BigDecimal:3463ce8,'-0.71104519E2',12(12)>}>
>> z.zips_within_miles(2).collect{|z| z.city}.uniq
=> ["BOSTON", "CHARLESTOWN", "ALLSTON", "BRIGHTON", "CAMBRIDGE",
"BROOKLINE", "BROOKLINE VILLAGE"]
```

With a variation on the preceding method, we can bestow upon any model that "acts as addresses" the ability to find instances within a given distance from a particular latitude-longitude coordinate. We add the following to the `ClassMethods` section of our `Addresses` plugin:

```
module ClassMethods
  def acts_as_address
    # validation / association code was here...

    # define the find_within_miles proc for all models that contain addresses
    find_within_miles = Proc.new do |zip, miles|
      z = ZipCode.find_by_zip(zip)
      !z ? [] :
      self.class.find(:all,
                      :include => :zip_code,
                      :conditions => ["miles_between_lat_long(?,
                        zip_codes.latitude, zip_codes.longitude) < ?",
                        z.latitude, z.longitude, miles])
    end
    self.send(:define_method, 'find_within_miles', find_within_miles)
  end
end
```

We can answer our question of which theatres are close by with very natural language:

```
Theatre.find_within_miles('02139', 10)
```

Strategy Pattern with Domain Tables

Another use of domain tables, when the number of records is tractable enough to be represented in code, is to point to collections of methods or data contained in classes, much as a trigger for the Gang of Four strategy pattern.

We will explore this idea with the payment types found in the **orders** table. We begin with the standard domain table refactoring performed earlier. Then, we'll enhance our solution by making use of ActiveRecord's single table inheritance, to achieve the Domain Table Strategy Pattern. We start out with our initial cut at the **Order** class, before we create the domain table for payment types. It looks very similar to our initial **Ratings** class, with an array containing the acceptable payment types to match the database constraint:

```
class Order < ActiveRecord::Base
  belongs_to :movie_showtime_id
  validates_uniqueness_of :confirmation_code
  validates_presence_of :confirmation_code,
    :purchaser_name, :payment_type,
    :credit_card_number, :credit_expiration_month, :credit_expiration_year

  PAYMENT_TYPES = ['Visa', 'MasterCard', 'American Express']

  def validate_payment_type
    unless PAYMENT_TYPES.include?(payment_type)
      errors.add('payment_type',
        "must be #{PAYMENT_TYPES[0..-2].join(', ')} or #{PAYMENT_TYPES[-1]}")
  end

  def validate
    validate_payment_type
```

```
    end
  end
```

Following the ratings example, we factor out the payment type into its own table, payment_types, and we insert the appropriate data for our domain of credit card processing:

```
create sequence payment_types_id_seq;
create table payment_types(
  id integer not null
    default nextval('payment_types_id_seq'),
  name varchar(128) not null unique
    check (length(name) > 0),
  primary key (id)
);

insert into payment_types (id, name)
  values(nextval('payment_types_id_seq'), 'MasterCard');
insert into payment_types (id, name)
  values(nextval('payment_types_id_seq'), 'Visa');
insert into payment_types (id, name)
  values(nextval('payment_types_id_seq'), 'American Express');
```

We also create a corresponding class, PaymentType, which contains constants for each payment type. Just as with the movie ratings, each of these constants contains the actual database record and can be treated like a real ActiveRecord object in our code:

```
class PaymentType < ActiveRecord::Base
  has_many :orders

  VISA = PaymentType.find_by_name('Visa')
  MASTER_CARD = PaymentType.find_by_name('MasterCard')
  AMEX = PaymentType.find_by_name('American Express')

  def validate_card_number(card_number, expiry)
    case self
      when VISA
        validate_visa_card_number(name, address, amount)
      when MASTER_CARD
        validate_master_card_number(name, address, amount)
      when AMEX
        validate_amex_card_number(name, address, amount)
    end
  end

  def process_order(name, address, amount)
    case self
      when VISA
        process_visa_order(name, address, amount)
      when MASTER_CARD
        process_mc_order(name, address, amount)
      when AMEX
        process_amex_order(name, address, amount)
    end
```

```
    end
  end
```

What's new here is that we've added some methods that must switch on the constant. Credit card validation is different for each credit card type, and the processing is often different also. There is likely to be a different processing provider for Visa than for American Express, and the API to secure the funds is likely to be different as well.

Whenever there are if-then-else or switch statements that switch on a type property repeated in many of a class's methods, it's usually an indication that we need subclasses to override some common method instead.

The astute reader might point out that we can avoid repetitive if-then-else clauses by applying some well-thought-out method-naming conventions, and create a dispatch mechanism. For example:

```
def process_order(*args)
  self.send("process_#{self.name.tableize}_order", *args)
end
```

While this will certainly will work, we are still left with three copies of each method in a single class—a recipe for confusion and bugs. Better is to effect a simple change with which we can turn our basic domain table into one that invokes Rails single table inheritance mechanism to pick the right methods for us. All we need is a **type** column that differentiates each record. Here is our **payment_types** table again, but we've renamed the **name** column to **type**, and to make single table inheritance work correctly, we modify our domain records slightly to insert types that are friendly to the Rails inflection mechanism ("American Express" is now one word):

```
create table payment_types(
  id integer not null
    default nextval('payment_types_id_seq'),
  type varchar(128) not null unique
    check (length(type) > 0),
  primary key (id)
);

insert into payment_types (id, type)
  values(nextval('payment_types_id_seq'), 'Visa');
insert into payment_types (id, type)
  values(nextval('payment_types_id_seq'), 'MasterCard');
insert into payment_types (id, type)
  values(nextval('payment_types_id_seq'), 'AmericanExpress');
```

The model class for **PaymentType** is now vastly simplified. We no longer have repeated switch statements. Instead we define stubs that throw an exception if the method is not overridden in a subclass, and we expect that subclasses will override each method. Also note that to load our constants, we now say **find_by_type** rather than **find_by_name**:

```
class PaymentType < ActiveRecord::Base
  has_many :orders
```

```
VISA = PaymentType.find_by_type('Visa')
MASTER_CARD = PaymentType.find_by_type('MasterCard')
AMEX = PaymentType.find_by_type('AmericanExpress')

def validate_card_number(card_number, expiry)
  raise "This method must be redefined in the subclass"
end

def process_order(name, address, amount)
  raise "This method must be redefined in the subclass"
end
end
```

The following is an example of one of the subclasses. In each one, we place the logic for the particular type of credit card:

```
class AmericanExpress < PaymentType
  def validate_card_number(card_number, expiry)
    # implement algorithm for card number validation
  end

  def process_order(name, address, amount)
    # implement credit card processing logic
  end
end
```

It's worth noting that now each constant not only points to a different object but also to an object of a different class. Notice the *script/console* output below and how it differs from the same exercise performed for the ratings:

```
>> PaymentType::VISA
=> #<Visa:0x3509c60 @attributes={"type"=>"Visa", "id"=>"1"}>
>> PaymentType::MASTER_CARD
=> #<MasterCard:0x3502eb0 @attributes={"type"=>"MasterCard", "id"=>"2"}>
>> PaymentType::AMEX
=> #<AmericanExpress:0x34fc0c4 @attributes={"type"=>"AmericanExpress", "id"=>"3"}>
```

Now within the order class, we can write very elegant and clear statements that delegate to the appropriate PaymentType subclass. Keep in mind that everything except credit card validation has been removed from the class definition below, to save space—you wouldn't remove them in practice:

```
class Order < ActiveRecord::Base
  def validate_credit_card_number
    unless self.payment_type.validate_card_number(
      credit_card_number,
      credit_expiration_month,
      credit_expiration_year)
      errors.add('credit_card_number', 'is invalid')
  end

  def validate
    validate_credit_card_number
  end
end
```

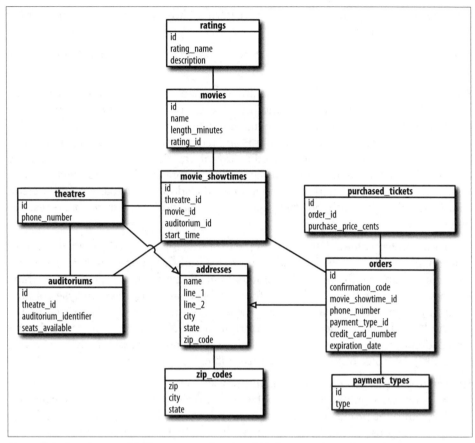

Figure 7-1. Our data model after creating domain tables for zip codes and payment types

Refactor from Day One

Our final data model, with addresses factored into their own inherited table, and with ratings, payment types, and zip codes moved into domain tables, is shown in Figure 7-1.

In terms of understandability, design elegance, and therefore maintainability, this is a much better design than we had at the beginning of this chapter. We haven't created any controllers or views yet, but that's OK—they are consumers of our models, and making changes to models becomes infinitely more difficult once active code is relying on them.

The real goal is to be able to spot opportunities for refactoring before design choices become entrenched in client code and before the design becomes problematic due to scale or lack of understandability, which leads to bugs. We are taking an intentionally slow and measured approach to data modeling here to point out patterns of refactoring that you should learn to spot in your own projects. Of course, we could have started with the "right" data model, but then the patterns of how to move from wrong to right would not have emerged.

Are there other opportunities for refactorings that may save us headaches down the road?

One possibility might be the credit card information stored in the orders table. Although it's not likely to repeat in another table, the binding of the information to the orders table may not be ideal. Imagine that not long after this site becomes a smashing success, we want to add member accounts and recall users' addresses and credit cards when they log in. Splitting out the credit card information into its own table named credit_cards will make it a breeze to later add a mapping table users_credit_cards, which will link the information together. Since the address is actually used for credit card verification, it's probably credit_cards that should inherit from addresses, not orders.

The phone_number column left behind in the theatres table is a good candidate for normalization as well. We may someday want to list multiple phone numbers, perhaps a local number and a toll-free number. Rather than adding a column each time we think of a new phone number we'd like to store, a table containing a number_type column, along with a join table theatres_phone_numbers does the trick much more elegantly. The credit card service that processes the payments might require a phone number for verification purposes as well, and we could easily reference the phone number with a foreign key reference from the credit_cards table.

How far to go in the first round of normalization and refactoring is a matter of judgment. In this book, we won't perform the refactorings we just listed, but only because we won't run into the problems we listed within this text. (Also, the examples would become monotonous.) However, if we were really building this site, it would behoove us to normalize as much as we could up front. While correct (and full) normalization can seem to result in an explosion of tables and therefore an explosion in the amount of work associated to write models and tests, in practice the up-front work proves minimal because each table and model class is simpler to write and easier to test. Fewer bugs tend to creep in, and when they do they are localized to a smaller subset of code, and are much easier to find.

CHAPTER 8

Composite Keys and Domain Key/
Normal Form

So far we have improved our data model and Rails model layer substantially from the small set of tables we began with. Specifically, we have:

- Added constraints everywhere
- Enforced referential integrity
- Added basic indexes
- Factored out repeated data model chunks with database inheritance, and created an analogous Rails plugin to facilitate reuse
- Factored out columns that were teetering on the edge of violating third normal form into fully fledged tables
- Created domain tables for our domain data, and analogous Rails models and constants

We have done quite a bit, but our data model is still not enterprise solid. In this chapter, we will discuss two related topics that can help us get closer to our goal. The first is the idea of keys made up of multiple columns, otherwise known as *composite keys*. The second is a topic that proverbial wars have been fought over, which boils down to whether primary keys should be simple *id* columns, as is the Rails default, or the more complex composite or *natural* keys, which rely on unique identifying information in the records themselves.

In Rails, as it comes out of the box, the decision to use *id* columns has been made for you. However, composite keys have inherent benefits over simple *id* keys. In reality, both conventions have pluses and minuses. In this chapter, we'll learn the pros and cons of each convention. We'll learn how to make composite keys work in Rails through use of a plugin. Then, we'll have our cake and eat it too by making both conventions coexist happily. We'll gain the benefits of each system without the addition of too much more work.

Let's begin by going over the benefits of an *id* column system.

The first and most obvious benefit is that it is sitting right there waiting for you to use it. The Rails associations mechanism—which allows you to define *has many*, *belongs to*, and *has and belongs to many* relationships—relies on *id* column primary and foreign keys. If you are prototyping a quick-and-dirty application, you can get going quickly without any hassle.

The second benefit is that an *id* column is an easy handle on a piece of data. For example, when editing the contents of a record via a web form, all of the values other than the *id* itself may be editable. There is no chance of the primary key of the object changing when it is edited, so logic involved in mutating that object is simple.

Conversely, editing a primary key can be tricky, because records in other tables may be referencing the primary key that is about to undergo a change. This is the third benefit: *id* columns provide a level of indirection to the real data. Because of that indirection, records in tables referencing a table with an *id* column do not need to be changed when the referenced record is updated. For example, let's say the primary key of our `ratings` table was not an *id* column but instead the `rating_name` column itself. The column `rating_id` in the `movies` table would now have to reference this column instead of the *id* column. If we then decided that PG-13 ought to have a `rating_name` of "PG13" rather than "PG-13," we would have to update every movie that referenced the PG-13 record in our `ratings` domain table—definitely something we would like to avoid if we can.

The final benefit is that the primary key for the next row to be added is always close at hand and is guaranteed to be unique. Either via database sequence, or serial column type, a built-in mechanism for uniqueness is responsible for generating the next key.

The preceding list seems like a lot of benefits. It's not so easy to simply list the benefits of using composite keys because, for one thing, you can't always use them. They serve a special purpose in maintaining data integrity. Whereas you can always slap an *id* column on a table, there isn't always a natural composite key available. However, when there is such a natural composite key present, ignoring it in favor of an independent single-column key can lead to big trouble.

When people argue that single-column primary keys are better than composite keys because of the long list of advantages mentioned earlier, they're missing the reality that special circumstances call for special measures. Problems arise when a situation requires composite keys but single-column *id* keys are used instead. The next section will show how we can pierce a giant hole in our movie showtime database's schema—which we thought we had locked down with full referential integrity—simply because we ignored a composite key.

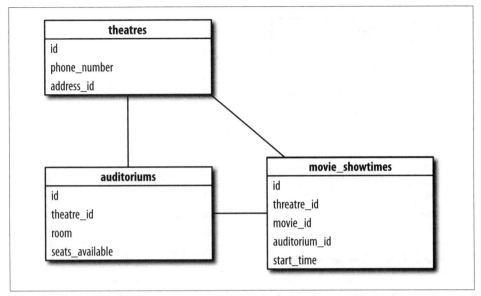

Figure 8-1. The auditoriums table and two related tables

Why Composite Natural Keys Matter

The first step in understanding the value of composite keys is knowing how to spot them. Figure 8-1 shows the `auditoriums` table along with two related tables, the `theatres` and the `movie_showtimes` tables.

We've defined the following references so far, indicated by the interconnecting lines above:

- `movie_showtimes(auditorium_id) references auditoriums(id)`
- `auditoriums(theatre_id) references theatres(id)`

But as we saw in Chapter 6, when we normalized on the `auditorium` column, we lost a reference from `movie_showtimes` to the theatres table. The reference was lost because it violated 3NF, but its absence is quite a nuisance. Simple queries such as "how many movies are playing in theatre *x* today?" become needlessly complex. We'd like to say:

```
select count(*)
  from movie_showtimes
 where theatre_id = ?
```

Instead, we need the following query:

```
select count(*)
  from auditoriums a,
       movie_showtimes ms,
 where ms.auditorium_id = a.id
   and a.theatre_id = ?
```

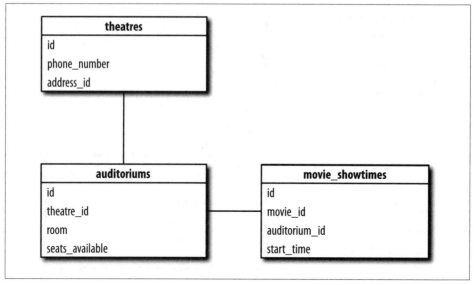

Figure 8-2. The movie_showtimes table with a reference to the theatres table; a violation of 3NF

Any query linking theatres to showtimes must go through the `auditoriums` table, which feels quite unnatural. It is extremely tempting to add the `theatre_id` column back to the `movie_showtimes` table, as shown in Figure 8-2. We'd then add this reference:

- `movie_showtimes(theatre_id) references theatres(id)`

Unfortunately, there is now a big referential integrity hole left wide open. Can you see it?

In this data model, a movie showtime can exist for which the auditorium does not exist in the theatre the movie is expected to play in. Consider the following data:

```
movies_development=# select id, name from theatres;
 id |        name
----+--------------------
  1 | Steller Theatre
  2 | Old Towne Theatre
(2 rows)

movies_development=# select * from auditoriums;
 id | theatre_id | room | seats_available
----+------------+------+-----------------
  1 |          1 | A    |             150
  2 |          2 | B    |             150
(2 rows)

movies_development=#
 select id, movie_id, theatre_id, auditorium_id from movie_showtimes;

 id | movie_id | theatre_id | auditorium_id
----+----------+------------+---------------
```

```
    1 |        1 |         1 |           2
 (1 row)
```

Our single movie showtime is playing in the theatre called Stellar Theatre and is show-ing in auditorium B. Unfortunately, auditorium B happens to be in Old Towne Theatre! This doesn't make any sense, yet it's perfectly valid based on our foreign key references and Rails associations. Even though we thought we had ensured referential integrity, we're actually still allowing for bogus data to enter our system. In *script/console*, we can cause nonsense to occur, as shown in Example 8-1.

Example 8-1. A functionally dependent reference can lead to bogus associations

```
>> t = Theatre.find_by_name('Steller Theatre')
>> puts t.movie_showtimes.first.auditorium.theatre.name
=> "Old Towne Theatre"
```

The reason this is happening is not because our references are wrong but because our primary keys are. Though the referential integrity of our data model is satisfied, the referential integrity of our problem domain is not. *id* columns do not always provide enough information to ensure referential integrity for interrelationships between mul-tiple tables. That's where composite keys come in.

Spotting Composite Keys

Simply put, a composite key is one that is made up of more than one column. But how do you determine what a composite key should be? Finding them actually turns out to be pretty straightforward.

First, let's examine the properties of a primary key. Actually, there is only one. A pri-mary key must be unique for all records.

This works in the opposite direction as well. If you have a real-world situation that has a uniqueness constraint on a set of columns, then in your data model, those columns are likely to be the right candidate for a composite key.When a primary key is based on attributes of the data that make it unique from all other data, the key is known as a *natural* key.

If we look back to our definition of the `auditoriums` table, we see that we did, in fact, have a unique constraint on the columns, (`theatre_id, room`). Certainly, it does not make sense for a single theatre to have two auditoriums called *A*. That would be most confusing. But this unique set of columns is also a great way to refer to the auditorium itself. Indeed, referring to an auditorium as "auditorium 'A' in theatre #1" is much more natural than referring to it as "auditorium #47," a number based solely on a sequence, which specifies nothing intrinsic about the auditorium itself. The former provides much more information, and as such, it provides much better guarantees for our referential integrity constraints.

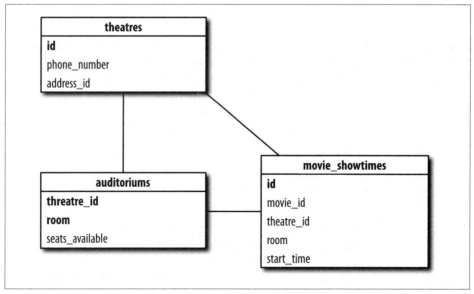

Figure 8-3. The auditoriums table with a composite key

Figure 8-3 reproduces the segment of our data model shown earlier, but we've removed the id column from auditoriums and replaced it with the more natural composite key. Primary keys are shown in bold.

In order to reference the auditorium from the movie_showtimes table, we need to reference both parts of the key. Therefore, we now have the following references:

- movie_showtimes(theatre_id) references theatres(id)
- movie_showtimes(theatre_id, room) references auditoriums(theatre_id, room)
- auditoriums(theatre_id) references theatres(id)

The new table definition is shown in Example 8-2.

Example 8-2. New definitions for auditoriums table with a composite key

```
create table auditoriums (
  room varchar(64) not null
    check (length(room) >= 1),
  theatre_id integer not null
    references theatres(id),
  seats_available integer not null,
  primary key (room, theatre_id)
);

create sequence movie_showtimes_id_seq;
create table movie_showtimes (
  id integer not null
    default nextval('movie_showtimes_id_seq'),
  movie_id integer not null
```

```
    references movies(id),
  theatre_id integer not null
    references theatres(id),
  room varchar(64) not null,
  start_time timestamp with time zone not null,
  primary key (id),
  foreign key (theatre_id, room)
    references auditoriums(theatre_id, room) initially deferred
);
```

It is now impossible for the inconsistent state demonstrated above to exist. Because the `theatre_id` column in `movie_showtimes` references *both* the `theatre_id` column in `auditoriums` *and* the `id` column in `theatres`, the three are guaranteed to be the same.

Atop the Shoulders of…

In Chapter 4, I discussed the idea of standing atop the shoulders of giants. Information architecture and database normalization techniques are highly developed areas of research. It should be no surprise that scholarly papers dealing with key selection go back more than 25 years. Here we have a perfect example of where we should not neglect to sit atop the shoulders of our predecessors.

In 1981, Ronald Fagin of IBM Research Laboratories introduced domain key/normal form (DK/NF) in his paper "A Normal Form for Relational Databases That Is Based on Domains and Keys," published in the journal *ACM Transactions on Database Systems*. In his paper, Fagin proved mathematically that a schema design in which keys are chosen as the smallest set of columns that naturally and uniquely identify a row of data absolutely prevents anomalies, such as the one we created earlier where a movie showtime could occur in an auditorium that didn't exist in the theatre the movie was set to play in. Sometimes these keys are a single *id* column, sometimes they are single columns that have intrinsic, natural meaning, and sometimes they are composite keys made up of mutiple columns. The overriding point is that there is no one-size-fits-all solution. Each table must be analyzed on a case-by-case basis to determine how it contributes to the whole of the schema.

The best relational databases we have today grew out of the research of past decades. Even a concept that may be taken for granted today, such as the ability to define a primary key based on multiple columns, is a database feature that grew up out of research such as Fagin's. While it's not surprising that over the course of decades scholars investigated these research areas and their findings made it into the database products we use today as fundamental features, it *is* surprising that many of these critical concepts are lacking from the core Ruby on Rails framework.

Many users of Ruby on Rails who are new to schema design take that lack of features as a cue that the concepts are not relevant or that they can live without them. Many more, if Rails is their first platform, may never have heard about DK/NF or natural keys and won't know of the benefits they are giving up by not using them when appropriate. Now that you know about natural keys, you don't have to be in this crowd of poor saps.

Migrating to Domain Key/Normal Form

Before we dive into the *how* of implementation, first let's get our schema into DK/NF so that we know *what* we are going to implement.

Often getting your schema into DK/NF can be an onerous task. However, because our schema was already properly refactored into third normal form, all that remains is the judicious selection of keys.

We've already handled the `auditoriums` table, which was an example of a table deserving of a composite key. Next, we'll look at tables that have single-column keys. We'll further break down the single-column case into two groups: primary key columns that should be left as monotonically increasing *ids* (the Rails default), and primary key columns that are candidates to be based on intrinsic, or natural, data. Then, we'll come back to the `auditoriums` table to see how to implement composite primary keys in Rails using a plugin. Finally, we'll look at the `movie showtimes` table, which is also a case of a table deserving a composite primary key, but we'll treat it as a special instance. We'll explain what heuristics should be used to decide when to not use composite keys, and instead of using a strict natural key, we'll introduce the concept of a Rails-DK/NF hybrid, which gives us the benefits of natural keys, but preserves some of the conveniences of Rails *id* columns.

Single column keys

The tables that hold movies, ratings, payment types, orders, ticket purchase line-items, and zip codes are examples of tables that have single column primary keys. As it happens, this is the majority of our tables, and this may be the reason why only single-column keys are available in Rails by default.

To decide whether a table's primary key should be a monotonically increasing (and therefore arbitrary) integer, we check to see if there is a more natural key. As we did earlier in this chapter, we do this by determining if there are unique constraints in the table other than the *id* primary key itself. Figure 8-4 shows all of these tables with the default Rails *id* column. Primary keys are in bold, and columns with a uniqueness constraint are in italics.

Examining these tables, we find that the `zip_codes`, `ratings`, and `orders` tables each have a single column with a uniqueness constraint apart from the primary key itself: `zip`, `rating_name`, and `confirmation_code`, respectively. Effectively, this means that there are two distinct ways to access a row of data, but the distinction is not meaningful. These columns can be merged into one without any loss of functionality in retrieving data. Because Rails doesn't actually care what kind of data is in the *id* column, and because you override the primary key's column name with the `set_primary_key`

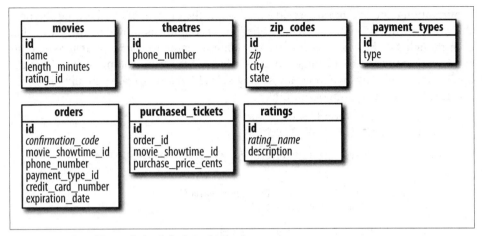

Figure 8-4. *The tables with the default Rails id column*

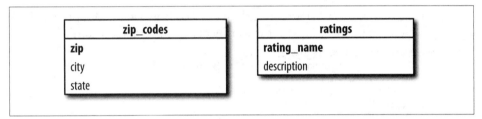

Figure 8-5. *Domain tables that may never be modified after an initial data load*

directive in your models, you also don't lose any built-in Rails functionality by merging the columns *and* choosing more descriptive column names than "id."

We already saw an example of this in Chapter 7, where we defined the primary key of the `zip_codes` table to be the `zip` column. For zip codes and ratings, which are domain tables and may never be modified after an initial data load, it's easy to forego reliance on the Rails mechanism for choosing new keys. These tables are shown in Figure 8-5, without the redundancy of two sets of unique columns.

Note that what we are doing here is only appropriate if the primary key is not likely to change, or at least if changes are infrequent enough that they aren't normal business use-cases within our application. For domain data, which—with the exception of zip codes—has a corresponding constant within the codebase, and for which we have no plans to build an edit interface, we can be reasonably assured that we are safe on this point.

For the `orders` table, the confirmation code also has no valid use case for change, so we can merge the `id` and `confirmation_code` columns. It may seem more difficult to break with convention, though, because we need to generate a special value before saving each record. But since we need to generate the confirmation code regardless of whether it is the primary key, it's no more difficult. In fact, we can easily generate a confirmation code in a `before_create` method in the `Order` class by hashing the next value of the sequence that would have filled the *id* column, as shown below.[*] Note that even though we changed the primary key column name to `confirmation_code`, Rails still forces us to refer to all single-column primary keys via a column called `id` at the application level. Thus when we are setting `self.id` below, we are actually filling the `confirmation_code` column of our table:

```
class Order < ActiveRecord::Base
  set_primary_key :confirmation_code

  has_many :purchased_tickets, :foreign_key => 'order_confirmation_code'

  def before_create
    next_ordinal_id = Order.connection.select_value(
      "select nextval('orders_id_seq')"
    )
    self.id = next_ordinal_id.crypt("CONF_CODE")
  end
end
```

The following output from *script/console* shows this code in action. Our primary keys are now beautiful random strings of text worthy of any confirmation code system:

```
>> o = Order.create({:movie_showtime_id => 1,
                     :purchaser_name => 'Joe Moviegover'})
=> #<Order:0x2553af0>
>> o.id
=> "COtW6pplX6z7o"
```

Adding dependent objects still works just as we expect:

```
>> o.purchased_tickets << PurchasedTicket.new(:purchase_price_cents => 650)
=> [#<PurchasedTicket:0x25166c8>]
>> o.confirmation_code
=> "COtW6pplX6z7o"
```

There are other benefits to having the natural key be the primary key, too. Consider the `orders` table, and the dependent table `purchased_tickets`, shown in Figure 8-6. On the left, we have Rails default *id* columns. On the right, the `orders` table has been updated to use the `confirmation_code` column as the primary key. Now, the `purchased_tickets` table has a `order_confirmation_code` column rather than an `order_id` column to reference the orders table. The added benefit is that if we have a confirmation number—likely to be provided by a visitor to our site to look up her order or to print out her tickets at a kiosk—we can select directly from the `purchased_tick ets` table. We don't have to first find the order record in the `orders` table, and then join against the `purchased_tickets` table to get the information we are looking for. When

---

[*] Note that `nextval` is a Postgres-specific command that generates the next value of a sequence. There is a method, `next_sequence_value`, which would have done this for us in a database-independent way, but Postgres support for this function sits in a patch awaiting merge to the Rails core as of this writing (Ticket #9178). If you're using Oracle, support is already there.

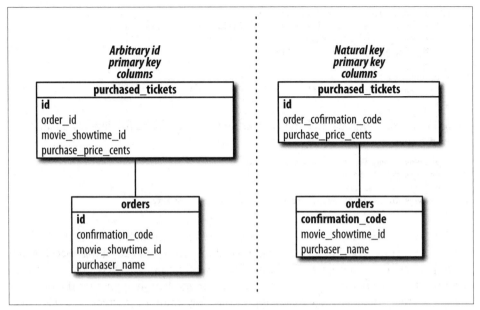

Figure 8-6. The orders table and its dependent purchased_tickets table

we removed the indirection *id* primary key column, indirection went away along with it.

The remaining tables, `theatres` and `movies`, keep the default *id* primary key column.

Using Composite Keys in Rails

Although Rails doesn't have built-in support for composite primary keys, there are two good methods for getting the benefits they provide. The first method is via a plugin by Dr. Nic Williams called, naturally, `composite_primary_keys`. The second is via a hybrid model—a Rails-DK/NF hybrid—discussed later in this chapter.

Using the composite_primary_keys plugin

The `composite_primary_keys` plugin is available at *http://compositekeys.rubyforge.org*. There you'll find more extensive documentation on how to use the plugin, but to install it as a gem, just type the following from the command line:

```
sudo gem install composite_primary_keys
```

Then add the following line to the end of your *config/environment.rb* file:

```
require 'composite_primary_keys'
```

Next, in your models, define the composite primary key with the plugin's pluralized analog to `set_primary_key`, `set_primary_keys`:

```
class Auditorium < ActiveRecord::Base
  # we do this because Rails inflection fails for this class name
  set_table_name 'auditoriums'
  set_primary_keys :room, :theatre_id

  belongs_to :theatre
  has_many :movie_showtimes, :dependent => :destroy
end
```

Then, in models that reference the composite key, specify the foreign key as an array of column names:

```
class MovieShowtime < ActiveRecord::Base
  belongs_to :movie
  belongs_to :theatre
  belongs_to :auditorium, :foreign_key => [:room, :theatre_id]
end
```

Working with models that have composite primary keys is straightforward; they behave just like regular models. Notice below that we don't need to do anything special when creating an Auditorium object. Similarly, when we create a MovieShowtime object, we don't need to specify the separate pieces of the foreign key. Just passing the object is enough for the plugin to pull out the appropriate key columns to create the reference:

```
m = Movie.create!(
  :name => 'Casablanca',
  :length_minutes => 120,
  :rating => Rating::PG13)
t = Theatre.create!(
  :name => 'Kendall Cinema',
  :phone_number => '5555555555')
a = Auditorium.create!(
  :theatre => t,
  :room => '1',
  :seats_available => 100)
ms = MovieShowtime.create!(
  :movie => m,
  :theatre => t,
  :auditorium => a,
  :start_time => Time.new)
```

Using a DK/NF-Rails hybrid

The next table we'll investigate is the movie_showtimes table. The combination of (movie_id, theatre_id, room, start_time) is certainly unique, and therefore it's a candidate to be a primary key. In fact, we have a greater constraint on showtimes than this: a movie cannot begin playing in an auditorium until the previous movie has finished (we'll see how to deal with this sort of constraint in the next chapter). But the decision to make a composite key a primary key is not based solely on whether the key is unique. The next question we must ask is whether changing the key is a valid use case or not.

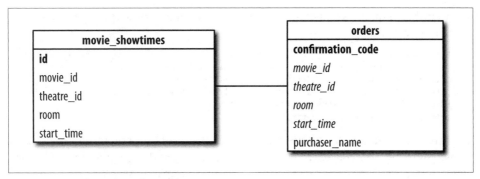

Figure 8-7. Updating the orders table

Are movie times set in stone once tickets have been purchased, or can the times be changed, patrons be damned? One school of thought would say the answer is yes. Why shouldn't a movie showtime be changeable?

On the other hand this may feel like a bait-and-switch operation to those who've already bought tickets, so another school of thought would say no. Once there is a dependent record—especially a dependent record that has been paid for, such as an order—the record cannot change. The appropriate course of action would be to mark the original record as cancelled, create a new one for the new time, and take action to refund the original ticket purchases. Patrons could then buy tickets to a different showtime if they so choose. That would certainly be fairer to patrons, and the database would then accurately reflect the events that transpired as well.

In the interest of a pure DK/NF data model, we would, therefore, define the full set of columns in the `movies_showtimes` table as a composite primary key. However, for the purposes of providing a breadth of examples, we'll say here that movie times *are* changeable. Although it's not impossible to make changes to a primary key, in practice it can be a bit more inconvenient to do so than it is for other columns. With ActiveRecord, it is actually impossible to change a primary key at all unless one resorts to custom SQL statements. Therefore, for those who are faint of heart when it comes to custom SQL, for now, we will retain our *id* column for `movie_showtimes`, but we'll also update the `orders` table to reference the rest of the columns, in addition to the standard Rails *id* column reference of `movie_showtime_id` (Figure 8-7). This will allow us the referential integrity benefits of a natural key while also maintaining some of the benefits of an *id* primary key: namely, it will be possible within Rails to make changes to the key without resorting to custom SQL.

Note that in order to add a foreign key reference from one table to another, the target columns of the constraint must constrained to be unique. This has two purposes. First, if there was no unique key, we could risk referencing more than one record, which would not be meaningful (in fact, it would be a bug, although MySQL allows such a relationship). Second, the unique constraint also adds an implicit index on the columns, which facilitates a quick internal database check to make sure the reference is valid.

Without the uniqueness constraint, we get the following error when we try to add the foreign key constraint:

```
movies_development=# alter table orders
  add constraint movie_showtimes_movie_theatre_room_start_time_fkey
  foreign key (movie_id, theatre_id, room, start_time)
  references movie_showtimes(movie_id, theatre_id, room, start_time);
ERROR:  there is no unique constraint matching given keys for
referenced table "movie_showtimes"
```

To correct this, we add the unique constraint on the rest of the columns in `movie_show` `times`: `movie_id`, `theatre_id`, `room`, `start_time`, and everything works fine. The two tables, `movie_showtimes` and `orders`, can be defined compactly as follows:

```
create sequence movie_showtimes_id_seq;
create table movie_showtimes (
  id integer not null
    default nextval('movie_showtimes_id_seq'),
  movie_id integer not null
    references movies(id),
  theatre_id integer not null
    references theatres(id),
  room varchar(64) not null,
  start_time timestamp with time zone not null,
  primary key (id),
  unique(movie_id, theatre_id, room, start_time),
  foreign key (theatre_id, room)
    references auditoriums(theatre_id, room) initially deferred
);

create sequence orders_id_seq;
create table orders (
  confirmation_code varchar(16) not null
    check (length(confirmation_code) > 0),
  movie_showtime_id integer not null
    references movie_showtimes(id),
  movie_id integer not null,
  theatre_id integer not null,
  room varchar(64) not null,
  start_time timestamp with time zone,
  purchaser_name varchar(128) not null
    check (length(purchaser_name) > 0),
  primary key (confirmation_code),
  foreign key (movie_id, theatre_id, room, start_time)
    references movie_showtimes (movie_id, theatre_id, room, start_time)
) inherits (addresses);
```

Making assignment easier with method overrides

One of the drawbacks of a hybrid model in which the natural key exists in addition to an arbitrary *id* column is that the columns must be assigned explicitly even in places where the Rails associations would normally do the magic for us. For example, ordinarily we would assume we could do the following to create an **order** object, assuming we already have a `movie_showtime` object in the variable *ms*:

```
>> o = Order.create!(
?>   :movie_showtime => ms,
?>   :purchaser_name => 'Joe Moviegoer')
```

This won't work with our hybrid model, however, because the columns `movie_id`, `theatre_id`, `room`, and `start_time` need to be specified as well. When not using the `composite_primary_keys` plugin, Rails knows only that the second line above implies the `movie_showtime_id` column's value. The rest of the values must be specified manually, as follows:

```
o = Order.create!(
  :movie_showtime => ms,
  :movie => ms.movie,
  :auditorium => ms.auditorium,
  :start_time => ms.start_time,
  :purchaser_name => 'Joe Moviegoer')
```

Note that we did get to skip the definition of the theatre because the auditorium composite key takes care of that for us.

We'd rather keep things simple, though. We really want Rails to accept the simpler syntax that we'd get if we chose to use the composite keys plugin, and with a little extra magic, we can get assignment to behave the way we expect it to.

In order to make this work, we use the `alias` method to save the old `movie_showtime=` assignment method under a new name, `old_movie_showtime=`. We then rewrite the original method to do all the assignments we expected it to do. Finally, we call the old framework method to be sure our method doesn't have any unintended side effects. Here is our method:

```
class Order < ActiveRecord::Base
  alias :old_movie_showtime= :movie_showtime=
  def movie_showtime=(ms)
    self.movie_id = ms.movie_id
    self.theatre_id = ms.theatre_id
    self.room = ms.room
    self.start_time = ms.start_time
    self.old_movie_showtime=(ms)
  end
end
```

Deferrable Foreign Key Constraints

Because natural keys are by definition not arbitrary—they are made up of the intrinsic information that identifies the row—care must be taken when changing that data. For example, if you sell a ticket for a movie showtime and then try to change the auditorium that movie is set to play in, you will immediately get a referential integrity violation exception from the database. The composite foreign key reference in the `orders` table will no longer have a corresponding row in the `movie_showtimes` table.

Deferrable constraints allow you to postpone the checking of foreign key relationships until the end of a transaction. Note that being inside a transaction is the key to deferrable constraints. You are only granted a short, closed period during which referential integrity can be violated. The following unit test illustrates how to change part of a key without violating referential integrity in dependent tables:

```ruby
def setup
  @m = Movie.create!(
    :name => 'Casablanca',
    :length_minutes => 120,
    :rating => Rating::PG13)
  @t = Theatre.create!(
    :name => 'Kendall Cinema',
    :phone_number => '5555555555')
  @a = Auditorium.create!(
    :theatre => @t,
    :room => '1',
    :seats_available => 100)
  @ms = MovieShowtime.create!(
    :movie => @m,
    :theatre => @t,
    :auditorium => @a,
    :start_time => Time.new)
  @o = Order.create!(
    :movie_showtime => @ms,
    :movie => @m,
    :theatre => @t,
    :auditorium => @a,
    :start_time => @ms.start_time,
    :purchaser_name => 'Joe Moviegoer')
end

def test_deferrable_constraints
  MovieShowtime.transaction do
    @ms.start_time = @ms.start_time + 1.hour
    @ms.save!
    Order.update_all(["start_time = ?", @ms.start_time],
      ["movie_showtime_id = ?", @ms.id])
  end
end
```

Of course, the test fails, since we haven't yet defined our foreign key reference to be deferrable:

```
ChakBookPro:chapter-7-dknf chak$ ruby test/unit/movie_showtime_test_case.rb
Loaded suite test/unit/movie_showtime_test_case
Started
E
Finished in 0.657148 seconds.

  1) Error:
test_deferrable_constraints(MovieShowtimeTestCase):
ActiveRecord::StatementInvalid: PGError: ERROR:  update or
delete on table "movie_showtimes" violates foreign key constraint
"orders_movie_id_fkey" on table "orders"
```

```
DETAIL:  Key (movie_id,theatre_id,room,start_time)=
(20,20,1,2007-12-16 00:53:49.076398-05) is still referenced from table "orders".
: UPDATE movie_showtimes SET "start_time" = '2007-12-16 01:53:49.076398',
"theatre_id" = 20, "movie_id" = 20, "room" = '1' WHERE "id" = 20
```

To create a deferrable constraint, simply append the keyword initially deferred when defining the constraint:

```
create table orders (
  confirmation_code varchar(16) not null
    check (length(confirmation_code) > 0),
  movie_showtime_id integer not null
    references movie_showtimes(id),
  movie_id integer not null,
  theatre_id integer not null,
  room varchar(64) not null,
  start_time timestamp with time zone,
  purchaser_name varchar(128) not null
    check (length(purchaser_name) > 0),
  primary key (confirmation_code),
  foreign key (movie_id, theatre_id, room, start_time)
    references movie_showtimes (movie_id, theatre_id, room, start_time)
    initially deferred
);
```

With our initially deferred foreign key, our unit test now passes:

```
ChakBookPro: chak$ ruby test/unit/movie_showtime_test_case.rb
Loaded suite test/unit/movie_showtime_test_case
Started
.
Finished in 0.093331 seconds.

1 tests, 0 assertions, 0 failures, 0 errors
```

Deferrable constraints solve the problem of "seldom changing." They give you cake and let you eat it, too. You can have true referential integrity, but you also are granted a window where referential integrity can be compromised—as long as you are using that window to make appropriate updates in dependent tables.

Note one caveat to this method of testing our deferrable constraint: deferrable constraints have meaning only within a transaction. Unit tests are all run within transactions to facilitate cleanup between each test run—all the effects of a unit test are rolled back before the next test is run. This means that, even if you forget to start and end your own transaction, the test will appear to pass even though the same code would throw a database exception elsewhere. This also, unfortunately, makes it impossible to write a negative unit test for deferrable constraints.

Understanding the Trade-offs

In this chapter, we've seen three variations on referential integrity. The first is based on the Rails default of *id* column primary keys. Through a rather simple example, we showed that single-column primary keys are not always enough to guarantee that a problem domain's referential integrity is maintained. We can easily be given a false sense of security that our data is protected when we have referential integrity constraints throughout a data model, but we run into problems when those constraints don't match the real-world constraints behind the problem. For those situations, only natural keys can give our data the protection it deserves.

We then saw two ways to implement natural keys. One method is a strict adherence to domain key normal form using the `composite_primary_keys` plugin. The other method is a hybrid that utilizes both Rails *id* columns for the primary keys but also enforces referential integrity with unique constraints and references on natural keys. The trade-offs between these methods are summarized in Table 8-1.

Table 8-1. Trade-offs of the methods for implementing natural keys

	Rails id columns only	Strict DK/NF with composite primary keys plugin	Rails-DK/NF hybrid
Supported out of the box	✓		✓
Domain-specific referential integrity		✓	✓
Natural key can be updated via Rails API	N/A		✓
Efficient use of indexes	✓	✓	
Ease of writing code	✓	✓	

The last two metrics, efficient use of indexes and ease of writing code, are worth discussing in more detail.

Efficient use of indexes

It's obvious that with the Rails-DK/NF hybrid, we need two sets of indexes and references as compared with a strict DK/NF data model. First, we need to index and reference the Rails *id* columns. We additionally need to place unique constraints on the natural key and then reference that key as well in dependent tables. This imposes a cost in our database in terms of both time and space. There is a time cost because each insert, update, or delete on a referenced table requires that two indexes be updated and checked. Inserts and updates to dependent tables also require two checks rather than one to be sure the reference is valid. It's worth paying this price only if the problem domain requires that the natural key be mutable. In our movie showtime example, we argued rather unconvincingly that this might be the case. We also presented a convincing argument that the natural key for showtimes be fixed, and that showtimes should be cancelled if, for example, the time needed to be changed and orders had already been placed. In many other real-world problems, it's similarly unwise to change natural keys once real-world dependencies are in play, as will often be the case.

Often newcomers to DK/NF are initially wary of leaving the well-understood behind. If you feel like you really need the security of being able to change natural keys through

Rails after dependent objects have been created, take a step back and re-examine the business case for doing so. As natural keys are those that map in some way to real life, in all but the most bizarre of circumstances, it makes more sense to deactivate old records and create new ones when this situation arises.

Ease of writing code

One of the major strength of Rails is that much can be said in very few lines of code, so conventions that reduce programmer efficiency should be anathema to a Rails programmer. As we saw, using the `composite_primary_keys` plugin does not require much in the way of additional code to make it work: just a single line in the class with the composite key to define it, and an extra parameter when defining associations in dependent classes. After that, coding proceeds as usual. In the Rails-DK/NF hybrid, we don't need any special definition for our natural key (other than database indexes and constraints), but because the relationship doesn't factor into the association relationship from Rails's point of view, we must constantly specify all of the natural key columns when creating objects that reference the key. That is, unless we override the association assignment method to make the assignments for us, but that too, is additional code to write.

While this is not exactly onerous, it should be considered when choosing to use the DK/NF-Rails hybrid over a strict natural key model.

Figure 8-8 shows the end product of this chapter's additions.

Exercises

1. Try to reproduce the anomaly demonstrated in Example 8-1. Convince yourself that with the correct composite keys, it is impossible.
2. Make a list of real-world queries that are simplified by a composite key reference from `orders` to `movie_showtimes`.

Refactor Steps

1. Examine each table. Are there any non-primary key columns that have a unique constraint, or which should have a unique constraint?
2. If you found places where you must add a unique constraint, add it:

   ```
   create unique index concurrently table_name_column_one_column_two_uniq_idx
       on table_name(column_one, column_two, ...);
   ```
3. Choose the next steps based on whether your unique constraint is based on one column or multiple columns.

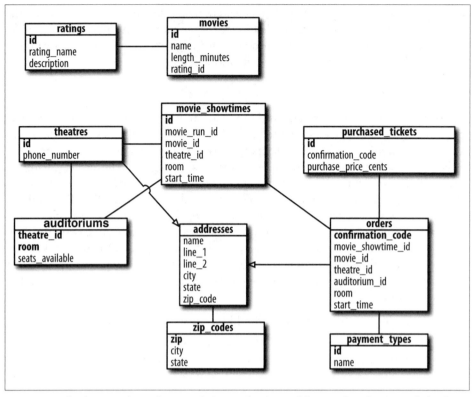

Figure 8-8. The theatre tickets schema with domain key/normal form and Rails-DK/NF hybrid

Single Column Refactor

1. In the table's model class, change the primary key column using `set_primary_key`:

   ```
   set_primary_key :unique_column
   ```

2. In tables that reference this table, add a column to reference the new key:

   ```
   alter table dependent_table
     add column referenced_table_unique_column coltype;
   ```

3. Fill the column with appropriate values:

   ```
   update dependent_table
     from referenced_table r
       set referenced_table_unique_column = r.unique_col
     where referenced_table_id = r.id;
   ```

4. Add the foreign key reference constraint to each dependent table:

   ```
   alter table dependent_table
     add constraint referenced_table_unique_column_fkey
       (referenced_table_unique_col)
     references referenced_table(unique_col);
   ```

5. Drop the original id column and reference:

```
alter table referenced_table
  drop column id;
alter table dependent_table
  drop column referenced_table_id;
```

6. Set the new column as the primary key:

```
alter table referenced_table
  add primary key(unique_column);
```

Multiple Column Refactor

1. Install the composite_primary_keys gem:

```
gem install composite_primary_keys
```

2. Load the gem in your application. In *environment.rb*, add the following:

```
require 'composite_primary_keys'
```

3. In the table's model class, change the table's primary key using set_primary_keys:

```
set_primary_keys [:col1, :col2, ...]
```

4. Follow the steps for single column refactor, starting with 2.

## CHAPTER 9

Guaranteeing Complex Relationships with Triggers

In this chapter, we'll go over an advanced technique for mapping tricky real-world referential integrity constraints to the data layer. This technique uses *database triggers*, which allow you to run arbitrary code to check that new data is valid before inserting or updating rows. We'll write a stored procedure that ensures an auditorium isn't double-booked and create a trigger that runs our procedure whenever a movie showtime is added or changed. I'll describe the basic structure of a function in Postgtres's procedural language PL/pgSQL, so you can start building your own functions for a variety of uses, and cover the special properties of trigger functions.

Constraint Checking with Triggers

As just noted, stored procedures that can be triggered when certain conditions in the database are met can allow you to check for and guarantee arbitrarily complex relationships. A number of times throughout this book, the issue of double-booking an auditorium has come up. This problem is not easy to avoid with simple foreign key or check constraints because the problem spans multiple tables. Auditorium bookings are recorded in the movie_showtimes table, but the length of a movie is recorded in the movies table (Figure 9-1).

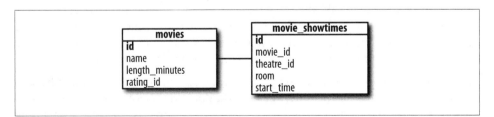

Figure 9-1. Auditorium bookings in movie_showtimes; length of movie in movies

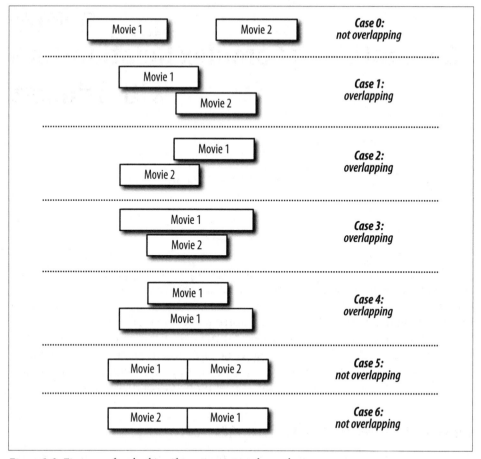

Figure 9-2. Five cases for checking if two time intervals overlap

There are also a number of cases to be considered to determine whether one showtime overlaps with another. Figure 9-2 shows these cases. The first case, Case 0, is the throwaway case: the showtimes do not overlap. In Case 1, the movies do overlap: Movie 2 starts after Movie 1, but before Movie 1 finishes. Case 2 is the same case with the movies reversed: Movie 1 starts after Movie 2, but before Movie 2 finishes. In Case 3, Movie 2 starts and ends while Movie 1 is playing. Case 4 is the opposite of Case 3: Movie 1 starts and ends while Movie 2 is playing. Finally, we also want to treat the edge cases of a movie starting exactly when another movie ends, which may be okay for a double feature with no intermission. Therefore, if a start time and end time are the same, it's OK, but if two start times are the same, it's not OK.

Examining all of these cases, we find the following statements hold true: if either the start or end time of one movie is between the start or end time of another movie, then the movies overlap. That is, unless the start time of one movie is equal to the end time of the other movie.

Rather than attacking this whole problem all at once, we work in stages. We begin by creating a small function called do_times_overlap, shown in Example 9-1. This method takes four arguments: start and end times for two intervals, respectively, and evaluates the expression we came up with earlier. The function also checks for invalid inputs, which can occur if an end time is before a start time.

Example 9-1. A PL/pgSQL function to determine if two intervals overlap

```
create or replace function do_times_overlap(
  start_1 timestamp with time zone,
  end_1 timestamp with time zone,
  start_2 timestamp with time zone,
  end_2 timestamp with time zone
) returns boolean as $$
begin
  if end_1 < start_1 then
    raise exception 'First end time is before first start time.';
  end if;
  if end_2 < start_2 then
    raise exception 'Second end time is before second start time.';
  end if;
  if start_1 = end_2 or start_2 = end_1 then
    return false;
  else
    return (start_1 between start_2 and end_2)
        or (end_1 between start_2 and end_2)
        or (start_2 between start_1 and end_1)
        or (end_2 between start_1 and end_1);
  end if;
end
$$ language plpgSQL;
```

The next order of business is to test this function. Does it work for all of these cases? Example 9-2 shows our test case class and all our tests, including tests that check that exceptions are thrown on invalid inputs. It may seem onerous or even wasteful to test such little pieces of code—indeed, the code to write the tests takes up twice as much space as the code we are testing—but it's worth it. In the interest of full disclosure, neither the PL/pgSQL function nor the set of test cases came out right the first time through when they were added to this example. It took a few iterations to get it all right, and writing the tests was instrumental in that process. I could have just tested the procedure ad-hoc—which is how much code is often tested—but as I changed the code to cover all cases or improve readability, I was able to quickly rerun the test cases, guaranteeing that after each change, all scenarios were covered. The result is not only a more complete test bed but also a correct and more complete function, which accurately accounts for all cases, even those I didn't think of right away.

Example 9-2. Tests for the do_times_overlap PL/pgSQL function, placed in test/unit/physical/
do_times_overlap_test_case.rb

```ruby
require File.dirname(__FILE__) + '/../test_helper'

module Physical
  class DoTimesOverlapTestCase < Test::Unit::TestCase

    def setup
      @start_1 = Time.new
      @end_1 = @start_1 + 1.hour

      @before   = @start_1 - 15.minutes
      @between  = @start_1 + 15.minutes
      @between2 = @start_1 + 30.minutes
      @after    = @end_1 + 15.minutes
      @after2   = @end_1 + 30.minutes
    end

    def do_times_overlap?(s1, e1, s2, e2)
      result = ActiveRecord::Base.connection.select_value("
        select do_times_overlap('#{s1}', '#{e1}', '#{s2}', '#{e2}')
      ")
      return (result == "t")
    end

    def test_do_times_overlap
      # case 0 - non-overlapping
      assert !do_times_overlap?(@start_1, @end_1, @after, @after2)
      # case 1 - movie 2 starts in the middle of movie 1
      assert do_times_overlap?(@start_1, @end_1, @between, @after)
      # case 2 - movie 2 ends in the middle of movie 1
      assert do_times_overlap?(@start_1, @end_1, @before, @between)
      # case 3 - movie 2 starts and ends during movie 1
      assert do_times_overlap?(@start_1, @end_1, @between, @between2)
      # case 4 - movie 1 starts adn ends during movie 2
      assert do_times_overlap?(@start_1, @end_1, @before, @after)
      # case 5 - non-overlapping - movie 2 starts right after movie 1
      assert !do_times_overlap?(@start_1, @end_1, @end_1, @after)
      # case 6 - non-overlapping - movie 1 starts right after movie 2
      assert !do_times_overlap?(@start_1, @end_1, @before, @start_1)
    end

    def test_exceptional_cases_caught
      test_for_db_error("Nonsense data was allowed") do
        do_times_overlap?(@end_1, @start_1, @before, @start_1)
      end
    end

    def test_exceptional_cases_caught_2
      test_for_db_error("Nonsense data was allowed") do
        do_times_overlap?(@start_1, @end_1, @after, @before)
      end
    end
```

```
    end
end
```

Anatomy of a PL/pgSQL Function

Next, we will write the function that will be triggered on inserts and updates, check_movie_showtime_overlaps. The actual definition of this function is shown in Example 9-3, but we'll start by going over the structure of a PL/pgSQL function in detail so that you can apply the lessons of this chapter to your own future, unknown situations.

Following is the basic structure of a PL/pgSQL stored procedure. Replaceable portions are in italics, and the rest of the code is common to all procedures:

```
CREATE FUNCTION myfunc(myparam sometype) RETURNS sometype AS $$
DECLARE
  local_variable sometype := default_value;
BEGIN
  -- procedure body goes here
  RETURN local_variable;
END;
$$ LANGUAGE plpgsql;
```

Aside from the basic structure, we see that a procedure has a name—our procedure is called *myfunc*—which we use to identify and also to execute it.

Procedures can also take parameters in a comma-separated list. Here we have a single parameter, *myparam*. Parameters also must have their type specified. Here we have used *sometype* as a placeholder for a real Postgres type. In practice, we would specify an actual type here: integer, varchar, etc.

Special types are available in PL/pgSQL procedures as well, which allow us to deal with entire rows of data. To specify that a type should have the structure of a particular table's row, you say *tablename%ROWTYPE*. If the structure does not match any particular table's row definition—for example, if the row is a result of a query that joins multiple tables—you can specify the type record, which is a generic container for a set of columns returned from a query.

We can also add comments to PL/pgSQL procedures. Comments are either SQL style, beginning with --, or C style:

```
/* This is a C style PL/pgSQL comment. */
```

Notice that we end the function by specifying the language. Postgres supports stored procedures written in a number of languages. Included in the core distribution is language support for stored procedures written in Tcl, Perl, and Python, in addition to the SQL procedural language PL/pgSQL. There are also a number of languages developed outside the Postgres core, which can be downloaded and set up alongside the built-in languages. These include PHP, Java, and Ruby. Although writing our procedures in Ruby is tempting, I don't do so in this book because PL/pgSQL is the most portable;

it matches Oracle's PL/SQL rather closely, so you won't have to do much relearning if you're writing your website atop Oracle rather than Postgres.

Regardless of which language you do choose, before you can write a procedure in that language, you must tell Postgres you are going to use it within your the database. You do so by issuing the `create language` command:

```
create language plpgsql;
```

You need to create a language only once for each database. A good place to put any language definitions you might have is at the start of your database install SQL script.

It's all strings

The entire body of a PL/pgSQL procedure is a string. In our preceding example, the string is delimited with double dollar signs (`$$`). We could have used the standard SQL string delimiter of an apostrophe (`'`), but then any apostrophes denoting strings within the procedure body would need to be escaped. This can get ugly, and it's also an easy way to write bugs. Therefore, in PL/pgSQL procedures, you can create as many unique string delimiters as you want, as long as they start and end with a dollar sign. `$$`, `$F$`, and `$FUNCTION$` are all valid delimiters. It's a good practice to avoid quoting your quotes, using single apostrophes only for innermost strings. The following shows assignment of a string containing an apostrophe to a variable:

```
CREATE FUNCTION myfunc() RETURNS void AS $FUNC$
DECLARE
    book text := $$'Scaling to Enterprise' by Dan Chak$$;
BEGIN
END;
$FUNC$ language plpgsql;
```

Local variables and assignment

Any local variables used within a PL/pgSQL procedure must be declared in the `declare` section. The syntax is:

```
varname <type> [:= default_value];
```

Once a variable has been declared, there are two mechanisms for assignment. One we've already seen: you specify `:=` after a variable name. You can follow `:=` with a literal, or with a SQL select statement. However, you drop the keyword `select`; it's implied when using this syntax:

```
varname := foo from bar where baz = 1;
```

The second assignment mechanism is `select into`. You specify a target variable followed by the query:

```
select into varname foo from bar where baz = 1;
```

The two methods are largely equivalent. The distinction occurs when you are selecting into a variable of type `record` or `%rowtype`; in these situations, you must use the `select into` syntax.

Blocks

PL/pgSQL is a block-level language. The structure of a block is:

```
DECLARE
    -- declarations
BEGIN
    -- code
END;
```

This looks much like our `do_times_overlap` method itself, and indeed, entire functions do comprise a block. You can embed blocks within other blocks if you are writing complex procedures and want to keep variables local to certain chunks of code.

Trigger-specific features

When writing a procedure that is to be used as a trigger, there are some additional things to keep in mind. First, such procedures must have `trigger` as their return type.

Next, in an insert or update operation, a special local variable `NEW` is available, which contains the row being inserted or updated. In updates, the variable `OLD` contains the original row that is about to be changed.

Triggers: fail safe versus fail fast

The return value of a trigger procedure determines what is ultimately stored in the database. If `NULL` is returned, no insert or update occurs. Otherwise, a record of the same structure as the row to be inserted should be returned, and that will be the record that is inserted. You can create a new record, or modify `NEW` in place and return it. These are ways to *fail safe* in the presence of some bad data. You know you don't want to commit the data to the database, but it's not critical enough in nature to put a halt to the application trying to do the inserts.

Most often, if you are using triggers to guarantee referential integrity, you'll want a hard stop that lets callers know explicitly that they're attempting something bad. Usually that signals a bug in software code that should be fixed. In these cases, you want to *fail fast*. To do so, you throw an exception, which will be rethrown to the application layer:

```
raise exception 'Exception thrown at %', now();
```

You can customize exception strings with substitutions. Within a string, you insert a % wherever you want to substitute text, and then add additional parameters for each substitution. We failed fast in our `do_times_overlap` function when end times were before start times. Indeed, this indicates some type of programming error, and we want to catch this as soon as possible. Otherwise, we will get unpredictable results from our procedure, and the bug may go undetected for some time, causing user frustration and compromising our data.

Conditionals

PL/pgSQL supports branching on conditional statements. The most common is an IF-THEN-ELSE structure, which is nestable. IFs must end with a matching END IF:

```
IF [conditional] THEN
  -- code
ELSE
  -- code
END IF;
```

Of course, there are additional conditionals in PL/pgSQL, as well as other control structures, and other language features in general. For complete documentation, see *http://www.postgresql.org/docs/8.2/static/plpgsql.html*. However, what I've just explained is enough to write and fully understand the procedure we'll write to guarantee movie showtimes do not overlap, shown in Example 9-3.

Example 9-3. The check_for_movie_showtime_overlaps PL/pgSQL trigger function

```
create or replace function check_movie_showtime_overlaps()
  returns trigger as $F$
declare
  new_end_time timestamp with time zone;
  conflicting_showtime record;
begin
  new_end_time := NEW.start_time +
      ((select length_minutes
          from movies
          where id = NEW.movie_id) || ' minutes')::interval;
  select into conflicting_showtime
         ms.*, m.*
    from movie_showtimes ms,
         movies m
   where ms.id != NEW.id
     and ms.theatre_id = NEW.theatre_id
     and ms.room = NEW.room
     and ms.movie_id = m.id
     and do_times_overlap(
         NEW.start_time,
         new_end_time,
         ms.start_time,
         ms.start_time + (m.length_minutes || ' minutes')::interval)
   limit 1;
  if conflicting_showtime is not null then
    raise exception $$This showtime overlaps with another showtime
in the same auditorium: '%' starting at %$$,
      conflicting_showtime.name, conflicting_showtime.start_time;
  else
    return NEW;
  end if;
```

```
end
$F$ language plpgsql;
```

To specify that a procedure should be executed as a trigger, we have to create the trigger on a particular table. We create a trigger as follows:

```
create trigger check_movie_showtime_overlaps_iu_trigger
    before insert or update
    on movie_showtimes
    for each row
    execute procedure check_movie_showtime_overlaps();
```

The final step would be to create unit tests—positive and negative tests and also tests that check for resilience against bogus inputs—for the `movie_showtimes` class. By now, you should be a pro at writing unit tests, so doing so is left as an exercise for the reader.

## CHAPTER 10

Multiple Table Inheritance

We've spent a lot of time on the idea of tweaking your data model until it's rock solid, impervious to application-layer bugs or a meddling Martha at the `psql` prompt. By now, you should feel like you're ready to practice referential integrity jujitsu or constraint kung fu. It may come as a surprise, then, to learn that there is a feature of ActiveRecord, *polymorphic associations*, that *depends* on breaking the referential integrity we've worked so hard to ensure.

Before you get your knickers in a knot, remember that ActiveRecord was primarily developed against MySQL, at a time when referential integrity was a "feature" that MySQL did not support. So it's understandable that some "features" crept into ActiveRecord and Rails that are not really features at all but actually Sdisasters waiting to happen.

In this chapter, we'll examine polymorphic associations, understand the problem they were intended to solve, and come up with a better solution that allows us to preserve referential integrity. We'll continue with our practice of pairing a powerful new pattern at the application layer with getting the most we can for free out of the data layer, allowing the two layers to work together side by side.

The Problem

Polymorphic association allows you to define a relationship between two tables without knowing ahead of time what one of the tables in the relationship is. This allows you to define "xor" relationships: "A has one of B or C but not both." Usually, it's assumed that B and C are of similar logical types, but just happen to be stored in different tables.

As an example, consider an object model for an employee who must choose between health plans of different styles, HMOs versus PPOs, as shown in Figure 10-1.

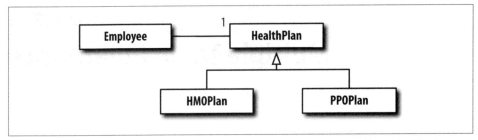

Figure 10-1. Object model for an employee associated with one of a set of different health plans

We see that in our object model, we want to differentiate between pan types. HMOs and PPOs definitely behave differently. We could still represent this at the data layer with a single table, using Rails' built-in single-table inheritance mechanism, but recognizing that HMOs are evil, the architect of this model chose to keep them separate.

Polymorphic associations to the rescue! Assuming we keep our health plan tables separate—one for HMOs and one for PPOs—we can define our `Employee` class like so:

```
def Employee < ActiveRecord::Base
  belongs_to :health_plan, :polymorphic => true
end
```

To specify an association is polymorphic, you say `:polymorphic => true` in an association definition. To support this, the `employee` table must look like this:

```
create table employees (
  id integer not null
    default nextval('employees_id_seq'),
  name varchar(64) not null,
  health_plan_id integer not null,
  health_plan_type varchar(32) not null
);
```

This trick is implemented in the data layer with two columns for the association. The first is the foreign key reference, `{foreign_table}_id`. The second specifies the table name of the foreign object: `{foreign_table}_type`.

This seems great—a veritable panacea to the problem of multiple table inheritance; unfortunately, the Rails approach to polymorphic associations is at odds with a design that hopes to enforce referential integrity. Because it's not known what table `foreign_table_id` refers to, it's not possible to add a foreign key constraint enforcing the relationship. This opens the design back up to the possibility of orphaned associations and generally invalid data. In fact, this construct is completely unconstrained at the application layer. You can assign any object into the `health_plan` attribute, not just `HMOPlan` or `PPOPlan` objects. What seemed like an elegant solution is suddenly a black hole for bugs.

In this chapter, we'll learn a better way to handle this sort of relationship. We'll start with a discussion of polymorphism in general. Understanding this important computer science principle will help us avoid abusing it. Next, we'll look at two mechanisms for inheritance: *single table inheritance* (STI) and *multiple table inheritance* (MTI). Rails supports STI out of the box. When you use it, you don't need a polymorphic association. Rails doesn't, however, support true MTI out of the box, and this is where polymorphic associations come into play; they attempt to solve that problem, but not very well. We'll see how to make MTI work in Rails, then learn how to make polymorphic associations work correctly in both the data and application layers in the section "XOR on Columns," later in this chapter.

With this technique, the relationship is just as easy to manage from the Rails application layer as polymorphic associations. We'll also have the added benefit that the database is put to work on our behalf to ensure the integrity of our data.

What Is Polymorphism?

Polymorphism is the property in a programming language that allows objects of different types to be substituted for one another in program flow without needing to know ahead of time what the object's type is.

Many people would take issue with that definition as overly simplistic. Indeed, most discussions about polymorphism are much more intricate because they get caught up in the syntax of a particular language and how you *achieve* polymorphism, as if it's an epic battle. This leads to discussion of the places where you can *have* polymorphism, followed by what hoops you must jump through to *get* polymorphism. In Ruby, polymorphism is everywhere, so it's much simpler.

Yes, polymorphism applies to methods as well as objects. For example, we could define a method plus, which just applies + to two parameters:

```
def plus(a, b)
  a + b
end
```

This method doesn't care what the types of a and b are. Method signatures are completely untyped. We also see polymorphism in the + operator itself. As long as it has meaning for the parameters, the method will work:

```
>> plus(1, 2)
=> 3
>> plus("hel", "lo")
=> "hello"
>> plus([1], [2])
=> [1, 2]
```

We can also demonstrate polymorphism at the object level; through inheritance, subclasses can take on specialized behavior not found in the base class:

```
class Animal
  def noise
    raise "Noise not defined for #{self.class}"
  end
end
```

```
class Dog < Animal
  def noise
    "Woof!"
  end
end

class Cat < Animal
  def noise
    "Meow!"
  end
end
```

We can now iterate over a list of animals printing out their noises:

```
>> [Cat.new, Dog.new].each{|a| puts a.noise}
Meow!
Woof!
```

We called the noise method on each object, and the right noise was made for each animal because the method was overridden in each class definition. In many languages, as well as in our preceding example, the language feature we used to implement polymorphism was inheritance. However, in Ruby, we don't need to use inheritance to get this behavior. We could have left the Animal class out altogether, as in the following, and the output of our puts loop would be identical:

```
class Dog
  def noise
    "Woof!"
  end
end

class Cat
  def noise
    "Meow!"
  end
end
```

In Ruby, inheritance is a mechanism for sharing common behavior, but it's not a prerequisite to achieve polymorphism. When we iterate over a list, there is no requirement that the list members be of the same type or inherit from a common ancestor (truth be told, all objects in Ruby *do* inherit from Object). In many other languages, class inheritance (or in Java, the use of *interfaces*) is how you achieve polymorphism with objects. Not so in Ruby, due to *duck typing*. In Ruby, you never specify the expected types of inputs to methods or their return values, nor do you specify the type of objects composing a list, hash, or other structure; as long as an object has the properties a caller expects it to have, everything just works. The distinction between polymorphism for methods as opposed to polymorphism for objects is blurred in Ruby. In most languages, the need for a distinction is borne out of implementation syntax. In Ruby, these syntactical considerations simply don't exist.

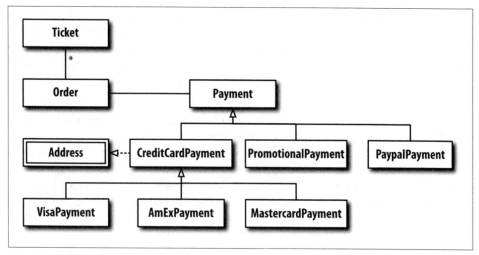

Figure 10-2. Logical model for the order payment system

Inheritance and Persistence

Aside from utility functions, most polymorphism in web programming *is* related to inheritance, be it strict class inheritance or implementation of interfaces through module includes.

The consideration, then, is how to store these hierarchies of objects in the database. Should the data be stored in a single table or in multiple tables? And if the latter, how do we do this in the context of Rails using ActiveRecord? In this chapter, we'll expand upon the payment data model we left off with in Chapter 5, reworking it to be more complete from the perspective of our real-world application. In doing so, we'll encounter a case of STI, which Rails supports by default. We'll also encounter an example of MTI.

Since our application is about to get rather complex, we begin by developing a logical model for the order payment system before we jump to the physical model.[*] The logical model is shown in Figure 10-2. We still have an order, which contains multiple tickets. However, we now split off the payment into its own class. We have three distinct types of payments: a credit card payment, as we had previously, a Paypal payment, and also a free promotional payment, which might be granted for entering a valid promotional code. The CreditCard class is a super class of three accepted card types: AmEx, Visa, and MasterCard. All credit card payments need address information, so the Credit Card class also implements the Address interface via a module include.

We have two inheritance hierarchies: one descending from CreditCardPayment and one descending from Payment. Logically there is no practical difference. The question to ask

---

[*] Logical versus physical models are dealt with in depth in Chapter 15.

when determining what type of *physical* inheritance to use (single- or multiple-table) is whether subclasses actually share any physical data. If all or even most of the data is shared from one subclass to the next, then single table inheritance is an appropriate choice. However, if the classes do not have much data in common, then multiple table inheritance (or even *no* inheritance at the data layer) is the right choice.

It's tempting to use single table inheritance for everything because it's built-in, but that would be a big mistake. When you use single table inheritance in cases where there is little data overlap, your data model becomes confusing; many of the columns are not intended to be filled except under certain circumstances—when the row is of the appropriate subtype. Similarly, the application layer becomes polluted with getter and setter methods for each physical column in the table; when viewed from the logical model's perspective, these columns and their getters and setters aren't intended to be there. When you use single table inheritance, the physical model of the data layer bleeds through to the logical model of the application.

STI also has another drawback: class names get saved to the database to identify the type of each row, linking code and data in a way that can have unexpected consequences as your application matures. One constraint you impose upon yourself by using STI is that your class names become more or less set in stone. If you decide to change them, you must update all the records that reference the original classes. On a production database with millions of records and active users, making such a change is practically impossible. It could take hours, and in the meantime, either your site slows to a crawl or it simply doesn't work because STI relationships can't be figured out.

Single Table Inheritance

We have recast our credit card model from Chapter 4. There we left off with credit cards implementing a sort of *strategy pattern*; credit card objects were constants whose methods could be applied to orders to get a job done, such as processing a payment. This time we'll take a different approach. Here, we've split off the payment information from the Order class. Each CreditCardPayment object will contain the data necessary to process a transaction: the credit card number, expiration information, and any address data necessary to authorize the transaction.

The object itself can take care of the processing, operating on its own local data. But there won't ever be any CreditCardPayment objects; the objects will be instances of one of the subclasses (MasterCardPayment, VisaPayment, and AmexPayment), which will define the particular behavior for processing transactions of that type. Because the types of information supplied by users to process a credit card payment is the same regardless of the payment type, this is a perfect case for single table inheritance. The physical single table that holds credit card payments for AmEx, Visa, and MasterCard is shown in Figure 10-3. The type column changes depending on which card type was chosen, specifying which class should be used.

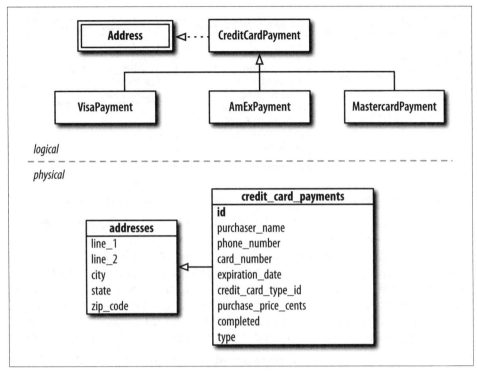

Figure 10-3. Logical and physical models for CreditCardPayment and its subclasses; physical model uses STI

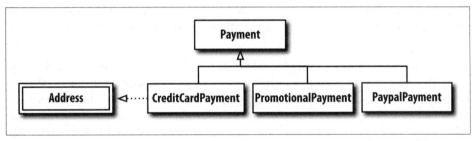

Figure 10-4. Logical model for Payment and its subclasses

Multiple Table Inheritance

Next we turn our attention to a very different case. We have defined three different methods for payment—by credit card, by Paypal, or by entering a promotional code—and we can imagine over time there may be even more payment options. New contenders such as Google Checkout or Amazon's payment system are likely future additions. Figure 10-4 shows this segment of our logical model.

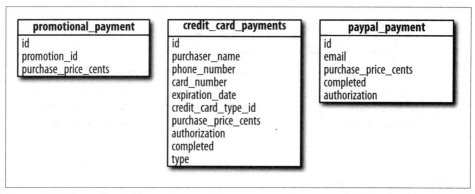

promotional_payment	credit_card_payments	paypal_payment
id	id	id
promotion_id	purchaser_name	email
purchase_price_cents	phone_number	purchase_price_cents
	card_number	completed
	expiration_date	authorization
	credit_card_type_id	
	purchase_price_cents	
	authorization	
	completed	
	type	

Figure 10-5. Physical model for our three payment types; no inheritance needed in the physical model

The physical models for these three classes is shown in Figure 10-5, along with all of their attributes. What we find when we look at these three payment subclasses is that they don't share much information in common between them. A Paypal payment might have the user's email address, as well as some returned authorization information from Paypal that means the payment was successful. A free ticket purchased via a promotional code might have a foreign key reference to the pertinent promotion (not shown). And standard credit card payment records will have all the credit card information necessary to process the transaction, and also any returned authorization information.

While the three subtypes of `CreditCardPayment` shared much in common, and were therefore ripe for single table inheritance, these three disparate payment types don't share much in common at all. They share the transaction amount, whether the payment was processed successfully or not, and if we stretch ourselves, the record *id* as well. Therefore, we keep these tables separate, but each model class will continue to inherit from the `Payment` class, so that we can continue to take advantage of the benefits of inheritance.

One problem we run in to, though easily solved, is that Rails assumes the table name associated with a class is based on the first class in the hierarchy to descend from `ActiveRecord::Base`. In this case it would be assumed that a table called `payments` existed, and that it contained a `type` column. This assumption is what makes single table inheritance work. When using multiple table inheritance, we need to tell Rails to use each subclass's own table, using the `set_table_name` directive in each subclass:

```
class Payment < ActiveRecord::Base
end

class PromotionalPayment < Payment
  set_table_name 'promotional_payments'
end

class CreditCardPayment < Payment
  set_table_name 'credit_card_payments'
end
```

```
class PaypalPayment < Payment
  set_table_name 'paypal_payments'
end
```

Our initial goal was to set up a relationship between the orders table and these payment types without using :polymorphic => true. Instead, we add to the orders table references to each of these tables. Example 10-1 shows the orders table with these references, each of which can support a true database-level constraint, unlike an application-level polymorphic assocation. Note that unlike most other references we have defined in this book, promotional_payment_id, credit_card_payment_id, and paypal_payment_id must all be nullable because only one of them should contain an actual reference at any one time. The challenge then, is how to make sure *only one* of the references is not null. We accomplish this with XOR on columns.

Example 10-1. Orders table with references to each subclass in a multiple table inheritance hierarchy

```
create table orders (
  confirmation_code varchar(16) not null
    check (length(confirmation_code) > 0),
  movie_showtime_id integer not null
    references movie_showtimes(id),
  movie_id integer not null,
  theatre_id integer not null,
  room varchar(64) not null,
  start_time timestamp with time zone,
  credit_card_payment_id integer
    references credit_card_payments(id),
  promotional_payment_id integer
    references promotional_payments(id),
  paypal_payment_id integer
    references paypal_payments(id),
  primary key (confirmation_code),
  foreign key (movie_id, theatre_id, room, start_time)
    references movie_showtimes (movie_id, theatre_id, room, start_time)
initially deferred
);
```

XOR on Columns

XOR, pronounced *"ex or"* is also known as *exclusive or*. It is a mathematical operator, meant to be applied to two inputs, which tests that one of the two values is true, but not both. Table 10-1 is a truth table for XOR.

Table 10-1. Truth table for two-value XOR

A	B	A XOR B
False	False	False
True	False	True
False	True	True
True	True	False

We could write XOR simply in Ruby:

```ruby
def xor(a, b)
  (a || b) && !(a && b)
end
```

It would also not be difficult to write this as a database check constraint. If we were only trying to guarantee the relationship that only one of `paypal_payment_id` or `promotional_payment_id` were not null, forgetting for a moment about `credit_card_pay ment_id`, we could create a constraint as follows:

```sql
alter table orders add constraint paypal_or_promotional_payment_xor
  check(
    (paypal_payment_id is not null or promotional_payment_id is not null)
     and not
    (paypal_payment_id is not null and promotional_payment_id is not null)
  );
```

However, the situation gets a bit more complicated when we move to a relationship with more than two columns. Strictly speaking, the mathematical definition of XOR for more than two values is not exactly what you might expect. Traditionally in mathematical contexts, XOR beyond two inputs is true if an odd number of values are true. For our purposes, we want a real *exclusive* or, meaning one and only one value is true. Therefore, for three values, a truly exclusive XOR would look like this in Ruby:

```ruby
def xor3(a, b, c)
  (a || b || c) &&
  !(a && b) && !(a && c) && !(b && c)
end
```

As we go up in the number of parameters, the first part of our expression, `(a || b || c)`, where we check that at least one value is true, expands linearly with the number of parameters. However, the second half of the expression, where we check that not more than one value is true, expands mathematically as the number of parameters *choose* two, written as shown here:

$$\binom{n}{2}$$

This means that we need to enumerate every pair that exists in the set, and that can be cumbersome to write. Cumbersome code tends to lead to coding errors, so we'd like to avoid that.

Instead we note a special property. If we convert values that are not null to 1, and values that are null to 0, and add these up, the property we want to maintain is true if the sum of these values is equal to 1.

We can convert an expression that evaluates to true or false to numerical values in the database using an integer cast. In Postgres, we would write this as:

```
(expression)::integer
```

An expression that evaluates to true is equal to 1 when cast to an integer, and a false expression evaluates to 0. So for three columns, only one of which should be null, we can cast the expressions to integers, and add them up. If the sum is equal to 1, then we know that only one column is not null. We add the following constraint to the orders table using this technique:

```
alter table orders add constraint payment_xor check(
  (credit_card_payment_id is not null)::integer +
  (paypal_payment_id      is not null)::integer +
  (promotional_payment_id is not null)::integer = 1
);
```

We now have the referential integrity we desired in the data layer. The next step would be to write database unit tests, which is left as an exercise. We'll skip ahead here to our next goal: easy-to-use polymorphic associations at the application layer, built atop our solid data model.

Elegant MTI in Rails

The physical data model we are left with now has three physical associations from our orders table to the various payment tables, shown in Figure 10-6. We would normally express such a relationship in Rails by creating a belongs_to relationship for each one:

```
class Order < ActiveRecord::Base
  belongs_to :credit_card_payment
  belongs_to :promotional_payment
  belongs_to :paypal_payment
end
```

Even though the physical model has three independent connections, application code is where we want to deal with objects the way our logical model dictates the objects fit together. Looking back at our logical model in Figure 10-2 (shown earlier), we see that an Order object has a Payment object. One nice aspect of the built-in polymorphic associations is that this relationship is created for you automatically; you can assign instances of any payment type directly into a attribute called payment, rather than having to explicitly assign into the attribute of the correct type, as we would have to do with three separate belongs_to declarations we wrote above.

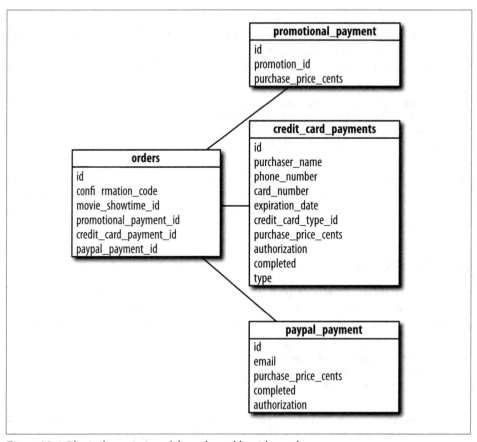

Figure 10-6. Physical association of the orders table with our three payment types

Luckily, we can get the behavior we want; we just need to create it ourselves. We'll use inheritance to accomplish this. The first step is to define our Payment class. It doesn't do much. It's purpose is to collect the subclasses somewhere; even though duck typing means our payment types don't have to descend from Payment to act like payments, we'll use the inheritance relationship to facilitate our implementation of MTI. The Payment class, therefore, is simply a shell:

```
class Payment < ActiveRecord::Base
end

require 'credit_card_payment'
require 'paypal_payment'
require 'promotional_payment'
```

Note that we also loaded each subclass using the require command. Generally, it's a bad idea for a parent class to know about its subclasses, but due to the way Rails loads code—only when it's needed—the subclasses may not get loaded in time for our needs here. We'll discuss how to get around this problem later in the book.

Example 10-2 shows how we go about creating an accessor, **payment**, which gives us the right object, regardless of which association is actually in use. Note that we could have written this method in a much simpler way, but we wrote it in a generic fashion so it could be applied to other classes, or be recast as a plugin, without much change. Writing it generically also allows us to introduce some advanced features of Ruby and Rails.

Example 10-2. Polymorphic accessor for multiple table inheritance

```
class Order < ActiveRecord::Base
  # assocations would go here...

  def payment
    # for a given class, returns the appropriate symbol
    # to pass to the ActiveRecord method reflect_on_association
    def reflection_symbol(klass)
      klass.to_s.split("::").last.underscore.to_sym
    end

    # for all subclasses of the given base class, returns a
    # list of defined associations within the current class
    def association_methods(mti_base_class)
      Object.subclasses_of(mti_base_class).collect{|p|
        assoc = self.class.reflect_on_association(reflection_symbol(p))
        assoc ? assoc.name : nil
      }.compact
    end

    # invoke each association method and return the first
    # that is not null
    association_methods(Payment).collect{|a|
      self.send a
    }.inject do |a, b|
      a || b
    end
  end
end
```

The above example of our **payment** accessor is rather complex, so we'll go through each piece in turn. If you are unfamiliar with any of the built-in Ruby or Rails methods introduced here, check the upcoming sidebar.

API Reference

Here are some Ruby methods:

array.collect {|item| block }→*an_array*
Invokes block once for each element of self. Creates a new array containing the values returned by the block:

```
a = [ "a", "b", "c", "d" ]
a.collect {|x| x + "!" }   #=> ["a!", "b!", "c!", "d!"]
a                          #=> ["a", "b", "c", "d"]
```

```
array.compact→an_array
```
Returns a copy of self with all `nil` elements removed:
```
[ "a", nil, "b", nil, "c", nil ].compact
                      #=> [ "a", "b", "c" ]
```

```
enum.inject {| memo, obj | block }→an object
```
Combines the elements of `enum` by applying the block to an accumulator value (memo) and each element in turn. At each step, `memo` is set to the value returned by the block. The first form lets you supply an initial value for `memo`. The second form uses the first element of the collection as the initial value (and skips that element while iterating).

```
# Sum some numbers
(5..10).inject {|sum, n| sum + n }  #=> 45
# Multiply some numbers
(5..10).inject(1) {|product, n| product * n } #=> 151200
```

And here are some Rails methods:

```
reflect_on_association(association)→AssociationReflection
```
Returns the `AssociationReflection` object for the named association (use the symbol):
```
# returns the owner AssociationReflection
Account.reflect_on_association(:owner)
# returns :has_many
Invoice.reflect_on_association(:line_items).macro
```

```
underscore(camel_cased_word)→String
```
The reverse of `camelize`. Makes an underscored form from the expression in the string. Changes `::` to `/` to convert namespaces to paths:
```
"ActiveRecord".underscore
        #=> "active_record"
"ActiveRecord::Errors".underscore
        #=> "active_record/errors"
```

```
Object.subclasses_of(*superclasses)→[Class]
```
Returns an array containing the subclasses of the parameters. The superclasses themselves are returned as well.

The first point to note is that we can define methods inside other methods. Notice that within the payment method, we've defined two additional helper methods, reflection_symbol and association_methods. The reason we did this is to limit the *scope* of these methods. By defining them within the payment method, which is the only place we need them, these methods are only accessible within that method, and they won't conflict with other methods that may have the same name. The more modules we mix in or plugins we use, the higher the risk of conflict and the greater the need for scoping.

Next let's look at the helper method reflection_symbol. This method would turn a class variable, such as CreditCardPayment, into the symbol :credit_card_payment. In this method, we've chained a number of methods together. The single line of code does quite a lot of things. Let's break it down:

- Starting with the input class, referred to locally within the method as `klass`, we cast the class name to a string with `to_s` so that we can use string operations.

- We then account for classes that are within modules, e.g., `SomeModule::CreditCardPayment`. The `split` method cuts our string everywhere that the split text is found, and returns an array, `["SomeModule", "CreditCardPayment"]`.

- The `last` method returns the last element of the array, which is the string representation of the class name we are interested in, `"CreditCardPayment"`.

- The `underscore` method transforms camel-case text into lowercase text separated by underscores everywhere there was a capital letter: `"CreditCardPayment"` becomes `"credit_card_payment"`.

- Finally, we turn this back into a symbol, using `to_sym`. The result is `:credit_card_payment`, which is the input expected by the Rails method `reflect_on_association`, which we'll deal with next.

The purpose of the `association_methods` method is to give us a list of the accessors for each subclass of the passed-in class, in this case `Payment`. Based on how we defined our associations for the three subtypes, we know that the methods are named `credit_card_payment`, `promotional_payment`, and `paypal_payment`. We could write a single-use method that returns this list. Instead of writing a single-use method that we would have to constantly update as we make changes, we instead write a general function that automatically gives us all the right associations. We don't want our code to break if we change the association definitions, or add or remove subclasses.

This method also looks complicated at first glance, but we'll examine it in detail as well:

- We start with the input, `mti_base_class`, which is the base class in the polymorphic association; `Payment` in this case.

- Rails extends the class `Object`, which is the base class of all classes in Ruby, with the method `subclasses_of`. As its name implies, this method returns all subclasses of the passed in class. This is the reason we needed to preload the subclasses of `Payment` ahead of time; if they aren't preloaded, this method returns an empty array. Passing `Payment` to `subclasses_of` produces `[CreditCardPayment, PromotionalPayment, ...]`. Note that this list includes all of the subclasses of `CreditCardPayment`, too.

- We then utilize the `collect` method on this array of classes, which allows us to run a block of code for each element. `collect` returns a new array where each element is the result of the code block run against each input element.

- Inside the code block, we run the ActiveRecord method `reflect_on_association`, which returns an object containing all the information Rails knows about the given association. For example, if we had given a custom name to the association, or if the foreign key is nonstandard, the information is contained in this return value. An example return object is shown in Example 10-3.

- We then check to see if there actually was an association defined at all. For example, the various subclasses of CreditCardPayment are included up to this point, but we didn't define an explicit association for each of them; they were included implicitly in the association with CreditCardPayment itself. If there was an association found, we call name on the association data, which gives us the name by which we can access the associated object. Otherwise, we return nil.

- Finally, we call compact on the result, so the nil values are removed. This method returns [credit_card_payment, promotional_payment, paypal_payment].

Example 10-3. A return value from reflect_on_association

```
>> Order.reflect_on_association(:credit_card_payment)
=> #<ActiveRecord::Reflection::AssociationReflection:0x24e13d8
@primary_key_name="credit_card_payment_id", @through_reflection=false,
 @active_record=Order,
@options={}, @class_name="CreditCardPayment", @name=:credit_card_payment,
 @macro=:belongs_to>
```

Finally, we can deal with the remaining code in the payment method, which makes use of these two helper methods, reflection_symbol and association methods:

- We start with the result of association_methods, which are the accessors for each association, as explained earlier.

- For each one, we call that method on the current object using send. The result is the associated object, if there is one, or nil if there isn't.

- We used collect, so the result is a new array of objects. All should be nil except for the association that actually exists.

- We could get the non-nil value out in a variety of ways. Above we saw compact, which would give us the non-nil values. Instead here we introduce inject, which allows us to apply an operator to the values of an array, two items at a time. Injecting || as we do here first applies || to the first two elements in the array. It then applies || to the first result and the third element, and so on. In other words:

    ((a || b) || c) || ...)

Evaluating this expression returns the first non-nil value encountered. This is the associated payment object that we are looking for.

It's another tribute to Ruby's compactness that it took more than two pages to explain a few lines of code. As you become more familiar with the entirety of the Ruby and Rails APIs and get comfortable using Ruby's powerful syntax, you can really say a whole lot with very little code.

In Example 10-4, we define the complementary method, payment=, which assigns the argument to the correct association assignment method. We won't go through it in detail; based on the explanation of the **payment** method, you should be able to understand it.

Example 10-4. Polymorphic assignment for multiple table inheritance

```
def payment=(p)
  def reflection_symbol(klass)
    klass.to_s.split("::").last.underscore.to_sym
  end

  def reflection_assignment_method(klass)
    Order.reflect_on_association(reflection_symbol(klass.class)).name.to_s + "="
  end

  self.send reflection_assignment_method(p.class), p
end
```

Factory Classes

Let's return to the **Payment** class. It's a very sad class, completely empty and with next to no purpose; however, we can give it a purpose by turning it into a factory class, utilizing another pattern in the famous Gang of Four *Design Patterns* (Addison-Wesley) by Erich Gamma et al. and making our MTI solution even more powerful and DRY.

A factory class is a class that has a constructor that returns instances of the correct subclass based on the inputs. Currently, if we have web forms with a radio selector for the payment type (Paypal, credit, or promotional), we'd have to write a case statement in every place we're processing the input in order to create an instance of the correct type. Same goes for the credit card type (Visa, American Express, or MasterCard).

Instead, we can localize this logic in the **Payment** class itself. Any code that needs a new payment object can pass in the appropriate information to the factory method and out will come an object of the correct type.

In the following code, we define a constructor, **new_payment**, for the **Payment** class:

```
class Payment < ActiveRecord::Base
  def self.new_payment(payment_type, credit_card_type)
    case type
    when 'paypal'
      PaypalPayment.new
    when 'promotional'
      PromotionalPayment.new
    when 'credit_card'
      CreditCardPayment.new_payment credit_card_type
    end
  end
end
```

Notice that if the payment is a credit card payment, we defer to a constructor within the **CreditCardPayment** class. That constructor might look like this:

```
class CreditCardPayment < Payment
  # other code ...
  def self.new_payment(credit_card_type)
    case credit_card_type
    when 'american_express'
      AmericanExpress.new
    when 'visa'
      Visa.new
    when 'master_card'
      MasterCard.new
    end
  end
end
```

Speaking of DRY, these classes are also a good place to keep a list of the allowable inputs to the constructor that can be used to build the dropdowns or radio button lists in our views. For example, the following array can be passed to `options_for_select` to create a credit card drop-down:

```
CREDIT_CARD_TYPES_FOR_SELECT = [
  ['visa', 'Visa'],
  ['american_express', 'AmericanExpress'],
  ['master_card', 'MasterCard']
]
```

We can then create a select box with the appropriate values for our constructor by calling `select_tag` and `options_for_select` like this:

```
<%= select_tag(
 'credit_card_type',
 options_for_select(CreditCardPayment::CREDIT_CARD_TYPES_FOR_SELECT)
) %>
```

Exercises

1. Write unit tests for the `orer_payment_xor` constraint. Ensure that the data layer prohibits any order with zero or multiple payments but accepts orders with a single payment.

2. Following the example laid out in this chapter, extend the MTI plugin with a `has_many` MTI association method.

3. What other methods are needed to create a complete MTI plugin? How would you implement them?

Refactor Steps

These sections break down the refactoring steps for you.

Refactoring STI

1. Examine each STI table in your data model. For each, determine how much data is really shared between the subclasses.

2. If the answer is "not much," or if different subclasses call for different constraints that are difficult to reconcile with each other, proceed with this multiple table inheritance refactoring.

3. Create a separate table for each class, custom fit to the class's needs.

4. Maintain the inheritance relationship in the model classes, but explicitly use the `set_table_name` directive in each class.

5. In the associated classes, replace built-in association declarations with the MTI-flavored ones developed in this chapter.

6. Run your tests.

Refactoring: polymorphic => true

1. Make a list of all the referenced types. You can find this list with the following SQL query, assuming the polymorphic type column is called *{foreign_table}_type* and the association exists in a table called **widgets**:

   ```
   select distinct foreign_table_type from widgets;
   ```

2. For each table referenced, add a column to the table with the polymorphic association (**widgets** here) that references the target table directly. The column should be nullable:

   ```
   alter table widgets
     add constraint specific_foreign_table_fkey
     (id) references specific_foreign_table(id);
   ```

3. For each table, set the reference. Keep in mind that your old data may have invalid references, which you should avoid copying:

   ```
   update widgets
      set specific_foreign_table_id = foreign_table_id
    where foreign_table_type = 'SpecificForeignTable'
      and exists (
   select true
     from specific_foreign_table sft
    where sft.id = foreign_table_id
   );
   ```

4. Once steps 2 and 3 have been repeated for all referenced tables, decide what to do with orphaned references. You may want to update them to a valid state or simply delete them. To delete them, delete rows where all of the specific foreign key references are `null`:

```
delete from widets where
 specific_foreign_table_1_id is null and
 specific_foreign_table_2_id is null and
 ...
 specific_foreign_table_n_id is null;
```

5. Add an XOR constraint to ensure future records will not become orphaned or invalid:

```
alter table widgets
  add constraint sft_1_thru_n_xor check (
  (specific_foreign_table_1_id is not null)::integer +
  (specific_foreign_table_2_id is not null)::integer +
  ... +
  (specific_foreign_table_n_id is not null)::integer) = 1);
```

6. Create a base class based on the original polymorphic association name, and derive all referenced classes from it.

7. Use the MTI plugin developed in this chapter to create the appropriate associations in the widget class:

```
belongs_to_mti :base_class_name
```

8. Run your tests.

## CHAPTER 11

View-Backed Models

Some concepts are extremely easy to explain in words, yet difficult to extract from a database. For example, on a ticket-purchasing site, it's pretty obvious that you need a way to quickly show visitors "current movies in my area." That is certainly an easy concept, but let's examine what it takes to get that kind of information out of our database.

"Current" means we need to be looking in the `movie_showtimes` table. We might define current to mean movies starting within a week.

Knowing the showtime isn't enough. We need to get the movie information, too. A showtime without the movie name isn't very useful. While we're at it, we probably need to know the rating and the length of the movie as well.

The request "in my area" means we need to know where the visitor is and where the movie theatre is. We can use the PL/pgSQL distance procedure `miles_between_lat_long` that we wrote in Chapter 6, but to do so we need data from the `theatres` table (the zip code) and from the `zip_codes` table (the latitude and longitude).

This represents a query with four tables: `movie_showtimes`, `theatres`, `movies`, and `zip_codes`. We *could* write an ActiveRecord query that could get us what we want:

```
MovieShowtime.find(:all,
  :include => [:movie, :theatre],
  :conditions => "
      movie_showtimes.start_time - now() < '1 week'::interval
    and movie_showtimes.start_time > now()
  "
)
```

The first problem we notice, as far as ActiveRecord die-hards are concerned, is that we've got some SQL peaking through here. There's no good way to say "current" in ActiveRecord parlance. The next problem is that we haven't accounted for "in my area" yet. To do that, we need to get to the `zip_codes` table through the `theatres` table, but that's not supported using the `:include` syntax. Certainly we don't want to get all of the current showtimes and then loop through them in the application layer to find the ones that are nearby. There are likely to be far more that aren't close than those that are so that would be inexcusably slow.

We can get to the zip code data using the `:joins` syntax, but this is just another mechanism to inject raw SQL through ActiveRecord:

```
MovieShowtime.find(:all,
  :include => [:movie, :theatre],
  :joins => "join zip_codes on (theatres.zip_code = zip_codes.zip)",
  :conditions => ["
        movie_showtimes.start_time - now() < '1 week'::interval
    and movie_showtimes.start_time > now()
    and miles_between_lat_long(
      zip_codes.latitude, zip_codes.longitude, ?, ?
    ) < ?
  ", request.latitude, request.longitude, request.miles]
)
```

It's getting pretty ugly, and this is with an example just complex enough to prove a point, yet simple enough to include in this book. A more complex, real-life query might extend more than half a page. Plainly speaking, this is *not* what ActiveRecord is good at. As soon as you have custom SQL in your ActiveRecord queries, you've lost one of the main benefits of ActiveRecord: queries are written to be database-independent.

Complex joins and complex conditions are never going to be easy to abstract away behind a simple-to-use library. In this case, with ease-of-use comes a loss of functionality. If we try to avoid SQL at all costs, using only the most well polished aspects of ActiveRecord, such as simple finds, and then take care of the joins and conditions in the application layer, we're going to pay dearly in performance costs. The database is optimized for these purposes, and the application layer is not.

We've hit upon a moment where SQL really wants to shine through. Here is an opportunity to sit upon the shoulders of giants, rather than try to hide the giant.

Luckily, we can restore order in the application layer by creating a view-backed model, which is the topic of the remainder of this chapter. And what's more, if we delegate this complexity to the database, we have further opportunities for performance enhancements that we wouldn't have otherwise. That's the topic of the next chapter: materialized views.

Database Views

There are two ways to think of a database view. The first way is as a named subquery, ready to be referenced in other queries. The second way is to think of it as a table that is defined by an algorithm—in the form of an SQL query—that can, with a few caveats, be treated like any other table.

Most people think of views by the second definition, but both are correct. In fact, you should be able to predict what the caveats mentioned in the table definition are by contrasting how a real table and a subquery can and cannot be used. Go ahead and think about it. The answers will be revealed in the section "Considerations" later in this chapter.

Creating a View

The syntax for creating a view is simple:

```
create view name as query;
```

For current movies, we would create the following view:

```
create or replace view current_movie_showtimes as
  select m.name,
         m.rating_id,
         m.length_minutes,
         ms.*,
         t.name as theatre_name,
         t.zip_code,
         z.latitude,
         z.longitude
    from movie_showtimes ms
    join movies m on (ms.movie_id = m.id)
    join theatres t on (ms.theatre_id = t.id)
    join zip_codes z on (t.zip_code = z.zip)
   where (ms.start_time - now()) < '1 week'::interval and ms.start_time > now();
```

Notice that lots of relevant data has been brought into the view from the referenced tables movies and theatres. The reason this is done is so that getting that information in the future doesn't require us to join against those tables for a second time.

It's also a good idea to select the primary key columns of tables, e.g., movies.id and theatres.id, so that it *is* still possible to do an ActiveRecord join later if necessary. In fact, the view just shown does implicitly select these columns; they are included in ms.*. Those columns exist in the movie_showtimes table as movie_id and theatre_id. When we see how to base an ActiveRecord model on a view in the next section, this will come in handy as it allows us to define associations just like in any other model. We'll gain flexibility at no additional cost.

Basing a Model on a View

Basing a model on a view is actually straightforward. The syntax is the same as it would be for a normal table. For the current_movie_showtimes table, our CurrentMovieShow time class is defined like this:

```
class CurrentMovieShowtime < ActiveRecord::Base
  belongs_to :movie
  belongs_to :theatre
  belongs_to :auditorium, :foreign_key => [:room, :theatre_id]
end
```

We also define the inverse relationships in the related classes. For example, in the Movie class, we have associations to both the MovieShowtime class as well as the Current MovieShowtime class:

```
class Movie < ActiveRecord::Base
  has_many :movie_showtimes, :dependent => :destroy
  has_many :current_movie_showtimes
end
```

The difference is that the relationship defined with the view cannot have a destroy dependency defined. You can only modify views by modifying the tables they depend on, so deleting from them would be meaningless (it would also cause an error).

The rest of the ActiveRecord magic still applies. You can access current showtimes directly through an association. For example:

```
cool_movie.current_movie_showtimes
```

You can also use all of the automatically defined ActiveRecord accessor on the Current MovieShowtime class itself as well:

```
CurrentMovieShowtime.find_all_by_theatre_id(@theatre.id)
```

Our original example of finding "current movies in my area" is now much simpler as well:

```
CurrentMovieShowtime.find(:all,
  :conditions => ['
    miles_between_lat_long(
      current_movie_showtimes.lat, current_movie_showtimes.long,
      ?, ?
    ) < ?
  ', lat, long, miles]
)
```

Because we defined this query within a class-level method, we can use it when traversing associations. For example, assuming we have a ZipCode object in the variable zip, we can find the current showtimes within 10 miles of that zip code with the following statement:

```
m.current_movie_showtimes.find_all_within_distance(
  zip.latitude, zip.longitude, 10
)
```

This results in only a single round trip to the database to get the results. The result objects are CurrentMovieShowtime objects, which have available all the movie and the-atre information as attributes, and also further support associations traversal to get at actual Movie and Theatre objects if needed.

Considerations

Although views are often thought of as "just-in-time" tables, and from Rails's perspective when creating models, we can treat views just like tables, *views are not tables*. I began this section stating that a view should be thought of as a named subquery. Let's take a very simple example and imagine that we defined a view, `view_of_movies`, which is essentially the same as the `movies` table itself:

```
create view view_of_movies as
select * from movies;
```

The view name, `view_of_movies`, is now a name for the subquery `select * from movies;`. If we wanted to do a simple select of all the records in this view, the query would look like this:

```
select *
  from view_of_movies;
```

But if we expand to show the subquery, we're actually doing this:

```
select *
  from (select *
          from movies);
```

Now it should become clear that many standard table operations won't work with views. Some operations that won't work on views include:

- Inserting
- Deleting
- Updating
- Referencing from another table
- Adding constraints
- Indexing

Although this seems like a long list of things you can't do, and it is, that's actually OK. These aren't disadvantages of views; they're just not what views are meant for. The word "view" itself implies that they are for looking at, not for modifying.[*]

Let's examine each of these constraints in turn and see what it means for our Rails application.

Insert, Update, Delete

Attempting to insert, update, or delete on a view triggers a database error. When you need to write data, you must do it against table-backed models. This means that view-backed models are not a replacement for table-backed ones. They must exist in parallel, and you must use the right one for the right circumstances.

---

[*] Note that the SQL standard *does* define certain scenarios under which you can insert, update, or delete from views, with the tables backing the views receiving the modifications behind the scenes. Some of these features are supported by Oracle. Postgres supports a more limited set using "rewrite rules." MySQL does not have support for this. Except under extremely rare circumstances, it's best to assume views are read-only, period, and move forward from there.

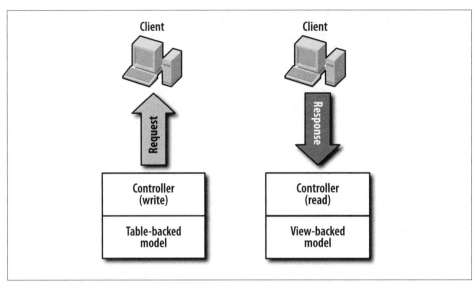

Figure 11-1. When to use view- versus table-backed models

When you are exclusively reading data, especially when reading data that matches the criteria imposed by the view's conditions, you should use the view-backed model. Some actions are only reads, such as a request that would display "current movies within my area."

If you are creating new data, use the table-backed model. An example of a write-only request might be "buy a ticket."

Some cases are less obvious. For example, in a request in the administrative interface, a single request may need to add a showtime, and then immediately return current movies at a theatre to show back to the administrative user. In this case, it's clear that you would use the table-backed `MovieShowtime` model to add the new showtime. When you're requesting data back out, you could use the `CurrentMovieShowtime` model to simplify the ActiveRecord query.

A good way to think about it is with these rules of thumb:

- If data is coming in, use a table-backed model.
- If data is going out, use a view-backed model.

These rules are shown in Figure 11-1.

References and Constraints

Views do not support references from other tables, nor do they support constraints. Using the named subquery model of views, the reasons why should be clear. But you don't need either operation.

The purpose of a reference is to ensure that data referenced from one table exists in another. A view is based on other tables, so the values you reference in a view should exist in the original table, too. If you are exclusively using a view, you may find that when you need a new reference, you instinctively think it should be added to the view. Instead, find the appropriate table the view is based on and reference that table instead.

Constraints are also unnecessary in a view. The purpose of a table constraint is to say that a row with certain properties is not valid and should not exist in the table. In a view, you can filter out invalid rows with the conditions of the view query. If you don't want rows with the property `column_a < column_b`, add that to the view's definition:

```
create view my_view as
select *
  from some_table
 where column_b >= column_a;
```

Indexing

The purpose of an index is to precompute the location of rows that meet a certain criteria in a table. When you select items out of a view, any indexes that exist on the base tables will still be used if possible. However, if you are computing a column of new values and want to filter based on that column, you're out of luck. Because views are just-in-time, data that did not exist in the base tables cannot benefit from indexes created on those tables. Each row must be computed and then selected or discarded, giving you the performance akin to a full-table scan.

Before getting disheartened, remember that without the view, the complicated Active-Record query has the same (or worse) performance. The original purpose of the view was to improve clarity in the application layer, not to boost performance. If you find that the query you turned into a view happens to be your application's biggest bottle-neck, there are additional options. The topic of the next chapter, materialized views, explains how you can, with some database wizardry, attain the benefits of views with the performance of fully indexed tables.

Exercises

1. Recast a complicated ActiveRecord query as a simpler query on a view-backed model. Now select the same information out of both, recording the time before and after. Repeat multiple times with each to eliminate the impact of disk and database caches. How does performance compare?

2. Using the same complex query and view from above, compare the database plans for each. In postgres, you can get a query plan with the command `explain plan query`.

3. Write a custom ActiveRecord extension plugin, `backed_by_view`, that when speci-fied, disables functions that would attempt to write to the view.

Refactor Steps

1. Locate complicated ActiveRecord queries that are repeated throughout your application. They don't have to be identical; "similar" is a high-enough bar.

2. Write a single SQL query that returns a superset of the data from the queries in the previous step.

3. Create a database view based on that query. Be sure to choose a name that abides by ActiveRecord naming conventions. Create a view with:

   ```
   create view viewname as query;
   ```

4. Create a model based on the view. Remember to carry over any associations from the base tables but omit destroy dependencies.

5. Within associated model classes, add associations for the new view-backed model. Again, omit destroy dependencies.

6. Replace the complicated ActiveRecord queries from the first step with more concise queries against the new view-backed model.

7. Run your tests.

## CHAPTER 12

Materialized Views

When you are not caching anything, every page load incurs the penalty of the queries required to make up that page. Initially, when you do not have much data and you do not have many users requesting pages, your application will be snappy. Unfortunately, with any amount of success, you eventually get hit with three problems seemingly all at once:

- Your application becomes popular and the traffic you need to handle has grown by orders of magnitude.

- As you sign new customers, gather data, and even simply exist, the amount of data in your database grows by orders of magnitude.

- Your application grows in complexity and more queries are required to render any given page.

Although most people would be envious of these problems (and the business side of your company would term them "successes"), you nonetheless have to find solutions.

Caching—the act of saving a queried or calculated result for future use—is not as simple and clear-cut as it sounds. A number of subtle issues surround correct caching, which go beyond picking a cache key and storing data in the cache behind that key. The first issue is freshness. Can your cache lag behind the true values of your data, or does it need to reflect the latest values? Next is correctness. If your goal is to keep the cache up-to-date, have you accounted for every situation where your cache needs to be invalidated or rebuilt? How do you know you've hit all of these cases? The final caching issue you must be aware of is the cost amortization of keeping the cache accurate. The purpose of caching is to reduce database load and speed up requests, but someone still must has pay the price for cache updates. Either the requestor who invalidates the cache or the next person to request the invalidated items will pay part or all of the cost. Choosing the wrong strategy for rebuilding can erase all of the gains that caching was meant to achieve in the first place.

In Chapter 11, we saw that a database view can be thought of as a named query. Even though a complex query can be hidden behind a simple view name, whenever you select from that view, you pay the price of database joins, subselects, filters, and functions that may be required to calculate the view results. A *materialized view* is a cached representation of a database view, stored in a regular table. Rather than query from the view with arbitrary complexity, with view materialization, an indexed table can be queried instead, with O(1) response time.

Chapter 19 contains an overview of caching at all layers of the application. In this chapter, we'll look in depth at caching on a single layer where we have already gained some experience: the database. The principles we will encounter at this layer are the same as those present at other layers of the application, but the database is the layer with the best tools for guaranteeing cache correctness. It is also the most mature and stable layer, so what you learn in this chapter can be applied to other caching problems for years to come, even as feature sets and APIs change for application layer caching solutions.

One way to look at database view materialization is that it is like the "wax on, wax off" exercise in *The Karate Kid*. It can appear painful and tedious, but when you are ready for your ultimate caching battle—where the tools may not be as thorough and you need to rely on your wits—having a nuts-and-bolts knowledge of caching via "wax on, wax off" practice will help you identify what elements may be missing from other caching at other layers, so you can be nimble as you come up with your own solutions. As you read this chapter, think beyond the database layer and identify analogs at the application layer to each situation, problem, and technique described.

Before proceeding, I'd like to give credit where credit is due, and pay tribute to Jonathan Gardner, who laid the groundwork for many who tread these waters in his online article, "Materialized Views in PostgreSQL."

Materialized View Principles

A materialized view is a *cache-complete* copy of your view. This means that every record in the original view appears in the materialized view. This is unlike an LRU cache, where items may expire from the cache if they are not used frequently, or if the set of data being cached exceeds the memory set aside for caching. In a cache-complete implementation, if an item is not in the cache, the application can assume it does not exist.

In this chapter, we will build a cache-complete materialized view for the current_movie_showtimes developed in the previous chapter. To create a materialized view, we put together a number of building blocks, which will be described in detail throughout this chapter.

The first building block is an initial view to be materialized, which ideally abides by some guidelines that ease materialization. We'll go through some slight modifications to our original view to get it into proper form before we begin.

Next is a target table in which we'll store the cached copy of the view. Unlike a view, which acts like a table, this is a full-fledged physical table, which means we can take advantage of indexing and other features available only with physical tables. In the game of performance enhancements, materializing the view is a big win in and of itself, but adding appropriate indexes hits a home run with the bases loaded.

After we have an initial snapshot in our target table, we'll need a *refresh function* that can update a single record in the materialized view when we detect a change in the base view. Sometimes we don't want to refresh right away—we instead want to put the compute cycles needed to refresh the cache off for the future—and for these cases, we'll create an *invalidation function* that marks a record as stale, but doesn't actually do the work of updating it.

We'll detect changes to the view by adding *triggers* to the base tables that make up the view. These triggers will—as the name implies—trigger either a refresh or an invalidation of the rows in our materialized view that are about to become out of sync.

Finally, we'll add some auxiliary views, including the *reconciler view*, on top of our target table to hide the fact that we've materialized the view at all. In addition to hiding our implementation from end users, the reconciler view will ensure that accurate information is always returned, even if parts of the target table have gone stale or are marked invalid.

A View to Materialize

First, we need something worth materializing. We'll start with our view from the previous chapter, but we'll make it a bit more complex so that we can explore a variety of caching techniques. Example 12-1 shows an extended version of our view, which incorporates the number of seats available in a theatre as `seats_available`, and the number of tickets purchased thus far as `tickets_purchased`. Since the purpose of this view is to show movie showtimes for which we can sell tickets, a filter has been added to the `where` clause to filter out showtimes that are sold out. Additions to our original view are shown in bold.

Example 12-1. A slightly more complex version of our original view from Chapter 11

```
create or replace view current_movie_showtimes as
  select m.name,
         m.rating_id,
         m.length_minutes,
         ms.*,
         t.name as theatre_name,
         t.zip_code,
         z.latitude,
         z.longitude,
         a.seats_available,
         coalesce(ptc.purchased_tickets_count, 0) as purchased_tickets_count
    from movie_showtimes ms
    join movies m on (ms.movie_id = m.id)
    join theatres t on (ms.theatre_id = t.id)
    join zip_codes z on (t.zip_code = z.zip)
```

```
      join auditoriums a on (ms.room = a.room and ms.theatre_id = a.theatre_id)
      left outer join (
   select count(*) as purchased_tickets_count,
          o.movie_showtime_id
     from orders o,
          purchased_tickets pt
    where pt.order_confirmation_code = o.confirmation_code
 group by o.movie_showtime_id
          ) ptc on (ptc.movie_showtime_id = ms.id)
    where (ms.start_time - now()) < '1 week'::interval and ms.start_time > now()
      and a.seats_available > coalesce(ptc.purchased_tickets_count, 0);
```

Let's pick apart some finer parts of this query to introduce some database concepts you may not be familiar with.

First, although normally you join against a table or view, you can also join against a named query. Indeed, recall from the previous chapter that a view is also nothing more than a named query. In this example, we've created a named query called ptc, for "purchased tickets count." It is a single-use named query. Unlike a view, this named query—ptc—has no meaning outside of this single place it is used; outside of the current_movie_showtimes view, it is out of scope. Of course, we could also cast ptc as a full-fledged view of its own with create view, and then we could join directly against the view. That would make current_movie_showtimes more readable and would also be a good idea if we wanted to use this subquery elsewhere. For now, we'll leave it as is and return to this idea when we talk about cascading materialized views.

Next, we've done a *left outer join* in our join against ptc. Unlike a regular join, which removes items for which there is no match between the two join tables, in a left outer join, every row from the table on the left remains regardless of whether there is a matching row from the table on the right. When there is no match, columns from the table on the right are filled with null values. In this example, if there are no tickets purchased for a given showtime, there would be no result row in the ptc subquery. However, we don't want to lose the fact that a showtime is current and has tickets available for purchase just because no one has purchased any tickets yet! That brings us to the third finer point of this query, coalesce.

The coalesce function takes an arbitrary number of arguments and returns the first one that is not null. Here, we're coalescing the number of ticket purchases—which will be null if none has been purchased yet—with 0, which is the actual value we want output when there aren't any tickets sold. So although a left outer join normally returns nulls when there's no match in the righthand table, we're substituting a value that makes sense for our domain.

Getting into Form

Although it is not technically mandatory to do so, it makes it a bit easier to implement a materialized view if every row from the view's main table is present in the view to be materialized. In order to accomplish this, we recast elements of the where clause into

Boolean columns in the table itself. Rather than filter out showtimes that aren't current, those showtimes will have a `false` entry in the `current` column, and movies that are current will have `true`. Likewise for sold out shows: they'll have a `true` entry in the `sold_out` column, and shows with seats available will have a `false` value there. Example 12-2 shows our rewritten view with the new columns in bold.

Example 12-2. where clause recast as Boolean columns to ensure every row from main base table is always represented

```
create or replace view movie_showtimes_with_current_and_sold_out_unmaterialized as
  select m.name,
         m.rating_id,
         m.length_minutes,
         ms.*,
         t.name as theatre_name,
         t.zip_code,
         z.latitude,
         z.longitude,
         a.seats_available,
         coalesce(ptc.purchased_tickets_count, 0) as purchased_tickets_count,
         ((ms.start_time - now()) < '1 week'::interval
and ms.start_time > now()) as current,
         (a.seats_available < coalesce(ptc.purchased_tickets_count, 0)) as sold_out
    from movie_showtimes ms
    join movies m on (ms.movie_id = m.id)
    join theatres t on (ms.theatre_id = t.id)
    join zip_codes z on (t.zip_code = z.zip)
    join auditoriums a on (ms.room = a.room and ms.theatre_id = a.theatre_id)
    left outer join (
  select count(*) as purchased_tickets_count,
         o.movie_showtime_id
    from orders o,
         purchased_tickets pt
   where pt.order_confirmation_code = o.confirmation_code
group by o.movie_showtime_id
         ) ptc on (ptc.movie_showtime_id = ms.id);
```

Note that in Example 12-2, we renamed the view from `current_movie_showtimes` to `movie_showtimes_with_current_and_sold_out_unmaterialized`. The element of the new name `with_current_and_sold_out` refers to the fact that we've shifted the where clause filters into columns on which we can later apply filters. We've also added the suffix `_unmaterialized` to signify that this is the version of the view that is still just a named query. In keeping with the idea that the caching implementation should be transparent to the user, by the end of this chapter, we'll have a new entity in our database called `current_movie_showtimes`. It will look and act just like our original view but will be orders of magnitude faster.

Another caveat worth mentioning is that the view to be materialized should be capable of having a primary key. This is another way of saying that there should be a one-to-one correspondence between the view and its primary base table and the primary base table needs to have a primary key. We've already helped guarantee this in our example

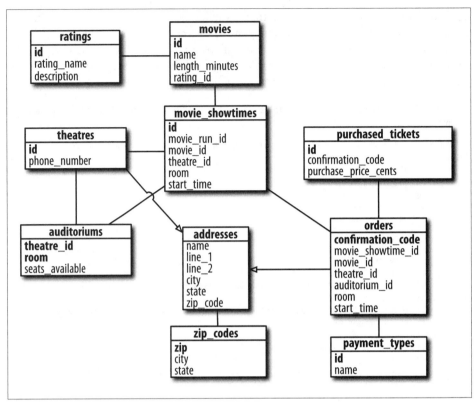

Figure 12-1. Schema from Chapter 8, for reference

by moving the where clause filters into columns and having only one row in the view per record from `movie_showtimes`. The *id* column from `movie_showtimes` will become the primary key of the materialized view. Figure 12-1 is a reproduction of our schema diagram from Chapter 8, which you can refer to as we go along.

The Target Table

A materialized view is created by taking an initial snapshot of the data in the unmaterialized view. Later we'll add triggers to monitor all of the tables that make up the view and update the view whenever there is a change. In this way, our materialized view always stays up-to-date.

To create the initial materialized view, we execute the following SQL:

```
create table movie_showtimes_with_current_and_sold_out_and_dirty_and_expiry as
select *,
       false as dirty,
       null::timestamp with time zone as expiry
  from movie_showtimes_with_current_and_sold_out_unmaterialized;
```

This statement creates a new table called `movie_showtimes_with_cur rent_and_sold_out_and_dirty_and_expiry` that is prefilled with all of the data from our view. Two columns have been added: `dirty` and `expiry`. The `dirty` column will be used to implement deferred refresh via the invalidation trigger. The `expiry` column will be used to deal with special cases where we can't count on a database event to trigger a refresh. How to use both of these columns will be explained in detail, but for now you can ignore them and think of the target table as a plain old table that happens to contain the result of our view. Example 12-3 shows the table described from a `psql` prompt.

Example 12-3. The physical table definition of our materialized view

```
movies_development=# \d movie_showtimes_with_current_and_sold_out_with_dirty_and_expiry
     Table "public.movie_showtimes_with_current_and_sold_out"
         Column          |            Type            | Modifiers
-------------------------+----------------------------+-----------
 name                    | character varying(256)     |
 rating_id               | character varying(16)      |
 length_minutes          | integer                    |
 id                      | integer                    |
 movie_id                | integer                    |
 theatre_id              | integer                    |
 room                    | character varying(64)      |
 start_time              | timestamp with time zone   |
 theatre_name            | character varying(256)     |
 zip_code                | character varying(9)       |
 latitude                | numeric                    |
 longitude               | numeric                    |
 seats_available         | integer                    |
 purchased_tickets_count | bigint                     |
 current                 | boolean                    |
 sold_out                | boolean                    |
 dirty                   | boolean                    |
 expiry                  | timestamp with time zone   |
```

Refresh and Invalidation Functions

The next piece of the puzzle is the `refresh` function. It takes as its argument the primary key of the materialized view. In this case, that key corresponds to the primary key of the `movie_showtimes` table. Whenever we detect that a row in our view is invalid, we run the refresh function on that row.

Example 12-4 shows our first pass at a `refresh` function. It accepts an integer parameter, the primary key of the materialized view. First, it deletes the old row keyed on that id. Then, it reselects the row with the same id from the unmaterialized view—which is real time and thus guaranteed to be accurate—and inserts it back into the materialized view. It also replaces the values in the `dirty` and `expiry` columns.

Example 12-4. A simple refresh function for a materialized view

```
create or replace function movie_showtimes_refresh_row(
  id integer
) returns void
security definer
language 'plpgsql' as $$
begin
  delete
    from movie_showtimes_with_current_and_sold_out_and_dirty_and_expiry ms
   where ms.id = id;
  insert into movie_showtimes_with_current_and_sold_out_and_dirty_and_expiry
  select *, false, null
    from movie_showtimes_with_current_and_sold_out_unmaterialized ms
   where ms.id = id;
end
$$;
```

Remember that the materialized view is just a table. You can modify it, thus invalidating the contents, and then run the refresh function on the modified rows to test that it sets them back to the correct values. Example 12-5 shows just that. We first find the movie name for the showtime with the *id* of 1, *Casablanca*. Next, we invalidate that record in the materialized view by changing the movie name to *The Godfather*. We check, and the materialized view indeed did allow us to change the record to an invalid value. We run our refresh function on that row, and when we select the name again, it has been restored to *Casablanca*.

Example 12-5. The refresh function patches an invalid row so that it matches the view

```
movies_development=# select name
movies_development-#    from
movie_showtimes_with_current_and_sold_out_and_dirty_and_expiry
movies_development-#  where id = 1;
    name
------------
 Casablanca
(1 row)

movies_development=# update
movie_showtimes_with_current_and_sold_out_and_dirty_and_expiry
movies_development-#    set name = 'The Godfather'
movies_development-#  where id = 1;
UPDATE 1

movies_development=# select name
movies_development-#    from
movie_showtimes_with_current_and_sold_out_and_dirty_and_expiry
movies_development-#  where id = 1;
    name
---------------
 The Godfather
(1 row)

movies_development=# select movie_showtimes_refresh_row(1);
```

```
movie_showtimes_refresh_row
-------------------------------

(1 row)

movies_development=# select name
movies_development-#   from
movie_showtimes_with_current_and_sold_out_and_dirty_and_expiry
movies_development-#  where id = 1;
    name
------------
 Casablanca
(1 row)
```

Of course, in this case, we knew that the record was invalid because we invalidated it ourselves. In practice, it won't be the materialized view that changes to bring the two out of sync but the unmaterialized one. We'll need to detect changes by watching all of the tables that make up the view with database triggers.

However, there are certain circumstances when observing changes in tables won't alert us to a change in our view. Such unobservable changes can arise from mutable functions being part of the original view definition. For example, if we had a column based on the random() function, our materialized view would always be out of sync. Such cases are rare, though. The most common mutable function is now(), which appears in our view in the definition of the current column. Before we build any triggers, we'll first see how to deal with these unobservable, time-based events.

Time Dependency

Although a seemingly random mutable function can be tricky to deal with, dealing with a time dependency in a view is straightforward.

The problem we are facing is that it is not a change in the contents of any table that changes the value of the current column in our view but simply the passage of time. In our original view, we have defined current to mean a showtime is in the future, and starts within one week. So with all else staying constant in our database, a showtime that is two weeks away should have a false value in current. After the passage of one week, it should switch to true. Another week later, back to false.

Because time always marches forward at the same pace, we know in advance the moment when the Boolean value in our materialized view needs to flip. If the showtime is far in the future, then current will become true one week before the start time of the showing. If the showtime is already current, it will become false when the present time is equal to the start time. And if the showing was in the past, it will never become current.

With this application-specific knowledge in hand, we can write a function that will tell us when a row in our materialized view should be considered invalid and in need of a refresh due to the need to update current. Example 12-6 shows this function. It takes an integer parameter referring to the primary key of our view. A local variable start_time is defined, which will hold the start time of the showtime in question. Then, within the function body, we select the start time from the view and put it in that variable. Then we run through the logic explained earlier to determine the moment in time that our record should be invalidated.

Example 12-6. A function to determine when a time-dependent row should expire

```
create or replace function movie_showtime_expiry(
  id integer
) returns timestamp with time zone
security definer
language 'plpgsql' as $$
declare
  start_time timestamp with time zone;
begin
  select into start_time ms.start_time
    from movie_showtimes_with_current_and_sold_out_unmaterialized ms
   where id = id;
  if start_time < now() then
    return null;
  else
    if start_time > now() + '7 days'::interval then
      return start_time - '7 days'::interval;
    else
      return start_time;
    end if;
  end if;
end
$$;
```

Armed with this new method, movie_showtime_expiry, we can construct a better refresh function that will insert the correct record expiration time into the expiry column rather than the null placeholder used in Example 12-4 (shown earlier). Example 12-7 shows our new function with the new elements in bold. Note that we've also modified the return type of the refresh function to return the expiration time. We'll use this later when we come to the reconciler view.

Example 12-7. A refresh function that calculates row expiry based on a showtime id

```
create or replace function movie_showtimes_refresh_row(
  id integer
) returns timestamp with time zone
security definer
language 'plpgsql' as $$
declare
  expiry timestamp with time zone;
begin
  expiry := movie_showtime_expiry(id);
  delete from movie_showtimes_with_current_and_sold_out_and_dirty_and_expiry
ms where ms.id = id;
  insert into movie_showtimes_with_current_and_sold_out_and_dirty_and_expiry
  select *, false, expiry
```

```
    from movie_showtimes_with_current_and_sold_out_unmaterialized ms
  where ms.id = id;
 return expiry;
end
$$;
```

We have introduced an inefficiency here. Can you see it? Because we want to return the expiry value—again, why we do this will become apparent later in this chapter—we have evaluated our costly unmaterialized view twice: first, in the call to `movie_show time_expiry`, which selects from the unmaterialized view; second, in the `refresh` function itself in the predicate of the select. Since our overarching goal here is to optimize, we'd rather not do twice what could be done once. Correcting this inefficiency is left as an exercise for the end of this chapter.

One last problem with time dependency is that our initial snapshot did not contain any expiration information. It would have helped to have our `expiry` function ready before we generated the snapshot, but we can update the entire materialized view with the following:

```
select movie_showtimes_refresh_row(id)
  from movie_showtimes_with_current_and_sold_out_and_dirty_and_expiry;
```

If we had the function available from the start, we could also have created our initial materialized view with a SQL statement that took the expiry into account:

```
create table movie_showtimes_with_current_and_sold_out_and_dirty_and_expiry as
select *,
       false as dirty,
       movie_showtimes_refresh_row(id) as expiry
  from movie_showtimes_with_current_and_sold_out_unmaterialized;
```

Who Pays the Price?

Nothing comes for free. Even if queries against a materialized view are fast (O(1) time) you still have a price to pay to keep the materialized view accurate. O(1) is nothing to shout about if the data you are retrieving is stale or invalid, and refreshing can be expensive. In fact, our `refresh` function makes it clear that the cost of refreshing is as expensive as the cost of querying our complex, slow, unmaterialized view. Therefore, it's important to minimize the amount of time you spend refreshing and also to refresh at times that are least likely to be burdensome.

When any table involved in the view definition changes, whether rows are inserted, updated, or deleted, you may have an event that requires an update to the materialized view. However, it may not be wise to update the materialized view at the first opportunity we have to do so.

Figure 12-2 shows three possible times when we can update our materialized view. The first is at the exact moment when a change to a base table record causes corresponding records in the materialized view to become invalid. These events are easily detectable through database triggers, and they are the topic of the next section. The second

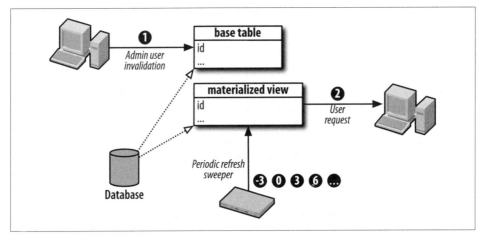

Figure 12-2. Timeline of refresh opportunities

detectable time we can refresh is when a user is making a request to the materialized view. If we know records are invalid, we can refresh them just before returning data to the user. The third opportunity for refresh is not detected but is forced through periodic update of rows known to be invalid. This method alone is not enough to ensure cache correctness, but in conjunction with the first two methods, it can help reduce the user-visible lag of refreshing invalid rows.

Before discussing in detail how to decide which refresh scheme is best for which circumstances, we need to clarify how, in the latter two refresh schemes, you would know whether a record is invalid or not. We've already seen how the `expiry` column can be used for this purpose for records with a time dependency. We need an analogous way to know when rows that we chose not to refresh at the time of invalidation are indeed invalid. This is where the `dirty` column, created in our initial snapshot, comes into play.

Example 12-8 shows a new method, `movie_showtimes_invalidate_row`, which sets the `dirty` column of a particular row to `true`. For triggered events where we decide not to call the expensive `refresh` function immediately, we can instead call this method, which runs in O(1) time. Now our second and third refresh opportunities—just before returning results to a user and the periodic refresh sweep—can check that a row is either dirty or has expired, and refresh only those rows.

Example 12-8. A function to mark a materialized view row as invalid

```
create or replace function movie_showtimes_invalidate_row(
  id integer
) returns void
security definer
language 'plpgsql' as $$
declare
  n_updates integer;
begin
  update movie_showtimes_with_current_and_sold_out_and_dirty_and_expiry ms
```

```
        set dirty = true
      where ms.id = id;
    return;
end
$$;
```

There are a number of considerations that go into choosing when to refresh. The first way of looking at the problem is in terms of who should pay the price. If you can split your users into two classes, admin users who are making the most changes to data, and customers, who are viewing that data, then the choice is clear. You're paying for customers and your employees are being paid to do their jobs, so in general the burden of update should be on the employee's shoulders.

However, in some cases, the relationships between the tables themselves play a role in determining whether it's appropriate to refresh immediately, while the actor is waiting, or to defer the burden to the viewer or the periodic sweeper. These relationships fall into three categories: 1:1 ("one to one"), 1:N, and N:1.

1:1 updates

In the first category, 1:1, every row you update in a base table corresponds to a unique row in the view. The most obvious example is the table from which the view gets its primary key, in this case `movie_showtimes`. If you update five records in the `movie_show times` table, five records change in the view and thus five records need to be refreshed or invalidated in the materialized view.

In this case, it usually makes sense to refresh the row in question right away, especially if only employees have the ability to invalidate the data. The additional time spent by the employee translates directly into time saved when rendering pages for your users.

1:N updates

For the second category, 1:N, an update of a single row in one of the base tables changes multiple rows in the view. For example, if we make a change to a movie or theatre, all of the rows for that movie or theatre change in our view. An update to a single row could require 100, 1,000, or even more refreshes or invalidations in the materialized view.

In this case, it's not obvious whether you should refresh rows immediately or invalidate them for a deferred refresh. Clearly, refreshing so many rows at once could seem beyond reasonable, even for someone on payroll. The statement "They don't pay me enough for this @!#%!" comes to mind. Factors affecting this decision are the number of rows likely to be invalidated at once, how many of these invalid rows are likely to be requested in a single request by a user, and how patient your employees are. If many rows are invalidated, but visitors request them one by one, it may make sense to have your site's visitors pay one row at a time rather than force employees to sit around waiting for a thousand records from a complex view to be refreshed. In the proceeding discussion of the reconciler view, we'll see how we can limit request-time refreshes to only those records that are being requested.

N:1 updates

Finally, in N:1 relationships, a number of updates to some base table corresponds to just a single row in the view. This type of relationship is generally found in aggregate functions. For example, in our view, each showtime record has a count of the number of tickets purchased in the `tickets_purchased_count` column. Whether we add 10 tickets to an order for a given showtime (one row per ticket), delete 10 tickets, or modify each of those tickets in some way, only one row in the view changes, and therefore only one record in the materialized view needs to be updated.

In this case, it is cruel and unusual to have the actor, generally your employees, pay the price of refresh N times when there is only one change to be made to the materialized view. Because each base table modification results in a trigger firing, if that trigger calls the complex `refresh` function, you will pay for the `refresh` function N times before the transaction is complete. Clearly, the result of refreshing once after all modifications are made is the same as refreshing N times, except that the latter case is a waste of time and more importantly, database resources. Therefore, in this case, the triggers related to N:1 relationships should invalidate materialized view rows for deferred refresh rather than perform the refresh in place. The cost to invalidate is negligible, and the heavier cost of refreshing need happen only once.

Triggered Refreshes and Invalidations

So far we have built a snapshot of our view at a given point in time, and we have created stored procedures that can be used to invalidate and refresh rows in the materialized view snapshot. Now it's time to build triggers that will refresh or invalidate rows automatically as changes are made to underlying tables.

In general, triggers follow these steps:

1. Determine if any change to the materialized view is necessary, and quit early if not.
2. Determine which rows, by primary key, need to be refreshed or invalidated.
3. Call the refresh or invalidate function on those primary keys.

Writing these triggers can be a tedious process because we need to account for inserts, updates, and deletes on all tables that make up the view. In this case, nearly all of our tables—six—are involved in the view in some way. With three functions per table for each insert, update, and delete, this could mean we need to write 18 trigger functions. Luckily, with some proper analysis, we can eliminate the need for more than half of these.

To facilitate this analysis, we create a reference table as shown in Table 12-1. We list each table involved in the view. For each table, we determine its relationship to the view: 1:1, 1:N, or N:1. Then, for each operation on the table, we first determine whether any action is needed at all, and if so, we choose whether we will refresh immediately, or defer the refresh by performing an invalidation operation. We'll examine each table in turn to see how we came up with the entries in this table.

Table 12-1. A summary of view base tables and how they relate to invalidation or refresh

Table	Relationship to view	Operation	Action needed?	Refresh	Invalidation
movies	1:N	insert			
		update	✓	✓	
		delete			
theatres	1:N	insert			
		update	✓	✓	
		delete			
movie_showtimes	1:1	insert	✓	✓	
		update	✓	✓	
		delete	✓	✓	
orders	N:1	insert			
		update	✓		✓
		delete			
ticket_purchases	N:1	insert	✓		✓
		update	✓		✓
		delete	✓		✓
auditoriums	1:N	insert			
		update			
		delete			

Movie Showtimes

As we've already discussed, the movie_showtimes table shares its primary key with the view, and therefore it has a 1:1 correspondence. When a new showtime record is inserted, we need to add that record to the materialized view. When a record is deleted, we need to delete the record. And when a record is updated, we need to update the corresponding record.

Example 12-9 shows three functions to handle each case of update, insert, and delete. There are three new features of PL/pgSQL relating to trigger functions worth noting here.

First, functions intended to be used in conjunction with table triggers must have a return type **trigger**. Second, functions called from triggers can implicitly receive two parameters: old and new. On an update, both of these are present, and old refers to the record before the update, and new refers to the record after the update. On an insert, only new is provided, and on delete, only old. Finally, we have used the keyword perform in our trigger functions. perform is used when you don't intend to store the result of a select statement. In these cases, you replace the keyword select with perform.

Note that in general, updates are a special case. If the record changes in such a way that the referenced primary key changes, we need to take action on both the old and new primary key.

Also note that the method names follow a particular pattern. First, we prefix them in a way that identifies the materialized view they are for: ms_mv_ for "movie showtimes materialized view." Then we identify the table this trigger function is for, here showtime as a shortened version of movie_showtimes. Finally, we append to the function name an identifier of whether this is the insert, update, or delete trigger with _it, _ut, or _dt, respectively. This pattern will be followed for all tables and triggers.

Example 12-9. Triggers functions for the movie_showtimes table

```
create or replace function ms_mv_showtime_ut() returns trigger
security definer language 'plpgsql' as $$
begin
  if old.id = new.id then
    perform movie_showtimes_refresh_row(new.id);
  else
    perform movie_showtimes_refresh_row(old.id);
    perform movie_showtimes_refresh_row(new.id);
  end if;
  return null;
end
$$;

create or replace function ms_mv_showtime_dt() returns trigger
security definer language 'plpgsql' as $$
begin
  perform movie_showtimes_refresh_row(old.id);
  return null;
end
$$;

create or replace function ms_mv_showtime_it() returns trigger
security definer language 'plpgsql' as $$
begin
  perform movie_showtimes_refresh_row(new.id);
  return null;
end
$$;
```

The naming convention just discussed was intended to help you identify which function is for which purpose, but from the database's perspective, these are just arbitrary names. For each function, we also need to add a corresponding trigger to the table itself so that the database knows which method to call when each particular event occurs. Example 12-10 shows how we add these triggers.

Example 12-10. Actual trigger declaration for the movie_showtimes table

```
create trigger ms_mv_showtime_ut after update on movie_showtimes
  for each row execute procedure ms_mv_showtime_ut();

create trigger ms_mv_showtime_dt after delete on movie_showtimes
  for each row execute procedure ms_mv_showtime_dt();

create trigger ms_mv_showtime_it after insert on movie_showtimes
  for each row execute procedure ms_mv_showtime_it();
```

Movies

The movies table, as noted previously, has a 1:N correspondence with our view. A change to a single movie affects all of the showtime records associated with that movie. Our trigger function must select a column of showtime *ids* for refresh. Because only an employee could change a movie record, an immediate refresh was chosen rather than an invalidation, which would make users viewing the site pay for the refresh.

Because a movie has no impact on our view until it has showtimes, we do not need a trigger on insert or delete of a movie. On insert, there can be no showtime records yet for that movie. On delete, there can be no records because of the referential integrity constraint, which guarantees that a showtime reference a valid movie. All of the movie_showtimes records would have already been deleted or updated to reference a different movie before a delete on movies could succeed, and the refreshes triggered after modifications to that table would have cleared all of the records from the materialized view. Example 12-11 shows the triggers for the movies table.

Example 12-11. Triggers for the movies table

```
create or replace function ms_mv_movie_ut() returns trigger
security definer language 'plpgsql' as $$
begin
  if old.id = new.id then
    perform movie_showtimes_refresh_row(ms.id)
        from movie_showtimes ms
      where ms.movie_id = new.id;
  else
    perform movie_showtimes_refresh_row(ms.id)
        from movie_showtimes ms
      where ms.movie_id = old.id;
    perform movie_showtimes_refresh_row(ms.id)
        from movie_showtimes ms
      where ms.movie_id = new.id;
  end if;
  return null;
end
$$;

create trigger ms_mv_movie_ut after update on movie_showtimes
  for each row execute procedure ms_mv_movie_ut();
```

Theatres

Our treatment of the `theatres` table exactly matches the treatment of `movies`. The theatres table also has a 1:N correspondence, so our trigger function must select a column of showtime *ids* for refresh. Just as with the `movies` table, referential integrity constraints prevent a theatre from being deleted while showtimes reference it, so we do not need a delete trigger function. Similarly, when a theatre record is first inserted, it has no showtimes and therefore cannot impact the view. Our single update trigger function is defined in Example 12-12.

Example 12-12. Triggers for the theatres table

```
create or replace function ms_mv_theatre_ut() returns trigger
security definer language 'plpgsql' as $$
begin
  if old.id = new.id then
    perform movie_showtimes_refresh_row(ms.id)
      from movie_showtimes ms
      where ms.theatre_id = new.id;
  else
    perform movie_showtimes_refresh_row(ms.id)
      from movie_showtimes ms
      where ms.theatre_id = old.id;
    perform movie_showtimes_refresh_row(ms.id)
      from movie_showtimes ms
      where ms.theatre_id = new.id;
  end if;
  return null;
end
$$;

create or replace trigger ms_mv_theatre_ut after update on theatres
  for each row execute procedure ms_mv_theatre_ut();
```

Orders

The `orders` table has an interesting relationship with the materialized view. It does not directly effect the view at all, but the records in `purchased_tickets`—which are linked to the `movie_showtimes` table through the `orders` table—do. Therefore, adding or removing an `order` record has no effect on the view, but a modification to the order that alters the showtime it is for—and transitively its associated tickets—does have an effect. Therefore, we need only an update function, and we need only to perform the refreshes or invalidations if the `movie_showtime_id` foreign key reference changes. Any other changes have no affect on the view. In this case, we have chosen to invalidate the row (see Example 12-13).

Example 12-13. Triggers for the orders table

```
create or replace function ms_mv_orders_ut() returns trigger
security definer language 'plpgsql' as $$
begin
  if old.movie_showtime_id != new.movie_showtime_id then
```

```
      perform movie_showtimes_invalidate_row(old.movie_showtime_id);
      perform movie_showtimes_invalidate_row(new.movie_showtime_id);
   end if;
   return null;
end
$$;

create trigger ms_mv_orders_ut after update on orders
   for each row execute procedure ms_mv_orders_ut();
```

Purchased tickets

Ticket purchases impact the purchased_ticket_count column of the view, but only the presence or absence of any given row is relevant. Therefore, we certainly need an insert and delete trigger for the purchased_tickets table. We do also need an update trigger, but it is constrained to take action only if there is a possibility that the tally for the ticket needs to be moved from one showtime to another. This is only possible if the ticket purchase is reassociated with a different order, which might be for a different showtime. Therefore, the update trigger takes action conditionally based on whether the order_confirmation_code foreign key column undergoes a change.

Because ticket purchases have an N:1 relationship with a showtime in our view (all the purchases for a showtime are counted and affect a single column in a single record) we call the invalidation function in our triggers rather than the refresh function. If 10 tickets are purchased, we want to refresh only once, not 10 times, since the end result is simply to increase the purchased_tickets_count column by 10. Calling the refresh function 10 times to increment the count one ticket at a time is a waste of time and resources. Example 12-14 shows the triggers for the purchased_tickets table.

Example 12-14. Triggers for the purchased_tickets table

```
create or replace function ms_mv_ticket_ut() returns trigger
security definer language 'plpgsql' as $$
begin
   if old.order_confirmation_code != new.order_confirmation_code then
      perform movie_showtimes_invalidate_row(o.movie_showtime_id)
         from orders o
         where o.confirmation_code = new.order_confirmation_code;
      perform movie_showtimes_invalidate_row(o.movie_showtime_id)
         from orders o
         where o.confirmation_code = old.order_confirmation_code;
   end if;
   return null;
end
$$;

create or replace function ms_mv_ticket_dt() returns trigger
security definer language 'plpgsql' as $$
begin
   perform movie_showtimes_invalidate_row(o.movie_showtime_id)
      from orders o
      where o.confirmation_code = old.order_confirmation_code;
```

```
      return null;
end
$$;

create or replace function ms_mv_ticket_it() returns trigger
security definer language 'plpgsql' as $$
begin
  perform movie_showtimes_invalidate_row(o.movie_showtime_id)
    from orders o
    where o.confirmation_code = new.order_confirmation_code;
  return null;
end
$$;

create trigger ms_mv_ticket_ut after update on purchased_tickets
  for each row execute procedure ms_mv_ticket_ut();

create trigger ms_mv_ticket_dt after delete on purchased_tickets
  for each row execute procedure ms_mv_ticket_dt();

create trigger ms_mv_ticket_it after insert on purchased_tickets
  for each row execute procedure ms_mv_ticket_it();
```

Hiding the Implementation with the Reconciler View

Now that we have defined our triggers, we have added yet another way for the materialized view to decay. The first decay mechanism was the expiry column, which allows
rows to declare when they should be treated as irrelevant. The second mechanism is
the dirty column, which our invalidation function sets to true when certain tables
receive updates.

Slowly but surely, our materialized view will become a minefield full of stale records
we need to avoid if we aim to present accurate data to database clients. Such a table is
by no means a drop-in replacement for the original view. Not only is the materialized
view slowly turning into garbage but also the interface is different. If selecting directly
from this table, a client must be careful to avoid stale or invalid rows. The logic that
was neatly contained within the view's where clause filters is now contained in columns,
which the client must explicitly filter on.

We will now plug up these holes, first ensuring that the data returned to clients is always
up-to-date. Then we'll give the original interface provided by the original view back to
the client. We'll hide the dirty and expiry columns and transform the current and
sold_out columns back into a filter.

We accomplish the first goal of always returning accurate data with the *reconciler
view*. We give this view the same name as our original, "well-formed" view from Example 12-2, but without the suffix _unmaterialized. It is simply called movie_show
times_with_current_and_sold_out. This new view is shown in Example 12-15. It is the

union of two select statements. The first returns rows from our physical materialized view table that are neither dirty nor expired.

The second part of this view contains the magic. It returns records that *look like* data from the materialized view, complete with a false dirty column, and an accurate expiry time. Recall when we built our `refresh` function in Example 12-7 (shown earlier), we constructed it so that it would return the expiry time of the new row being inserted. That was not without purpose; we make use of that behavior here to create a complete yet functional façade for the materialized view, which hides the mixture of accurate, expired, and dirty rows. When we call the `refresh` function, it both fills in the `expiry` column accurately, but more importantly, it refreshes the expired or dirty row.

This is as close as we get in this book to pure magic. *The process of requesting rows from the reconciler view refreshes the expired rows in the materialized view.* The reconciler view, then, is nearly our end-state view. Although it does have two additional columns that our original view did not—`expiry` and `dirty`—it is essentially a drop-in replacement for the view we started out with in Example 12-2 (shown earlier), as it is always accurate.

Example 12-15. The reconciler view provides just-in-time cache-correctness

```
create or replace view movie_showtimes_with_current_and_sold_out as
select *
  from movie_showtimes_with_current_and_sold_out_and_dirty_and_expiry
 where dirty is false
   and (expiry is null or expiry > now())
 union all
select *,
       false,
       movie_showtimes_refresh_row(w.id)
   from movie_showtimes_with_current_and_sold_out_unmaterialized w
 where id in (select id
                from movie_showtimes_with_current_and_sold_out_and_dirty_and_expiry
               where dirty is true
                  or not(expiry is null or now() <= expiry));
```

 In the reconciler view, we use `union all` rather than `union`. A SQL `union` returns only unique rows. To do so, the result rows must be first be sorted, followed by a unique operation to filter out any duplicate rows. Since we aren't expecting any duplicate rows, using `unique` can be much more efficient if we're requesting a large number of rows from the reconciler view at once.

You may have noticed that the way we implemented the reconciler view, with its selection from the unmaterialized view *and* a call to the `refresh` function for each invalid row, actually evaluates the unmaterialized view twice for each invalid row that needs to be updated. This is unfortunate, but it is still a vast improvement over an evaluation of the unmaterialized view for every page request. Of course, nothing is impossible, and therefore writing a reconciler view that does not evaluate the unmaterialized view twice is not impossible. However, such an implementation is beyond the scope of this book and strays from our purpose here: that is, the fundamentals of materialization and cache correctness. A more complete materialized view implementation is available at this book's website, located at *http://enterpriserails.chak.org*.

You may also be wondering, when you select from the reconciler view, how many rows are refreshed? Are all of the expired and invalid rows refreshed, which could be quite costly, or just the ones that influence the query? In fact, it is the latter. Example 12-16 shows a set of SQL queries to illustrate this. First, two rows in the materialized view are manually set to be dirty. Then, one of those rows is requested from the reconciler view. Finally, the `dirty` column of both rows is selected directly from the materialized view. Only the one we selected from the reconciler view has been refreshed, and it now has a `false` value in the `dirty` column.

This property of the reconciler view plays a big role when you're choosing between invalidation or refresh for 1:N table relationships. If it's common for rows to be selected from the materialized view in small chunks rather than all at once, you can amortize the full refresh of a 1:N invalidation over a number of future site visitors. Alternatively, the user who invalidated the rows—often an employee—must pay the price of refreshing N rows all at once.

Example 12-16. When selecting from the reconciler view, you pay only for refreshing the rows you select

```
movies_development=#
  update movie_showtimes_with_current_and_sold_out_and_dirty_and_expiry
    set dirty = true
  where id in (1, 2);
UPDATE 2

movies_development=#
  select *
    from movie_showtimes_with_current_and_sold_out
  where id = 1;
(1 row)

movies_development=#
  select id, dirty
    from movie_showtimes_with_current_and_sold_out_and_dirty_and_expiry
  where id in (1, 2);
 id | dirty
----+-------
  2 | t
  1 | f
(2 rows)
```

Periodic Refreshes

In Figure 12-1, I alluded to a periodic refresh activity. Now that we have seen the reconciler view, such an activity is trivial to implement. That activity is simply the variation on the bold portion of the reconciler view in Example 12-15. We simply need to select the refresh function on all of the rows that are expired or dirty. This can run via a cron job at a given internal to alleviate some of the burden imposed on site visitors whose requests go through the reconciler view. If the refresh function is called between an invalidation operation (either explicit or implicit due to an expiration date passing) and a request, then cron pays rather than the next visitor (see Example 12-17).

Example 12-17. A refresh function to be run periodically

```
select movie_showtimes_refresh_row(w.id)
 from movie_showtimes_with_current_and_sold_out_and_dirty_and_expiry w
where dirty is true
   or not(expiry is null or now() <= expiry));
```

Completing the circle

Our reconciler view, although it is a nearly identical drop-in replacement for our well-formed view from Example 12-2, is not the same as the view we began with in Example 12-1, current_movie_showtimes.

At this point, it is not hard to create a new view with the same name that has the same output, but is based on the materialized view. We just request all rows except dirty and expiry from the reconciler view. We also omit our Boolean columns from the new view and instead use them as filters. Example 12-18 shows the new definition of our original view. Now we've come full circle.

Example 12-18. A view indistinguishable from our original current_movie_showtimes view but based on the reconciler view

```
create view current_movie_showtimes as
  select name,
         rating_id,
         length_minutes,
         id,
         movie_id,
         theatre_id,
         room,
         start_time,
         theatre_name,
         zip_code,
         latitude,
         longitude,
         seats_available,
         purchased_tickets_count
    from movie_showtimes_with_current_and_sold_out
  where current is true and sold_out is false;
```

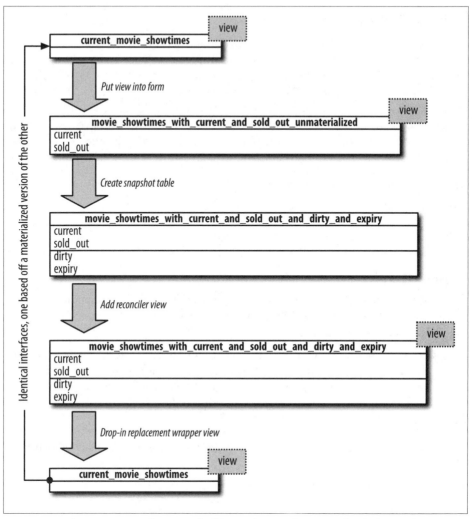

Figure 12-3. The progression of views and tables to abstract the materialized view implementation from clients

Figure 12-3 shows the progression of views, tables, and wrapper views we created to completely hide the implementation of our materialized view from clients.

Cache Indexes

Our materialized view implementation is actually rather useless if we do not add indexes. Although we don't need to evaluate the complex view query when we query the materialized view, without indexes, each request would need to run a full table scan to return any results. Indexing makes queries by *id* or by one of our original filters close to instantaneous.

There is a minimal set of indexes we need on a materialized view. First, we need to index the primary key column. It's fine to do this by creating an explicit primary key. Next, we need to add indexes on the `dirty` and `expiry` columns, since they are part of the `where` clause of the reconciler view. Indexing these columns keeps that part of our implementation fast. Finally, we should index the filters that we recast as columns, `current` and `sold_out`, since it's likely we'll be filtering on these columns frequently. Apart from this set—the primary key, the invalidation implementation columns, and the filter columns—you can index any columns in your materialized view that your application will select or filter on. The creation of our primary key and indexes is shown in Example 12-19.

Example 12-19. A minimal set of indices on a materialized view

```
alter table movie_showtimes_with_current_and_sold_out_and_dirty_and_expiry
  add primary key (id);

create index movie_showtimes_with_current_and_sold_out_dirty_expiry_idx
  on movie_showtimes_with_current_and_sold_out_and_dirty_and_expiry(dirty, expiry);

create index movie_showtimes_with_current_and_sold_out_current_idx
  on movie_showtimes_with_current_and_sold_out_and_dirty_and_expiry(current);

create index movie_showtimes_with_current_and_sold_out_sold_out_idx
  on movie_showtimes_with_current_and_sold_out_and_dirty_and_expiry(sold_out);
```

Results

The results of using a materialized view rather than an unmaterialized one are quite impressive. In Example 12-20, a select from both for current, non-sold-out showtimes is analyzed.

First, the count of records in each table is selected to give you an idea of how much data we are dealing with. In fact, it is not too much data compared to what a real production site selling tickets for all theatres and all movies nationally might have in its database. Our data set likely accounts for a day or at most a week's worth of accumulated data on a real system.

Next, we select all of the current, non-sold-out showtimes from the unmaterialized view. On a Dual Core 2.1 Ghz MacBook Pro, the query takes 1.16 seconds. Next we issue the same select against the materialized view. It takes 0.013 seconds. With this dataset, selecting from the materialized view is almost 100 times faster. As the dataset grows, the time required to select from the unmaterialized view increases, while the time to request from the materialized view remains nearly constant.

Example 12-20. Comparison of runtimes on a view versus a materialized view

```
movies_development=# select (select count(*) from movies) as movies,
                             (select count(*) from theatres) as theatres,
                             (select count(*) from movie_showtimes) as showtimes,
                             (select count(*) from orders) as orders,
                             (select count(*) from purchased_tickets) as tickets;
 movies | theatres | showtimes | orders | tickets
--------+----------+-----------+--------+---------
     44 |        6 |     20201 | 218593 |  218591
movies_development=# explain analyze
   select id
     from movie_showtimes_with_current_and_sold_out_unmaterialized
    where current = true
      and sold_out = false;
Total runtime: 1158.617 ms

movies_development=# explain analyze
   select id
     from movie_showtimes_with_current_and_sold_out
    where current = true
      and sold_out = false;
Total runtime: 12.553 ms
```

Cascading Caches

In Example 12-2, we joined against a named query subselect to create our view. We noted that this query could also be recast as a full-fledged view in its own right. By extension, it could also be recast as a materialized view.

If that were the case, we would be cascading two materialized views. The inner materialized view would be concerned with orders and ticket purchases, and the outer view would no longer need to watch those tables directly. Instead, the outer materialized view would maintain triggers on the inner materialized view.

Working this way can reduce the complexity of any given materialized view. It also speeds up the inner view, for cases where there are other uses for that data. Implementing a cascading materialized view is left as an exercise for the readers.

Exercises

1. Write a stored procedure that verifies a one-to-one correspondence between rows in the materialized "reconciler" view and the unmaterialized view.

2. Using the stored procedure from Exercise 12-1, write a series of unit tests that modify records—one at a time as well as simultaneously—and then assert the validity of the reconciler view.

3. It was noted that our `refresh` function does extra work to calculate and return the `expiry` value. Write a new `movie_showtime_expiry` stored procedure that takes `start_time` as a parameter and returns an expiry value *without* selecting from the unmaterialized view.

4. Rewrite the snapshot creation query and the refresh function to use the new procedure you wrote in Exercise 12-3. Time the snapshot creation and refresh operations with both methods. Which set is faster and by how much?

5. Following the procedure outlined in this chapter, create a materialized view for `ptc`, the named subquery from Example 12-2. Then rewrite the triggers for the main materialized view to use this new physical table. How do you propagate invalidations?

## CHAPTER 13

SOA Primer

Service-oriented architecture (SOA) is a concept that seems to be almost universally misunderstood. Especially in the era of Web 2.0 and web services, the definition of true SOA services has been muddled. I have encountered people who think they have a service-oriented architecture but don't. I've encountered people who have stumbled upon a service-oriented architecture in solving an architectural scaling problem but didn't know the architecture they had invented had that name. "That's what all those people talking about SOA are talking about? That's easy!" Because SOA is a buzzword, no one wants to admit that they don't know what it means.

Many application developers are unfamiliar with true SOA because the need for it enters late in an application's lifecycle. It is often only when a company has matured to enterprise level that the old, tried and true, "monolithic" approach to building websites can no longer cut it. The single web application and single database of the monolithic architecture at some point cannot stand up to the demands of the company's success, and a wholly new architecture is needed to meet the challenge. Usually that architecture is SOA.

But what *is* SOA? When is it useful and what are the advantages? The goal of this and the following chapters is to lift the veil of confusion surrounding "services" as they relate to service-oriented architecture. We'll start with the *what*. What does a service-oriented architecture look like? Then we'll look at the *why*. What are some common situations where a SOA solution is appropriate and likely to be successful? Finally, we'll look at the *who*. Who uses SOA and how can it benefit your organization?

We'll save the *how* for the next chapters.

What Is SOA?

SOA is a way to design complex applications such that the complexity is more manageable. This is accomplished by splitting out major components into the building block of SOA, which are individual services.

Before defining that building block, the services, first let's look at an analogous architectural jump that you're no doubt already familiar with: object-oriented programming (OOP). OOP , initially introduced in the 1960s and 1970s in Simula 67 and Smalltalk, swept the software development scene in the mid-1990s with C++, when programs were getting too large and complex to be maintained in procedural programming languages such as C. In procedural programming, you have large amounts of data, and lots of methods that process the data managed by the application. All functions are globally accessible, as is most data. Organization is imposed through naming conventions; for example, `new_movie` and `delete_movie`, rather than the more object-oriented `Movie.new` and `Movie.delete`. Eventually, as program size increases, procedural programs becomes increasingly fragile. It is especially difficult for multiple programmers to be working on the same procedural application at the same time because so much of the program—both methods and data—are more or less global in nature. It's challenging for developers to avoid stepping on each other's toes, as it's not always clear where one program module ends and another begins.

Object-oriented programming solved this problem by separating collections of methods and data through language mechanisms rather than through convention. While convention can be powerful, it can also be strayed from, while language rules are hard and fast. In object-oriented programming, lines are drawn between different types of data and their related methods.

For each type of data, a class—one of the building blocks of OOP—is defined. That class contains all of the data and data structures particular to that type of data. Also, any methods that are related to the data are packaged up in the class as well. Various amounts of the class's data (often all of it) and methods (often a good deal of them) are declared to be *private*, which makes that data and those methods off-limits to the rest of the program and to developers working in other parts of the application. In this way, the language itself leads to an architecture within an app, which makes it easier for developers to organize their work.

What's left after all of this information-hiding (public methods and data) defines the API of the class. The API is the contract of the class and also the barrier. It is a contract because it says, "Provide me with these inputs, and I will provide you with these outputs." It is a barrier because it is the only way—albeit indirectly—to access the class's private methods and data. You can only access a class's data in ways that the public API allows.

SOA follows a similar jump in the level of organization as did object-oriented programming from procedural programming. But Ruby is already an object-oriented language, so what is SOA jumping *from*? In this context, object-oriented programming is to SOA as procedural programming is to *monolithic application design*.

Before we go further, monolithic application design must be defined. In fact, it is everything that has been discussed in this book up to this point. In monolithic application design, all of the functionality of a website is contained in the same code base

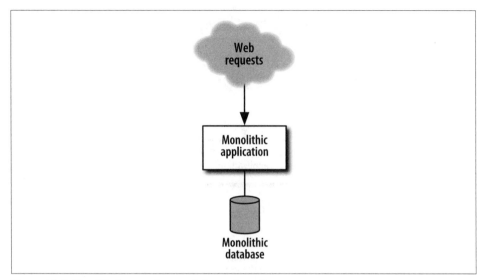

Figure 13-1. Simplified view of a monolithic web application

and runs in the same process on the web server. Figure 13-1 illustrates this concept. All of the data is contained in a single database—the monolithic database—or is otherwise accessible in some way, without restriction, from the monolithic application. This should sound familiar because this application design is the sole subject of virtually every Rails programming book in print today.

Now that we know what a monolithic application is, we should define a *service*—the building block of SOA. Recall that in object-oriented programming, a class represents a slice of an overall application represented by a data type and all the methods related to that data. SOA is analogous: a service is a slice of a website related to a particular set of functionality and the related data.

The difference between the object-oriented and the service-oriented analogies is how you access the APIs of different objects or services. In an object-oriented program, objects pass messages to each other, but the message passing occurs within a single process on a single machine. In a service-oriented architecture, individual services pass messages back and forth, but they do so over the network.

So what does a service look like? Actually, it can look like anything. Just like a class in object-oriented programming is defined by its API, and everything else is hidden behind a layer of abstraction, so too with a service. What's behind the API is anyone's best guess, and to gain the benefits of modularity, such details should be the service client's most remote concern. Of course, there is a template for the structure of a service that will be adequate for most problems. That architectural template at a very high level is shown in Figure 13-2.

Hopefully, it is not too shocking that the high-level architecture of a service looks remarkably similar to that of the monolithic application. Similarly, the code within a class

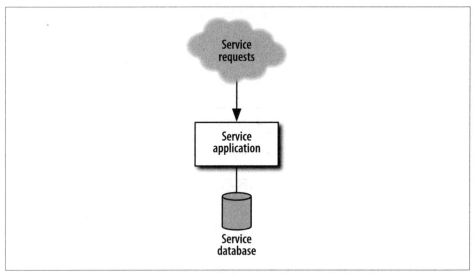

Figure 13-2. Simplified view of requests to a SOA service

in object-oriented programming doesn't look much different from code in functional programming. In SOA, it's not the structure of any particular service that matters, but rather the fact that the application has been organized into a number of simpler, more understandable components, each separated from the others, and communicating via well-defined, public APIs.

And, of course, Figure 13-2 presents a drastic over-simplification of a service "template." In Chapter 14, a lower-level template will be provided for a Rails XML-RPC service based on ActionWebService, the preferred mechanism for most SOA services. In Chapter 17, REST services will be introduced.

The great news is that if you do follow the service templates described in this book, all of the concepts already covered remain applicable. The design principles of a monolithic application and of a service within a service-oriented architecture are nearly identical.

Why SOA?

Many scenarios lead naturally to the need for a service-oriented design. Some scenarios, like a shared resource, demand it. Other scenarios, like the need for massive scaling, can be helped by a service-oriented architecture because a SOA design naturally segments databases. It also reduces local complexity, which can make a caching scheme easier to implement, further enhancing scalability. The notion of reducing local complexity can be a goal in and of itself, for which SOA is the means. In this section, each of these scenarios is explored in detail.

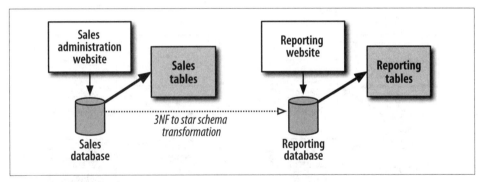

Figure 13-3. Two databases in our system

Shared Resources

Imagine that you are building a site that sells widgets. For that site, you'd have a database full of sales data, both products and orders. Next imagine that you took my advice in Chapter 4 and did not attempt to report directly out of the sales database. Instead, you created a separate *data warehouse* database, which transformed the 3NF or DK/NF sales and orders tables suited for Online Transaction Processing (OLTP) into a star schema, which is better-suited for Online Analytical Processing (OLAP). This setup is shown in Figure 13-3. Each of these databases has a front-end interface for employees to access the contained data, be it sales data in the sales administration website or aggregate reports in the reporting website.

There's an additional wrinkle, though. Each front-end website needs to look up access control information to validate that the users who are logging in and carrying out actions are authorized. There are numerous solutions to this problem, each of varying merit. We'll look at two candidate solutions that fail our litmus test for "enterprise" before settling on—and in the process defining—a service-oriented solution.

Synchronized tables

In Figure 13-4, we've seemingly solved this problem by reproducing the access control tables in both the sales and reporting databases. Each website is essentially its own monolithic application, with direct access to all the data it needs in its own local database. This works for a while, but now new employees need to be added to both databases through each front-end. Similarly, whenever an employee changes her password on the reporting site, she needs to remember to change her password on the sales site, too. Keeping two sets of passwords in sync might not seem too onerous, but three sets of synchronized data gets daunting, and 5 or 10 sets of data for each user to manually keep in sync is downright ludicrous. This solution doesn't scale with the business.

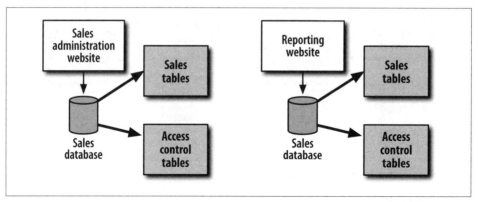

Figure 13-4. Attempting to solve the access control problem by replicating tables

A shared database

Figure 13-5 illustrates another attempt at solving the problem of shared data. This time, we've gotten around the problem of keeping multiple databases in sync with each other. We've moved the access control tables out into a third database, which each site accesses to authorize users.

This technique is DRY in that we don't need to repeat user data in each database. However, at the code level it's not very DRY at all. Each website needs to duplicate the logic for authorizing a user and any other logic associated with those tables. If we find a bug in one site's authorization implementation, we have to correct the code not only in that site but in every site that uses the access control database tables.

Similarly, if we make a change to the table structure to improve performance or to allow for a great new feature, we need to modify every application that authorizes users to remain compatible with our changes. Again, in our example of two sites, this may not seem too onerous, but with 10 applications you're out of luck. Propagating the changes through software code is difficult enough. In a production environment, you'll also have to roll out a very well-planned strategy to avoid needing a site outage to commit your database changes.

A third problem with this setup is that it makes correct caching impossible. Imagine that you've got tons of traffic coming to your sites, and each request needs to check authorization data. All that authorization activity is becoming a strain on the database. Fortunately, the list of authorized users is relatively small, so you decide to cache the entire users table in Memcache, clearing all users' entries on appropriate events: when they change their password, or when an administrator deletes or changes their account in some meaningful way. Of course, the sales and reporting websites are completely unrelated code bases, so they don't share the same Memcache cluster. Having shared memory between distinct applications is to be avoided under all circumstances, as there is never any guarantee, express or implied, that one application won't manipulate that memory in a way that is counter to the expectations of another application. For

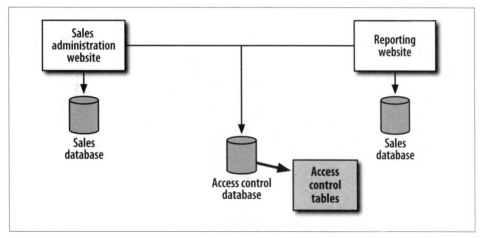

Figure 13-5. Attempting to solve the access control problem by splitting common tables off into a new database

example, two applications may choose the same cache key for different types of data, leading an application to load and display incorrect data, or to fail completely.

Therefore, with shared memory spaces out of the question, maintaining correct caches between separate applications requires that "appropriate events" for clearing each site's user cache must be broadcast somehow from application to application so that a deleted user is deleted from the perspective of *all* caches. With our current design, when a user is locked out of one site, he can continue to access other sites until the bogus Memcache entries expire due to the course of time. The broadcasting necessary to keep the caches maintained by completely separate applications in sync would be difficult to implement and is not worthwhile, as better alternatives exist.

A service-oriented architecture

We finally come to the third and final solution to our problem of sharing user authorization information. This one avoids duplication in databases and in code. It abstracts database changes away from the clients of those tables so that code changes to support a schema change need to be made only in one place. Finally, this solution does not pose a problem for maintaining cache correctness, as the previous attempt did. In fact, this solution is ready-made for horizontal scaling. The solution is—you guessed it—an access control *service*.

Figure 13-6 shows the service in the context of our other two applications. It is a complete Rails application, but rather than serve web pages, it accepts *service requests* from other applications for a predefined API and returns *service responses*. In this example, the service supports a method `authorize()`, which would return true or false to the application trying to authorize the user. The makeup of the tables in the access control database is completely abstracted by this method. We could change the database

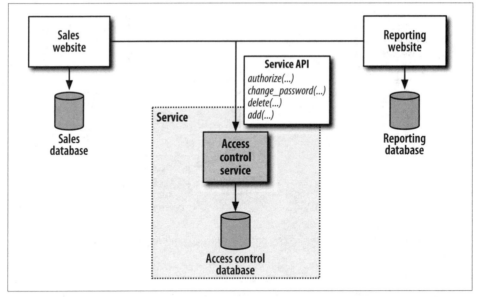

Figure 13-6. Solving the access control problem by introducing a service layer

schema completely or even replace it with an LDAP database; so long as the *implementation* of the `authorize()` method within the service is updated, all of our client applications—here, the sales and reporting sites—can continue to authorize users without needing to make any changes.

In this example, we have extracted not just the repeated database tables, but also the repeated application code, all into a single place: the service. The service publishes an API or a set of methods to which it can respond. In a sense, a service API is just like a model class in a Rails application, but the methods execute on a remote server.

Reduce Database Load

The database is usually the first bottleneck to show up in a project, and it is also generally the most persistent. You can add as many application servers as you want, but you are stuck with a single database server to handle all of your SQL queries.

Luckily, the amount of time spent processing SQL queries can be greatly reduced through a variety of techniques available to the application developer:

- Analyze slow queries with a query planner. Add indexes to speed up slow queries, or rewrite the queries to use already existing indexes.

- Recast expensive queries as database views. Then materialize those views for faster access, as described in the previous chapter.

- Replace database queues with external queues mechanisms such as Amazon's Simple Queue Service (SQS).

Unfortunately, database tuning can seem like a constant uphill battle. Every new batch of code you release is likely to contain new SQL queries. Often, you won't even explicitly know what those queries are when you're releasing them because the SQL will be hidden behind the abstraction of ActiveRecord magic in Ruby code. Ideally, all of your database queriesuse indexes; however, new queries may mean new indexes are necessary. In your development or staging environments, where there's less data in the database and less traffic, the queries—while slow—may seem to be an acceptable speed. You may not feel the pain of missing indexes until the queries are out in production and massive amounts of traffic are suddenly getting slammed against a query that runs too slowly in the context of your production database and all its contained data.

Similarly, a change in the application may lead users to implement a feature they didn't before. A slow culprit query may have been in your application all along, but growing popularity may cause it to hose your entire site.

Slicing and dicing

One of the biggest benefits of a service-oriented architecture is that it allows you to bend the rule that says you can have only one database server serving traffic. A service represents a vertical slice of your site's functionality, from the database up to the service API itself. This means that each separable slice of functionality can persist its data in a separate database on a separate physical machine. If you have two services, such as a Product Service and an Orders Service, each handling roughly half of the database load, then by splitting the application into a service-oriented architecture, you can—at the expense of added hardware—reduce database load by 50%. While some may take issue here and point out that a second database server may be expensive, whereas making software faster is free, in practice the cost of hardware pales in comparison to the cost of a good software developer's time.

To illustrate this, let's take the example of the monolithic application we developed in the first half of this book, shown in Figure 13-7. There are two components, the Rails application, with code for dealing with movies (our product), and for taking orders for movie tickets.

There are two good ways to split up this monolithic application. The first step is to simply slice the database in half, leaving the movie information in one database and the order information in another. Then model classes relating to orders are moved into their own new application, the Orders Service. A service API exposes the methods of those classes. Anywhere that model classes related to orders were referenced in the original application (now the Movies application), they are now delegated via the service API to the orders application. This architecture is shown in Figure 13-8.

The other way to split up a monolithic application like this is to make *everything* a service. The `movies` application and the `orders` application are both services: a Movie Service and an Order Service, respectively. Each contains only the logic pertinent to its

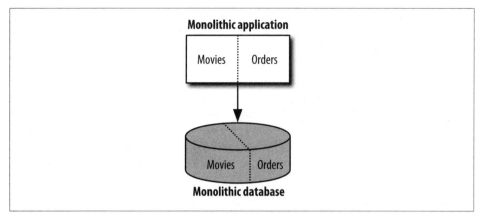

Figure 13-7. A monolithic application serving two functions

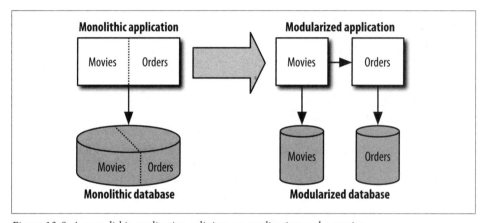

Figure 13-8. A monolithic application split into an application and a service

own mission: movies and showtimes or orders for some type of product. Gluing the services together and providing the HTML web interface for customers is a thin front-end, which has controllers and views but no database. The thin front-end provides the user experience, but all the hard work is done behind the scenes by the services. This architecture is shown in Figure 13-9 and is the architecture preferred in this book.

It should be noted that with this architecture, movies and orders are completely de-coupled. This means that the Order Service can be written to be completely generic and be reused regardless of what product is being sold. If your company starts selling video games or music, the Order Service shouldn't need to be rewritten to support new types of products.

One anti-pattern that is *not* a service-oriented architecture but still splits the database, is shown in Figure 13-10. Here, the tables related to movies have been separated from the tables related to orders, and each set is placed in a separate database. This *does*

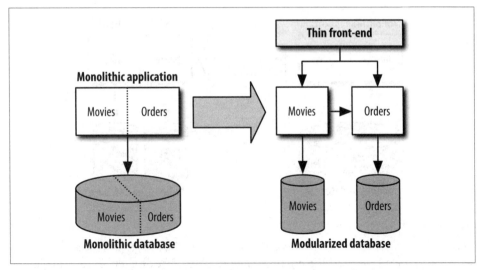

Figure 13-9. A thin front-end backed by two services in a service-oriented architecture

solve the initial problem of reducing database load. However, it is an anti-pattern because a vast many parts of your application stack no longer work as intended.

The first problem is that Rails classes can no longer behave as you would expect them to. Our monolithic application has a `has_many` relationship between movie showtimes in the Movie Service and orders in the Order Service. This is perfectly valid from the perspective of Rails. However, as soon as you execute any of the following queries, you hit a wall:

```
movie_showtime.orders
order.movie_showtimes
Order.find(:all, :include => :movie_showtime)
```

Second, the databases can no longer maintain referential integrity. While this is true of the SOA examples in Figures 13-8 and 13-9, the applications have been decoupled and there can no longer be any expectation of referential integrity *between* the services (of course, referential integrity would be maintained within each service). In Figure 13-8, there is no `has_many` relationship in Rails between movie showtimes and orders because neither Rails application knows about both models. An order, in the decoupled Order Service, would maintain an *external foreign key* that the thin front-end would know is related to a movie showtime.

In Figure 13-10, showtimes and orders *are* represented by models in the same Rails application, which means the tables backing the models must maintain referential integrity. However, the split database guarantees that referential integrity cannot be enforced. In essence, this architecture removes even the possibility of maintaining referential integrity, although the application can still be written in a way that assumes it. This is the antithesis of the entire first half of this book.

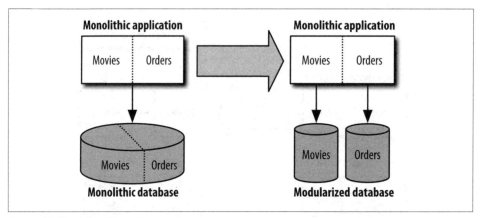

Figure 13-10. A database split anti-pattern

You may be asking yourself why it is OK to lose referential integrity in the architectures shown in Figures 13-8 and 13-9, but not in Figure 13-10. The difference is that in Figures 13-8 and 13-9, there can be expectation of referential integrity to begin with. Because the applications are split along the same lines as the database, there are no database-related model classes for the tables that exist in the other applications' database. Each table's model classes exist in the service application sitting atop the physical tables. Within the tables, rather than have traditional foreign keys where there can be an expectation of a join, we'll store *external foreign keys*. These will be understood to exist in a separate system, and to access the related data, a service call will be required, not a join or other SQL lookup. However, because we're dealing with an external system at the application level, we don't assume that the data must be present. Instead, the service can return the equivalent of a 404 Not Found error, and the calling application should be written to gracefully handle such a scenario. In Chapter 15, when we build an XML-RPC services that talk to each other, we'll get a taste for how this works.

The myth of database replication

A common counterargument to SOA as a solution for managing database load is the contention that databases can be replicated to balance load, just like application servers. Except in rare read-only situations, nothing could be further from the truth.

Why is this so? First, let's examine the problem (database load) and the proposed solution (database replication). Figure 13-11 shows two configurations. On the left, a single database is connected to two application servers. We find that the database is heavily loaded, so we attempt to rectify the problem by replicating the database. In reality, we would want to direct all writes at the master and allow both the master and the slave to handle reads; in this diagram, for simplicity, we have directed half of the traffic to the master and half of the traffic to the slave.

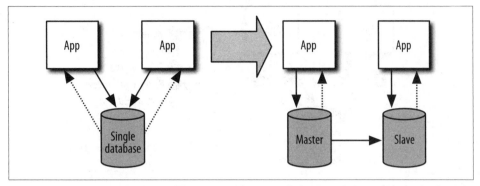

Figure 13-11. A database under load from two applications; the load is split by replicating the database

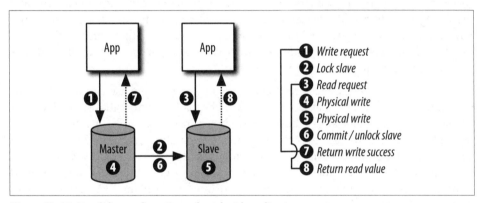

Figure 13-12. Breakdown of a write and read with replication

This looks like it should work. However, there is always a trade-off between speed and consistency. If you have one or more slave machines that need to maintain the same data as the master, and you expect query results to be consistent, you will pay a heavy price in waiting for the databases to get synchronized—including network overhead—before you can trust any data retrieved from any slave machine.

Figure 13-12 shows the steps required for a write to the master database followed by a read of the same data from the slave database. With a replicated database, there are additional network operations to lock the slave database, send the data to be written over the wire, and then unlock the slave database. This blocks not only the read on the slave, which cannot return a value until the master has unlocked it. It also blocks the write on the master. The write cannot be deemed successful until it has been propagated successfully to all slaves.

Figure 13-13 shows the same scenario but with a single database. Here, there are no network operations to synchronize databases for writes because there is only a single database. A read following a write returns immediately after the write is deemed

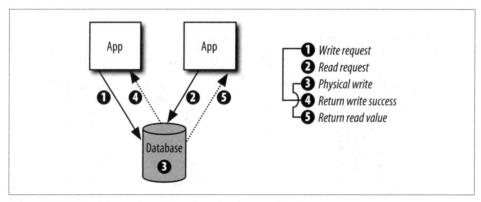

Figure 13-13. Breakdown of a write and read without replication

successful locally. In this scenario, there are two steps between initiating a write and the write succeeding, and two steps between initiating a read and obtaining the result. Further, none of these steps requires a network hop. On the other hand, with a replicated database, it takes six steps after the write is initiated for the write to succeed. The read waits for five steps before returning a result.

So in a situation where writes are frequent, replicating a database can actually slow your application down rather than speed it up. The load on the database machines may appear to be lower, but that's because the machines are sitting around waiting for locks to be lifted and data to pass over the network. The database in Figure 13-13, while it appears from CPU and disk metrics to be more heavily taxed, will actually be outperforming the replicated database because it is much more efficient. It doesn't sit around waiting for others to catch up but rather slogs forward using all the CPU and disk cycles it can to serve application requests.

Scalability II: Caching Is Tricky

Centralizing the logic for a single "concern" of our application into a single place also eases our problem of cache correctness and horizontal scaling. To scale horizontally, we need to ensure that the database is not our bottleneck and that we can handle more load simply by adding more application servers. To accomplish this, we need to cache data somewhere.

But caching can be a tricky proposition. Before relying on a cache, we need to be highly confident that the data in the cache is accurate. A service-oriented architecture can help us gain that confidence. Because all access to the data in question must arrive through the service API, we don't have to look very far to find all the places where the data may change. This makes it much easier to cache data at the right times and be reasonably assured that we're clearing our cache at the right times, too.

While correct caching in a monolithic application is certainly possible, correctness is harder to guarantee because there's much more code around that has the potential to

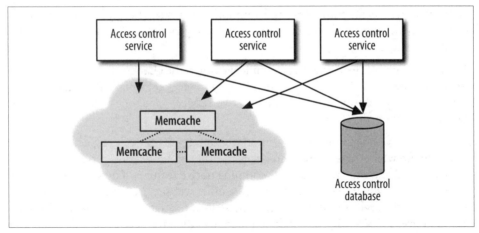

Figure 13-14. A service can scale horizontally while maintaining a provably correct cache

do something bad and *break* the cache correctness. In the monolithic application, any code, at any time, can access and modify the access control tables—or any other tables in the database, for that matter. You may have spent a lot of time in a monolithic application, carefully designing an abstraction for authentication that relies on caching to boost performance, but one day a new programmer comes along and forgets to use your abstraction. He accesses the database tables directly, and suddenly your carefully crafted authorization API no longer works as expected. Data has changed underneath the caching abstraction and the cache no longer matches the actual data. In a service-oriented architecture, such a catastrophe is impossible because only the authorization service itself has direct access to the authorization tables. There is a physical separation of the data belonging to one service from all other services and applications. There is no opportunity for unrelated code to make modifications to a service's data.

Just as the monolithic application can be run on multiple servers to balance load, the service application can run on as many physical machines as necessary to handle the load of all the client sites that need to authorize users. Each machine would have a Memcache server contributing to a shared cluster. Whereas we would not allow a heterogeneous set of applications to participate in the same Memcache cloud to cache and expire user data, we now have a single code base for authorizing users contained within the service, so the problem disappears. Figure 13-14 shows a service cluster of three machines, all running the access control service and a shared Memcache cluster.

Reduce Local Complexity

When your application is designed as a set of services and service consumers, your organization—i.e., your company or business unit—gains something that is lacking in a company whose software is monolithic. Your business organization gains team modularity along the same module splits as your software. This is a good thing because modularity gives teams autonomy, and autonomy means less need for communication to get any particular job done. That can spell huge productivity gains for the organization as a whole.

How is this possible? Consider the example we began the chapter with: a sales site and a reporting site, both clients of an authentication service. Let's make this example a bit more realistic by splitting the sales site into two services: one for product information and a second for order data.

The services have a plain old HTML interface for administrative uses, accessible only within the firewall. These admin interfaces use the authentication service to validate employees and grant them access to the administrative features. The services also have a "service API," which a single front-end consumer website consumes, combining the features of both services to present a unified view of the data to customers. When the front-end needs to access product data, it contacts the Product Service. To build and execute an order, it contacts the Orders Service.

All of this is hidden from the site's visitors, but it is plain as day to those developing the website. There are five clearly delineated compartments of code:

- Authentication service
- Product service
- Orders service
- Reporting website
- Externally facing consumer website

This translates into five teams of developers. Because the services all have well-defined APIs, consumers of the services don't need to talk to the service teams unless the API is no longer satisfying their needs. Similarly, service teams can work within their code base without worrying that their changes may result in unknown consequences for others. As long as the service continues to behave as specified by the published API, clients of the service can remain blissfully ignorant of any architectural changes going on within the service. Thus, every team can innovate within their own bubble in a way they could not when all the source code and database tables were intertwined in a monolithic application. The same was true in the 1990s with the collective leap from procedural to object-oriented programming. And we've said nothing about the dramatic reduction in overhead accrued while resolving source control conflicts in a monolithic environment where everyone is simultaneously modifying the same files. Figure 13-15 shows an example of a Rails service split, with admin functionality contained within the service applications.

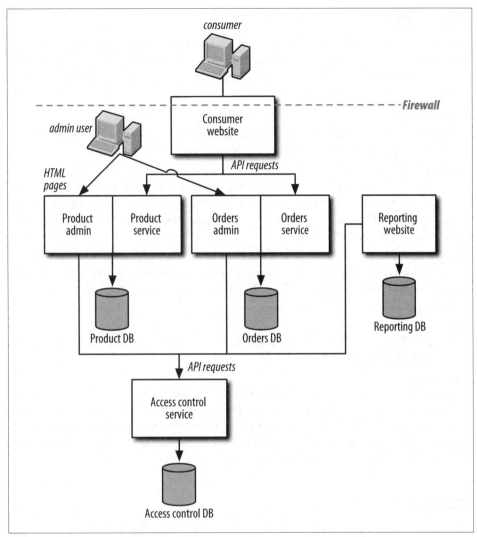

Figure 13-15. A likely Rails service split, with admin functionality contained within the service applications

In Summary

Simply put, a service is a vertical slice of functionality: database, application code, and caching layer. *Within* a service, you should follow the same principals of design that we covered in the first half of this book. Externally, the service-oriented architecture provides a number of additional benefits:

Understandability

> Each service is responsible for a single business function. The amount of code is minimized to a quantity understandable by a single person.

Isolation

> A service's application code is separated and isolated from all other application code. Its database is separate from other services' databases. Only the service application itself has direct access to its persistence and caching layers. A service is a gatekeeper for its data.

Uniform access

> A service is accessed through a published API, and likewise, it accesses other services through their published APIs. The API is the only interface to access a service's data.

Trust

> A service lives inside the firewall, and it trusts any client that has physical access to make service requests.

Scalability

> Isolation and uniform access means that cache correctness is much easier to guarantee. The number of places where persisted data can change is reduced to the service code. Thus, the use of caching can be maximized, which reduces demand for database resources, and in turn allows the application to scale to greater loads simply by adding more application servers.

Exercises

1. Examine your application for vertical slices of functionality. Which are good candidates to be separated out as services? Why?

2. For each candidate service identified, what database tables drive the functionality?

3. For each table, what are the foreign keys in and out of the service? How might you deal with foreign keys in isolated databases?

## CHAPTER 14

SOA Considerations

A service-oriented architecture (SOA) prescribes very little about service implementation. The only thing that can be inferred from a design being SOA is that different concerns are handled by different applications, and those applications pass messages back and forth. What language a particular application is written in, what messaging transport applications use to communicate, how the messages are structured, and even what is in the messages is up to the software architect.

That said, you don't need to start from scratch determining a byte order for your transport layer each time you write a service. There are a handful of industry-standard approaches for service-to-service communication that you can take advantage of to get rolling right away. The two most popular have been XML-RPC and SOAP, and more recently, REST.

In this chapter, we'll examine the pros and cons of each approach. However, before comparing and contrasting REST, XML-RPC, and SOAP—an endeavor that generally pleases no one and disgruntles everyone—we'll first go over two sets of properties for a good service design. In the first set are properties that ensure your service is maintainable and interoperable with current and future clients. The second set is guidelines for keeping a service lean and fast.

Service Considerations

As has been mentioned, a service is accessible only through its API. The service, via this contract, is the gatekeeper of any data it manages. This leads naturally to two desirable properties. The first is that the implementation *within* the service should be completely abstracted from the clients. The implementation—be it software code, database table layout, or even physical composition—is free to change as long as the API's contract is maintained, without disruption to the client. The second property is that the service API should be accessible to as many types of clients as possible. Because the service is the gatekeeper, it should be in a common language that is accessible to many types of clients. Let's look at each of these two properties more closely.

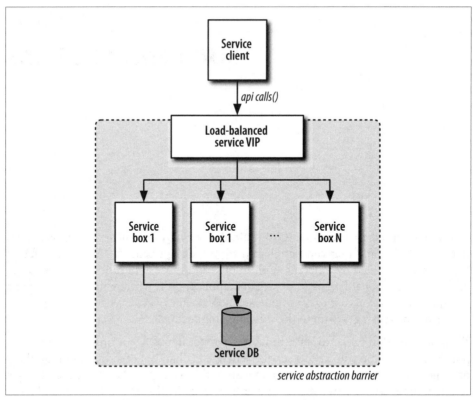

Figure 14-1. Service abstraction barrier

Implementation Details Are Hidden

Just as in object-oriented programming (OOP) the implementation details of a class are hidden behind its public interface, in a service-oriented architecture the details of each service should be hidden behind its public service API. Figure 14-1 shows an example service, which is made up of a number of service machines ("box 1" through "box N") and a database. The first level of abstraction belongs to the load balancer. A load balancer hides the detail that there are a number of servers by creating a virtual IP (VIP) and spreading traffic among the service boxes to balance load. It should be possible for any request to be handled by any service box. It should also be possible for any service box to be shut down (taken "out of service") without disruption to the service's clients. This implies that each service request must be stateless. The ability of a request to the service to succeed cannot depend on the request being directed to the same service box as previous requests. If this were the case, any in-process request sets that are bound to one back-end service server would be aborted if that service box was taken out of the rotation. On the other hand, if any service box can handle any service request, a change in the configuration of the service's hardware will go unnoticed by clients.

This is in contrast to the accepted (but problematic) convention of many user-facing websites, which maintain a *session* object for each visitor to the site. The session object often contains lots of information that is critical to serving subsequent requests to the user. If the sessions are stored locally on a particular web server, a user's traffic must always be directed to that server for the session to be maintained and utilized. This is commonly supported by load balancers via "sticky sessions," in which the load balancer issues a cookie to users on their first request, and then uses that cookie to direct subsequent requests. When that server is shut down for a software upgrade, or is lost due to a hardware failure, all browsing by users who were being directed to that server by the load balancer is disrupted.

One way to get around lost session-state on a single server is to store sessions in a shared location. This, of course, has its own problem because the session store becomes a single point of failure. In general, this is to be avoided. In Rails 2.0, sessions data can be stored in cookies maintained by the client's browser, which removes the burden from your application servers. For back-end service boxes, the solution is to design an API in which each request is independent of every other request.

Principle 1

A service should be internally fault-tolerant. This is accomplished by load balancing and statelessness between requests.

The second abstraction barrier lies with the API itself. The API hides the implementation details of the application code. The API is truly a contract: a guarantee to clients that they can communicate with the service in a specific way, and get specific results. Once the contract is published to clients, via WSDL (Web Service Description Language) for XML-RPC or SOAP services, or via WADL (Web Application Description Language) for REST services, it should never change.[*] The only acceptable time an API may change is in a major publicized version. However, even under the condition of a version change, generally the old version of the API should continue to be supported for some time to give clients an opportunity to upgrade to the new version without loss of service. Changing the contract because it makes changes within the service more convenient is unacceptable once clients are consuming the service API. Changes that are not backward compatible are guaranteed to break all clients' implementations.

The psychological way to enforce the immutability of a service API, in some organizations, is to have software developers write their W*DL files by hand, and then generate stub application code based on the W*DL. Application developers then fill out the stubs to instrument the application. A change to the W*DL requires regenerating stubs and losing large chunks of prewritten code, a strong deterrent. On the other hand, many frameworks, including Rails, generate WSDL on the fly based on methods written by

---

[*] From here on out, except when specifically referring to WSDL or WADL, the notation *W*DL* will be used, to denote that either service contract type is applicable.

developers.[†] This can cause an apparently innocuous change in a method signature to have a pervasive effect on the interoperability of the service with all of its clients. In such an environment, where W*DL is generated from code rather than vise versa, developers must be aware of what changes will affect the service API and be disciplined to avoid doing so.

Principle 2

The service API, except under major version changes, must not change. Changes must occur *within* the application but not be visible to service clients.

API Is Accessible

For service clients to make use of the service easily, the service API must be accessible. The first principle of accessibility is that the API is published and documented. Published, in this sense, means the API is available in a machine-readable format so that clients can automatically generate their own interface to the service. They can send messages to the service and process results without needing to first obtain a custom client library. As noted, W*DL service description files are the standard way to publish the service's API contract. When they are available on the network at a predetermined and permanent URI, the service API is said to be *discoverable*.

Principle 3

The service API should be discoverable via a network accessible WSDL or WADL description file.

Documented means there is some way for developers to understand the API and its effects. A W*DL file is a complete description of the service, and both formats support comments mixed into the XML descriptions of the API. Tools exist to transform machine-readable W*DL files into human-readable documentation that is easier on the eyes than raw XML.

In a perfect world, all of your services and service clients would be Rails applications. However, in a real enterprise environment, the clients of a service are likely to be written in a variety of languages, using a variety of technologies. Your organization may have legacy applications that are still maintained but aren't likely to be rewritten in Rails any time soon. You may inherit applications through a merger or acquisition and have a need to integrate a .NET- or Java-based application with your own services. Rails is an excellent framework for web application development, but it may one day be superceded by an even better framework. And finally, some clients may not be web

---

[†] Rails does not generate WADL as of version 2.0.

applications at all, and in those cases, Rails may not be the right choice for implementing the new clients.

All of this means that, as mentioned earlier, rather than design a communication mechanism from the byte-ordering on up, it's important to use a technology that already has wide support and easily integrates into a variety of other technologies: Java, .NET, C++, etc. XML-RPC client libraries are available on nearly every platform, and a growing number of platforms are beginning to support REST in some way. Various degrees of SOAP functionality are also available on many platforms.

Principle 4

The service should communicate in an industry-standard way so that clients written in any language or with any framework can participate.

API Design Best Practices

So far, four principles of service design have been laid out. Now we turn to the API itself, and define four guidelines for an API design that will ensure your application maintains a high level of user-perceived speed. The jump from monolithic application design to service-oriented design is not without trade-offs. In exchange for reduced local complexity and other benefits of a modular SOA design, you give up locality of information. Because the overall architecture no longer features a single application directly connected to a database, overhead is imposed in the form of network messaging between services. This overhead can either be detrimental to performance or it can be barely noticeable if the API is designed to minimize overhead.

Four guidelines described below can help keep the overhead in the "barely noticeable" category. Note that these guidelines may seem contradictory at times. That is why they are guidelines rather than rules. An appropriate balance must be found between each of the guidelines, based on the situation at hand.

Send Everything You Need

In object-oriented programming, it's a best practice to have lots of small methods that each perform a small function and return a small piece of data. Within an application, method calls are cheap, so writing small methods that are easily testable is often desirable. In a service-oriented architecture, on the other hand, method calls are processed remotely within the service, and therefore any call incurs the overhead of the network. Rather than issuing lots of finely grained method calls, as we might within an object-oriented program, it can be much more efficient to get all of the data necessary in one shot.

For example, imagine we want to render a page for a movie along with the showtimes in a particular location. The following calls seem reasonable if the entire application is running on a single machine:

```
@movie = Movie.find(params[:id])
@rating = Rating.find(@movie.rating_id)
@showtimes = MovieShowtime.find_all_by_movie_id_and_location(@movie.id, params[:zip],
  :include => :theatre)
```

In a scenario where each method call incurs network overhead, the preceding would require at least three network operations. If our network API did not allow theatre information to be included with a showtime as is possible with ActiveRecord, we would incur 3 + N network operations, where N is the number of showtimes found for our movie. The service client code might look something like this (service calls are in bold):

```
@theatres = Hash.new
@movie = MoviesClient.getMovie(params[:id])
@rating = MoviesClient.getRating(@movie.rating_id)
@showtimes = MoviesClient.getShowtimesByMovieAndLocation(@movie.id, params[:zip])
for showtime in @showtimes do
  if !@theatres[showtime.theatre_id]
    @theatres[showtime.theatre_id] = MoviesClient.getTheatre(showtime.theatre_id)
  end
end
```

Code styled this way would certainly put the overhead of our service API into the detrimental rather than barely noticeable category. If we know ahead of time that clients of our service will frequently request information about movies within a certain location, and theatre, movie, and rating details will often be required, we can design the API to return all of this information within a single request. Rather than have very fine-grained API methods, we could define a method that given a movie *id* and a zip code would return movie information, the rating description, showtimes, and theatre information all in one request:

```
@showtime_data = MoviesClient.getShowtimeData(movie_id, zip)
```

The @showtime_data variable would then be a hash or struct, as shown in Figure 14-2. The hash has a :movie field, which contains the rating information, denormalized into a rating field. The hash also contains a :showtimes field, which is an array, one element per movie theatre. Within that array, each element has members describing the theatre, and a member, :showtimes, which is another array, one element per showtime at that theatre. This data structure, while more complex than each of its component parts as described in the physical ActiveRecord models of the back-end service, is just what the average client needs to display movie showtimes to a user. This data structures is therefore part of the *logical model* of our application (Figure 14-3). Logical models are the topic of the next chapter.

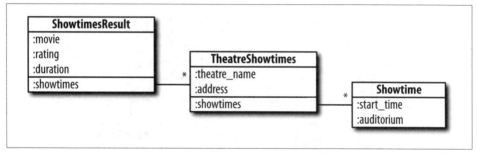

Figure 14-2. *A result object for the getShowtimeData method, which returns all needed for displaying showtime information in a single request*

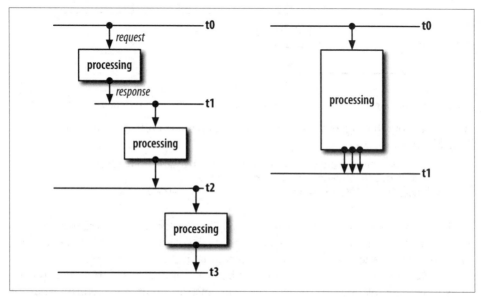

Figure 14-3. *Finding the correct grain for the logical model reduces the number of service calls*

API Guideline 1

Design the API with a granularity of data that minimizes the number of requests a client must make in the common case. The goal is one service request per client action.

Limit Round Trips

In some cases, we need the result of a first service request in order to build all of the parameters needed for a second service request. For example, on a shopping website, after placing an order, we might want to display additional items that the user may be

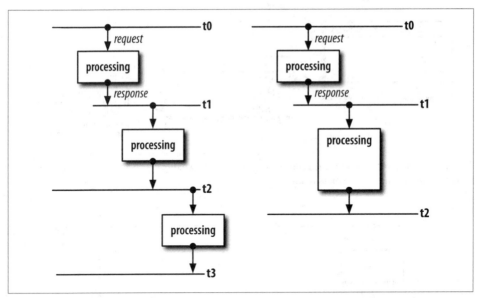

Figure 14-4. Limiting the number of round-trips reduces overall communication penalty

interested in purchasing, based on the purchasing habits of others. It might look something like this:

```
order_status = ShoppingService.complete_order(credit_card_info, @items)
if order_status == ShoppingService::ORDER_SUCCESS
  related_items = ShoppingService.get_related_items(@items)
end
```

While having these two API methods—`complete_order` and `get_related_items`—makes perfect sense, calling them this way incurs the overhead of two service requests when the order is successfully completed, resulting in slower user-perceived performance. If we know ahead of time that it will be common for clients to request related items after completing an order, we can instead alter the return type for `complete_order` such that it returns not only a status value, but also an array of related items if the order is successful. This results in the same amount of processing on the service side, but the client does not incur the overhead of two round-trips to the service (Figure 14-4).

Therefore, when designing an API, it's necessary to think carefully about how it will be used. You don't need to foresee every possible use, but today's common cases are likely to be tomorrow's as well. In this example, it wouldn't make sense to *remove* `get_rela ted_items` from the API. There will certainly be times when it is convenient to call that service method independently from placing an order. However, if we can guess what most clients will want to do after placing an order, it makes sense to be proactive and get the data to the client right away.

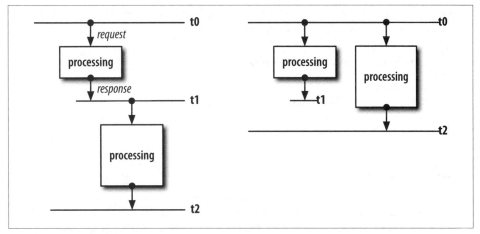

Figure 14-5. With parallelized requests, the cost is the time of the slowest request

API Guideline 2

Requests should not depend on the results of other requests. Rather than requiring a client to chain multiple requests to get the data it needs, guess what is needed and provide it up front.

Look for Opportunities for Parallelization

Even with the first two guidelines in hand, it will often not be possible or even desirable to get everything needed from a service in a single request. The service may be responsible for retrieving a number of unrelated types of information that would not be logical to return together. In such cases, it makes sense to make multiple service requests, one for each distinct type of information. But this doesn't mean we need to suffer the overhead of multiple round-trips. If the inputs to one method call do not depend on the result of another, we don't need to wait for the first request to return data before making the second request. Instead, we can dispatch all of the unrelated service calls all at once, and then wait for them all to return before proceeding.

Figure 14-5 illustrates the time savings that can be realized by dispatching multiple requests at the same time. Here only two requests are shown, but the benefits increase with the number of requests that can be parallelized. When the requests are chained, you pay the price of each request, plus accumulated overhead for each call. When the requests are dispatched simultaneously, you pay the price of the longest running service call and overhead for only one network operation.

For example, if we are making one request to the movie service to get showtime data, and another request to an ads server to get third-party offers to display, we can make them in parallel. Normally, we would see the following code:

```
@showtime_data = MoviesClient.getShowtimeData(movie_id, zip)
@advertisements = AdsClient.getAdsByLocation(zip)
```

However, since we know the requests are unrelated, we can dispatch them both at once, and then wait for the results. The code might look like this:

```
t1 = Thread.new do
  @showtime_data = MoviesClient.getShowtimeData(movie_id, zip)
end
t2 = Thread.new do
  @advertisements = AdsClient.getAdsByLocation(zip)
end
t1.join
t2.join
```

API Guideline 3

Where multiple service requests are required, encourage and support parallelization. Make the cost of communication with a service equal to the slowest service operation, rather than the sum of all service requests.

Send as Little as Possible

The guidelines just described were not created in a vacuum. I learned guidelines 1 through 3 while working at Amazon.com (*http://amazon.com*). We had very tight service level agreements (SLAs) regarding how long any page could take to load to ensure that the site would feel as fast as possible. This translated into SLAs for services; to be included on a page that should take one second to render, the service call might, for example, need to guarantee delivery of data in 0.25 seconds. These tight requirements led to service API designs in which round-trips were limited, more than enough information was always returned to callers, and parallelization was possible and widespread. Caching was also key, as it removed the database as a bottleneck and prevented requests times from suffering as traffic increased.

When I brought the three guidelines I gleaned from my time at Amazon to the Rails world, I was rudely awakened. At Amazon, we wrote back-end services using C++ and Java, so the services themselves were very fast. As I have already mentioned, Ruby is not a fast language. In Chapter 2, we saw that the extensive processing of data can be extremely costly—even something as simple as instantiation of ActiveRecord objects where hashes will suffice. There, we shaved 50% off the time of an ActiveRecord query by preventing the results from being unmarshalled into heavy objects.

It turns out that translating data to and from service calls can be an expensive operation as well. Request results are commonly sent from server to client as XML data. So first imagine the overhead incurred translating database results to ActiveRecord objects. Then add to that the overhead of marshalling those objects into XML. All of this is time spent in the slowest part of the system—Ruby—and the results can be surprising. We designed one API method, which followed guideline 1 and returned a very large chunk of data. On the back-end service, this data was cached, so we cut out database time. Retrieving the data from the cache was instantaneous. However, due to the sheer size

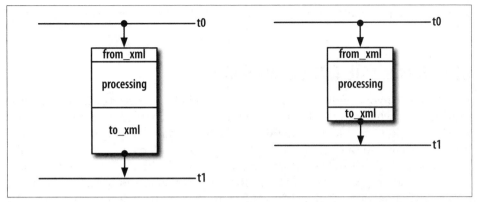

Figure 14-6. Limiting the amount of data to be marshaled to XML can reduce response times dramatically

of the data and the amount of XML processing that was required to generate the service response, the service request was consistently taking 12 seconds to process.

From that experience, we came up with the fourth and final guideline, illustrated in Figure 14-6 (which can seem to be in direct conflict with guideline 1).

API Guideline 4

Avoid expensive XML serialization and deserialization costs by sending as little information as necessary in any given request.

While the guidelines seem to conflict, they actually don't. Let's say a movie has show-times and reviews. Guideline 1 encourages us to use an API that returns all of this data together because it's likely it will often be shown together on the same web page. But it's unlikely that any web page on our site would contain *all* of the information about the movie, *all* of the showtimes, and *all* of the reviews in their entirety. That would be too much information and would be almost universally considered a poorly designed web page.

Guideline 4 does not restrict what kinds of data we send back, but *how much*. For example, if there are hundreds of movie reviews, it's unlikely that we need them all when we're requesting details about the movie itself. Returning five is probably suffi-cient, as long as there's another API method that does let us get them all if we want to. Similarly, when returning related "follow-on" data that's likely to be useful per guide-line 1, it's often a good idea to return this data in an abridged or summarized form. On the movie's "gateway page," which would link to all showtimes and all reviews, the first few sentences of the first five reviews are probably all that's needed. Similarly, a list of local theatres, without actual showtimes, is enough detail. From there, a user might click a link to see all showtimes or all reviews, or click a "read more" link on a particular spotlighted review to get the full text of just that review. With this in mind, guidelines 1 and 4 could be restated together as, "Send everything you need, but no more."

REST Versus XML-RPC Versus SOAP

We now come to one of the great battles being fought by designers of service-oriented architectures: which protocol is best? The three main contenders in this arena are SOAP, XML-RPC, and REST. Even within the Rails community, the answer has not been consistent. Up to version 2.0, ActionWebService, which makes it easy to make XML-RPC and RPC-based SOAP services, was included with the core of Rails. In version 2.0, it was dropped in favor of ActiveResource, which provides facilities for working with REST services. XML-RPC, SOAP, and REST all provide a means to an SOA end; they all facilitate lopping off a vertical slice of an application and providing remote access over the Internet. And with some allowed deviances from pure REST (or "*high REST*," as some call it), any of these three alternatives can be equally well suited to the task of representing any given API.

What differentiates the protocols is the ethos of how a remote protocol should behave and how it should be used. The cultures that have grown around each protocol reflect different views of how systems should be interconnected. In this book, I will take the universalist and also universally contrarian view and suggest that there is no single best protocol and the decision of which to use should be based on the problem at hand. Each design problem is unique: some problems are more easily solved with a REST interface, while others are more easily solved with an RPC-style interface.

Although the Rails community is putting its full backing in REST-based approaches, widespread REST-based services are not yet to be found. Part of this scarcity is related to a dearth of tools. As tools evolve, REST may in fact be *the* answer to the question *Which protocol?* Until then, we must remind ourselves that in the enterprise practicality is at least as important as purity.

The remainder of this chapter will explore the difference ethos of the three protocols. We'll also explore the scenarios—regarding problem space and audience—when one protocol can make more sense than another.

XML-RPC

RPC stands for remote procedure call, and XML-RPC is a protocol for making procedure calls remotely, using XML to encode the parameters on the way in and the return values on the way out. The notion behind XML-RPC is very simple and straightforward. A service server implements a method. A service client invokes that method, which results in a network request to the server over HTTP. The server executes the method and returns the result of the invocation.

In XML-RPC, services define an *endpoint URL*, which clients access to make their requests. The method the client wishes to invoke, as well as any parameters required by the method, is part of the XML payload of the request, which is an HTTP POST.

Virtually every language has an XML-RPC client library available, which makes XML-RPC a good choice when clients will be written in disparate or even unknown languages. In the age of Web 2.0 and rich JavaScript clients, it's good to know that even JavaScript applications can consume XML-RPC services.

The ethos behind XML-RPC, as the name implies, is procedural. The methods typically seen in an XML-RPC API are action-oriented: `get_movie()`, `get_showtimes()`, `place_order()`, and so on.

Implementing an XML-RPC client in Rails, as well as many other frameworks, is as easy as falling off a horse. The ActionWebService gem, which was included in the core of Rails up to version 2.0, makes it trivial to define an XML-RPC service and automatically publish a WSDL file describing the methods available to clients.

Before moving on, it's worth noting that a major benefit of an XML-RPC-style interface is the ease with which you can hide implementation details from clients. Normally, this might be something you would assume as a property of any SOA service, especially after reading the previous chapter. However, the property of abstraction must be noted due to the way many Rails-based REST services are being written these days. These implementations are sacrificing the very desirable property of *decoupling* that maintaining a solid service-based abstraction barrier would provide, a significant basic advantage of SOA.

In XML-RPC, the scope of what the procedures defined as part of the API can do is limitless. For instance, the API need not have a one-to-one relationship with the physical data model. It may initially, if your logical model does not differ greatly from the physical tables, but the API is free to diverge without consequence as you change the internals of your service but maintain your original API for legacy clients.

In addition to not being tied to a data model in general, an XML-RPC method implementation need not be tied to a particular table or even a particular row in a table. Exactly the opposite is true: a method can access whatever it wants, wherever it wants to (within the convinces of the host language, of course). For example, the following would be a perfectly acceptable XML-RPC method call, even though it clearly affects multiple rows in a table on the server:

```
BankAccountService.transfer_funds(acct_1, acct_2, amt)
```

Note also that the implementation of this method on the server absolutely requires a database transaction to ensure that a race condition doesn't corrupt the account balances (see Chapter 1 for a refresher on why). The following could be disastrous if executed on the client without a means of defining a transaction on the database connected to the bank service server:

```
bal1 = BankAccountService.getBalance(acct_1)
bal2 = BankAccountService.getBalance(acct_2)
BankAccountservice.setBalance(acct_1, bal1 - amt)
BankAccountservice.setBalance(acct_2, bal2 + amt)
```

It's important to note this example up front to illustrate how easy it is to define the kind of API necessary to solve a problem with XML-RPC, which is completely flexible regarding the methods that can be defined. As we will see in our discussion of REST, with "pure REST" it can be quite difficult to design an API that allows for a transaction on the server side, as in our first example shown earlier. Of course, there are solutions to this problem in the REST world, which I will describe in turn as well.

SOAP

SOAP is an incredibly versatile protocol for building a variety of service-oriented architectures, including some architectures not covered in this book. Originally SOAP stood for Simple Object Access Protocol, but as the breadth of the SOAP specification ballooned, the W3C dropped the words behind the acronym. Indeed, the number of layers added atop SOAP are staggering; they include such additional specifications as WS-Addressing, WS-Security, WS-Polling, WS-Eventing, WS-Enumeration, WS-Reliable Messaging, and more. This conglomeration of specifications, collectively known as WS-*, has been affectionately named "WS Deathstar" by SOAP's numerous critics.

While SOAP as an idea has great promise, the problem is that it's difficult to find a complete implementation of the SOAP standard anywhere on the planet. Microsoft's and some of Java's development environments make it somewhat easy to create SOAP services that utilize these higher-level parts of the SOAP protocol. However, when you use these service-builders and the more esoteric parts of the SOAP specification, you're limited to other Microsoft and Java clients to consume the services. You don't ever see SOAP services of this nature accessible as "web services" for public consumption because almost no one could actually make use of them.

In my own experience, the designers of SOAP systems fall into two camps. In the first camp are seasoned and battle-trained software architects. They understand the inaccessibility that SOAP engenders, but they don't care because they are solving a technical problem internal to their own organization, and they are their own clients. There's nothing wrong with these people or their SOAP services; likely you'll never have to tangle with either. The second camp doesn't understand the interoperability problems they will soon face with non-Microsoft clients, but they end up with a SOAP service anyway; they hit a pretty button in a Microsoft IDE and the choice is made for them. With no offense intended to those in the former camp, I find that most SOAP users fall in the latter.

As it happens, the majority of SOAP use out there is simply as a wrapper for performing remote procedure calls, just like XML-RPC, except at a slightly higher cost. Because SOAP *could be* so much more versatile, there is a bit more overhead in the message envelopes in SOAP than there is with plain old XML-RPC. Indeed, the SOAP client and server implementations available in Ruby are also based on ActionWebService, and only RPC-style SOAP functionality is provided. When using ActionWebService, you don't really make a choice at all regarding whether you are creating an XML-RPC or a SOAP-based service. Because only the RPC subset of SOAP is implemented, you're making both at once.

To the Rails developer, XML-RPC and SOAP are functionally equivalent, although XML-RPC might be slightly faster in practice. Because in the end SOAP offers the Rails developer nothing she isn't already getting with XML-RPC, SOAP won't be discussed any further in this book.

## CHAPTER 15

An XML-RPC Service

This chapter demonstrates how to build an XML-RPC service in Rails using Action-WebService. Like the rest of this book, this chapter won't simply drive through the mechanics of setting up a service. Building on Chapters 11 and 12, you'll learn not only how to make a Rails app communicate with another Rails app—that's easy—but also how to build an infrastructure for services that makes your application enterprise-solid. That involves properly abstracting your database schema—the physical data model—from your logical model. Enterprise-solid also means knowing where to put all of your service code so that your application remains coherent. But first, you need to get set up with ActionWebService, which can be tricky in Rails 2.0.

ActionWebService and Rails 2.0

As noted before, in Rails 2.0, ActionWebService was relegated from the core to plugin status. As of this writing, simply installing the ActionWebService gem does not work as expected with the following:

```
gem install ActionWebService
```

You may want to try installing the gem like this anyway. The warning signs that the plugins are still not fully integrated are errors such as "Uninitialized constant Action-WebService". If you want to wait until you've got some ActionWebService code in place before hacking up your installation, feel free to come back to this section later. In any case, rest assured that the following steps will get you going with ActionWebService in no time. Note that this procedure assumes you have previously frozen your Rails distribution in *vendor/rails* by running:

```
rake rails:freeze:gems
```

First, from the *vendor/rails* directory, type:

```
svn co http://svn.rubyonrails.org/rails/ousted/actionwebservice
```

This checks out the ActionWebService code, in essence, promoting it back to "core" status. Next, above the `Rails::Initializer` code, add the following code, shown in Example 15-1.

Example 15-1. First set of modifications to environment.rb needed to get ActionWebService working in Rails 2.0 and higher

```
class Rails::Configuration
  attr_accessor :action_web_service
end
```

Just below, within the `Initializer` section, add the code in Example 15-2.

Example 15-2. Second set of modifications to environment.rb needed to get ActionWebService working in Rails 2.0 and higher

```
Rails::Initializer.run do |config|
  config.frameworks += [ :action_web_service]
  config.action_web_service = Rails::OrderedOptions.new
  config.load_paths += %W(
    #{RAILS_ROOT}/app/apis
    #{RAILS_ROOT}/app/controllers/services
    #{RAILS_ROOT}/vendor/rails/ActionWebService/lib
  )
```

Finally, in order to make use of the test scaffolding, which allows you to invoke XML-RPC requests using your web browser, you'll need to patch the file *ActionWebService/lib/action_web_service/scaffolding.rb* under *vendor/rails*. Change line 114 from:

```
content = @template.render :file => default_template
```

to:

```
content = @template.render({:file => default_template, :use_full_path => false})
```

You're now ready to get started writing your first service.

Creating an Abstraction Barrier

In the first half of this book, we concentrated on third normal form (3NF) and domain key/normal form (DK/NF). In this chapter, we'll move away from this normalization restriction when we create an object model. That may sound surprising, given the emphasis placed on normalization at the data layer, but as we'll see, normalization won't help us here.

Before we proceed with creating an object model, we first need to understand what one is and what it's not. Therefore, we need to take another look at ActiveRecord, from the perspective of the application as a whole. Once we've done that, we'll see how an object model fits into the picture.

ActiveRecord As the Physical Model Layer

Think back to earlier chapters in this book and recall your thoughts as a simple schema turned into what at first glance may have seemed like an overly complex one. In many ways, that more intricate data model was easier to deal with because it removed the possibility of recording or producing incoherent data, which itself is no picnic to deal with.

Often developers shy away from highly normalized schemas because the abundance of tables and relationships seems too distant from the end result they hope to display on a web page. The data presented to users on web pages is usually not normalized, and if you work from display to schema, it will seem onerous (or even pointless) to obsessively normalize your data.

Such a perspective seems hard to argue against; what's missing is a key element of data-driven website design. That element is the object model: the layer of abstraction *above* the physical layer. Its job is to make web pages easy to display. It was never claimed by anyone, anywhere, that a physical model's purpose is to make web pages easy to display. The schema of the physical model maintains data integrity in your database, *period*. It's the object, which has yet to be fully explained, that model maintains sanity—your sanity—in your presentation layer.

If you were born and bred on Ruby on Rails, you may be wondering why you have not heard of this distinction before. The reason you have not read about the difference between physical models and logical models in Rails is that Rails does not distinguish between them.

In Rails, the mantra is "convention over configuration," and most tutorials are focused on showing the quickest way rather than the best or most scalable or maintainable way. Part of this ethos is an insistence that "magic" is good, especially at the data layer, where in Rails there is next to zero configuration. Since you don't have a step in which you declare the nitty-gritty of your data model, the hope is that you can get started writing object model code right away in ActiveRecord models. That is the promise. But here are those words again: *object model*. Now we're saying that ActiveRecord isn't for object model code but for physical model code. So what does belong in ActiveRecord models, if not object model code? What are they for?

In fact, there is quite a bit of "configuration" required in Rails on top of your data model. First, you do still need to tell Rails which tables exist by creating model classes based on ActiveRecord::Base for each table or view. You do need to define what relationships exist between those tables with `has_one`, `has_many`, `belongs_to`, and `has_and_belongs_to_many`. You also need to define validation for data-passing through ActiveRecord model classes to prevent invalid data from being saved: e.g., `validates_uniqueness_of`, `validates_presence_of`, `validates_numericality_of`.

Once you have put all of this information into your ActiveRecord model classes, what you have, in essence, is a directory full of database configuration. Convention saves you the necessity of declaring class names and foreign key column names. Of course, you are free to specify them, and you need to if you must stray from convention or are working with a legacy schema. But no matter how you look at it, the reality is that you have written quite a bit of configuration, it just was written in Ruby rather than in XML files.

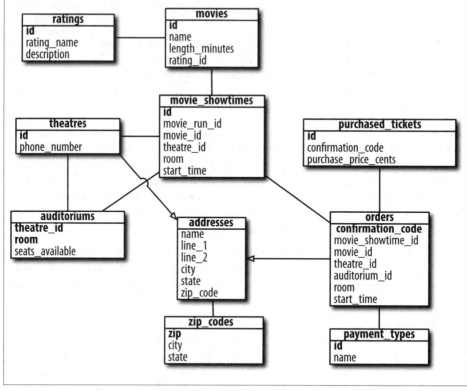

Figure 15-1. A review of our DK/NF movie showtimes schema

The normal Rails convention would be to place application logic into ActiveRecord models, but this blurs—in fact, it *removes*—the line between the physical and logical models. This gets to the heart of why inexperienced database schema designers are uncomfortable with 3NF and DK/NF when viewed from the application layer, where they are most at home. They ask, "I have to design my UI with *this?*" Thankfully, the answer is no.

Before we move on to the object model layer, let's first review our data model as we left it in Chapter 8. Figure 15-1 shows the schema, which has a one-to-one relationship with our ActiveRecord model classes. Review it, as soon we will be layering on top of it.

The Object Model Layer

Between the data layer (represented by ActiveRecord models) and the display layer, there is an object model layer that represents the problem the way it is natural to think about it. An object model need not be in 3NF or DKNF. As mentioned, the physical layer's purpose is to maintain order at the data layer, whereas the object model's purpose (based upon the assumption that the physical layer is doing its job) is to

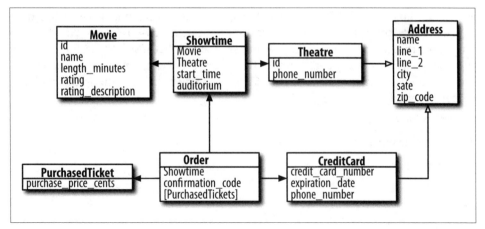

Figure 15-2. Movie tickets object model

maintain sanity at the application layer. In other words, it maintains sanity for the application developer.

The object model for the movies portion of our schema might look like Figure 15-2. It is vastly simpler than our physical model, but it still contains all of the necessary information to:

- Display current movies
- Display details about a particular movie
- Display details about a particular theatre
- Display movies in a given location
- Place an order

Note the many things that we don't care about here:

- The rating information is repeated in every movie object
- There is nothing to constrain the auditorium of a showtime to any set of actual auditoriums in a theatre
- There are no "domain" objects to constrain values, such as ratings or zip codes
- There are no foreign keys but rather object-oriented "container" relationships

But at this layer, we don't need to worry about any of this because the physical ActiveRecord layer is worrying about it for us.

Think of it this way. First, we created a solid data model, keeping in mind that the database is a true piece of the application whole. At the physical layer, we were concerned with translating this rock-solid layer into ActiveRecord models that would give us easy access to our data from Ruby. The next step is to translate ActiveRecord layer objects into something that is easily accessible for passing through the service and for building UIs.

When building an XML-RPC service in Rails, we create object model classes based on `ActionWebService::Struct`. These classes translate data from ActiveRecord models into something that can be returned through our service API. Because Ruby is not a strongly typed language, and many consumers of XML-RPC services *are*, you need to define the types for all data members in `ActionWebService::Struct` classes. You do this with the `member` keyword:

```
member name, :type
```

The allowable types are:

- `int`
- `string`
- `base64`
- `bool`
- `float`
- `time`
- `date`
- `datetime`

And of course, another `ActionWebService::Struct` class is an acceptable type as well.

For now, let's focus on the classes related to displaying movies and showtime information, and for the moment put orders aside. We can define our classes as in Example 15-3.

Example 15-3. Class declarations for the MoviesService object model, lib/movies_service.rb, or in plugin

```ruby
module Logical
  class Movie < ActionWebService::Struct
    member :id,                  :integer
    member :name,                :string
    member :length_minutes,      :integer
    member :rating_id,           :string
    member :rating_description,  :string
  end

  class Address < ActionWebService::Struct
    member :line_1,              :string
    member :line_2,              :string
    member :city,                :string
    member :state,               :string
    member :zip_code,            :string
  end

  class Theatre < ActionWebService::Struct
    member :id,                  :integer
    member :name,                :string
    member :phone_number,        :string
```

```
      member :address,             Address
  end

  class Showtime < ActionWebService::Struct
    member :movie,                 Movie
    member :theatre,               Theatre
    member :start_time,            :datetime
    member :auditorium,            :string
  end
end
```

Here we have declarations of our classes, but no definition of how they work. What we have in Example 15-3 is very much like a header file in a C++ program. We've defined the structure of our data, but not how it works. This "header file" will have a special location in our architecture, but for now, if you want to get started following along, place it in *lib/* so that Rails will automatically load it. We'll move it later, when we come back to the header file analogy in our discussion of the *service plugin*. But first, let's add some logic to the `Movie` class so that we can instantiate one based on data fro ActiveRecord objects. Example 15-4 demonstrates.

Example 15-4. Logical model for a movie, app/models/logical/movie.rb

```
module Logical
  class Movie < ActionWebService::Struct
    def self.get(physical_movie_id)
      return nil if !(m = Physical::Movie.find_by_id(physical_movie_id)
      Movie.new(:id => m.id,
                :name => m.name,
                :length_minutes => m.length_minutes,
                :rating_id => m.rating.id,
                :rating_description => m.rating.description)
    end
  end
end
```

This file, *movie.rb*, gets placed in a new location in our application under the models directory. Notice that we have placed the class in the module `Logical`. Just as our physical models were in a module called `Physical` and went in the directory *app/models/physical/*, this class and other class definitions for our object model classes will go in *app/models/logical/*.

You may have noticed that we just defined the class `Logical::Movie` twice: once in the file *lib/movies_service.rb* and again in *logical/movie.rb*. This is not a problem because in Ruby you can reopen classes as many times as you like to add more methods or data. However, while this is fine as a Ruby practice, reopening a model class in this way does create a problem within the Rails framework. When your code looks for the `Logical::Movie` class the first time, it will have already been defined from within the *movies_service.rb* file. That prevents the Rails auto-loader from looking for the file in *models/logical/*. Rails has already loaded our declarations in the "header" file, but to make Rails do what we expect and load the definitions as well, we need to explicitly instruct Rails to load the logical model class definitions. We do that by adding the following lines at the bottom of *application.rb*; this is similar to the method we used to make Rails play nice with our multiple table inheritance mechanism in Chapter 10:

```
Dir["#{RAILS_ROOT}/app/models/logical/*.rb"].each { |file|
  require_dependency "logical/#{file[file.rindex('/') + 1...-3]}"
}
```

You may be wondering why we don't just put the declaration and definition of each class in the same file. Hang on to that thought, as this structure will make sense when we arrive at creating the service plugin.

Before we do that, since we have written a new type of class, let's do the right thing and test it. Testing logical models is no different than testing physical models, which we've already done quite a bit of. Example 15-5 shows a simple test that retrieves a Logical::Movie object and checks through a series of asserts that the logical model matches the corresponding physical models.

Example 15-5. A unit test for a logical model class

```
require File.dirname(__FILE__) + '/../../test_helper'

class MovieTestCase < Test::Unit::TestCase

  def test_logical_movie_get
    p = Physical::Movie.create!(
      :name => 'When Harry Met Sally',
      :length_minutes => 120,
      :rating => Physical::Rating::PG13)
    l = Logical::Movie.get(p.id)

    assert l.name == p.name
    assert l.length_minutes == p.length_minutes
    assert l.rating_id == p.rating.id
    assert l.rating_description == p.rating.description
  end

end
```

As expected, our simple test passes:

```
chak$ ruby test/unit/logical/movie_test_case.rb
Loaded suite test/unit/logical/movie_test_case
Started
.
Finished in 0.013015 seconds.

1 tests, 4 assertions, 0 failures, 0 errors
```

The definition of our other object model classes proceeds similarly. Example 15-6 shows the definition of the Logical::Theatre class. Notice how on the way from the physical to the logical model, we moved the address information from the class itself into a substructure.

Example 15-6. Logical model for a theatre, app/models/logical/theatre.rb

```ruby
module Logical
  class Theatre < ActionWebService::Struct

    def Theatre.get(theatre_id)
      p_t = Physical::Theatre.find(theatre_id)
      a = Logical::Address.new(
        :line_one => p_t.line_1,
        :line_two => p_t.line_2,
        :city => p_t.city,
        :state => p_t.state,
        :zip_code => p_t.zip_code)
      Logical::Theatre.new(
        :id => p_t.id,
        :name => p_t.name,
        :phone_number => p_t.phone_number,
        :address => a)
    end

  end
end
```

Figure 15-3 shows how the physical and logical models fit together. At the very bottom is the database, with a 3NF or DK/NF schema. Attached to the database are Active-Record models. All SQL queries occur at this layer and this layer only. The ActiveRecord models have two clients. On the right, ActionController classes intended for internal administrative use access them. On the left, the ActionWebService stack accesses the ActiveRecord models. First there is a translation layer from physical to logical model with the `ActionWebService::Struct` classes. The external-facing API deals in these logical object models. Neither the ActionController classes nor the ActionWebService classes ever access the database directly; they always go through the ActiveRecord layer. Each layer sees only the data directly below it. Now that we have a logical model layer, the next step is to define the ActionWebService API.

Defining the API

There are four components to a Rails service. We've already defined part of our logical model layer—the `Movie`, `Theatre`, and `Showtime` `ActionWebService::Struct` classes. Now let's look at the other three pieces so that we can begin making actual service requests.

The first is the API, which defines which methods are available to clients. Your API files go in the directory *models/apis*. You can split up segments of your API into multiple API files, just as you can split up different actions into multiple ActionController controllers. For now we'll define a single, simple API called `MoviesApi`. Our API declaration is shown in Example 15-7. This API declares two methods (`get_movie` and `get_thea tre`), which allow for retrieval of a `Movie` or `Theatre` object by ID.

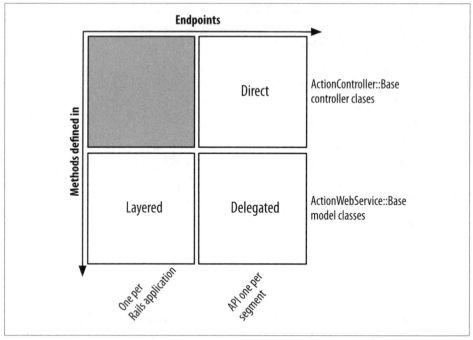

Figure 15-3. The pieces of a Rails XML-RPC service application

Example 15-7. An API definition for MoviesApi, models/apis/movies_api.rb

```
class MoviesApi < ActionWebService::API::Base
  api_method(:get_movie,
             :expects => [:movie_id => :int],
             :returns => [:movie => Logical::Movie])

  api_method(:get_theatre,
             :expects => [:theatre_id => :int],
             :returns => [:theatre => Logical::Theatre])
end
```

A few points are worth noting here.

First, we define each API method with the method api_method. It has three parameters. The first parameter is a symbol defining the method name. The second is an array defining the parameters the method expects. The third is an array defining the return value. The method name is required, but the expects and returns parameters can be omitted if the method takes no parameters, has no result, or both.

Note that each element of the expects and returns arrays is a one-item hash. Although this is not required—you are free to list only the types—this syntax is recommended, as it is self-documenting.

The third thing to notice in this code is that when declaring one of our logical model types as a parameter or return value, we need to provide the module name as well as the class name. This is because the API class is in global scope.

The second component of our XML-RPC service is the API implementation, which actually assigns code to each API method. These implementation files, which are based on `ActionWebService::Base`, are analogous to regular ActionController controller files. By default they should be placed in the *app/models/services* directory. However, functionally these classes are controllers, so instead we can put them in a more sensible directory by modifying the Rails load path. We already did this in Example 15-2 (shown earlier) when we added *app/controllers/services* to the load path list.

Example 15-8 shows our API definitions for MoviesApi. Note that we must declare which API we are implementing using the `web_service_api` method.

Example 15-8. controllers/services/showtimes_service.rb

```
class MoviesService < ActionWebService::Base
  web_service_api MoviesApi

  def get_movie(movie_id)
    Logical::Movie.get(movie_id)
  end

  def get_theatre(theatre_id)
    Logical::Theatre.get(theatre_id)
  end
end
```

The third and final component of putting together our XML-RPC service is defining a controller that passes service requests through to the ActionWebService. The endpoint URL is still just a URL to Rails, so we need a proxy class that translates requests destined for an ActionController class into those that can be handled by our service. Example 15-9 shows how we define such a class, which is placed in the standard *app/controllers* directory.

Example 15-9. controllers/movies_service_controller.rb

```
class MoviesServiceController < ApplicationController
  web_service_dispatching_mode :layered
  web_service_scaffold :invoke
  web_service :movies_service, MoviesService.new
end
```

Each line in this class deserves an explanation.

The first line, a call to `web_service_dispatching_mode`, defines the type of dispatching. In ActionWebService, three types are supported: `:direct`, `:delegated`, and `:layered`. We write our Rails code identically for delegated and layered modes, but for `direct` mode, we define methods directly in ActionController controller classes, not in a separate implementation model as in Example 15-8. The second difference is in the number

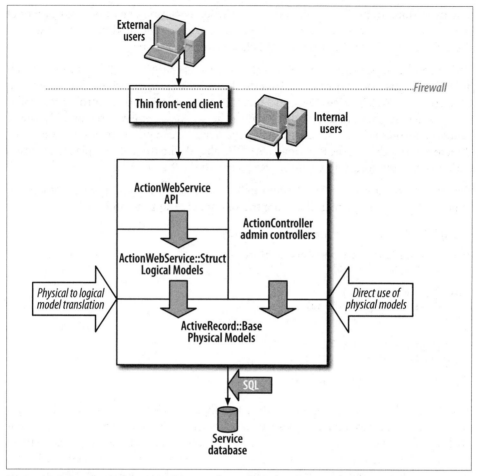

Figure 15-4. Summary of ActionWebService dispatch modes

of endpoint URLs. For direct and delegated modes, we have a different endpoint URL for each controller or API model class we define. In layered mode, there's a single endpoing URL, and the API intended to be accessed is specified by the client in a protocol specific way. For XML-RPC, that's done by prefixing the method name with the API name and a period. Figure 15-4 summarizes these differences.

In practice, the differences between the modes is not significant. In this book, we'll use layered mode. Having a single endpoint URL makes life easier for non-Rails clients, and separating some logic between controllers and models can give us some additional flexibility.

The second line contains a call to `web_service_scaffold`. Like ActionController scaffolding (which should never be used outside of testing), this generates a series of web pages where you can test your web service via a web browser. The parameter defines the URL where the scaffolding will be found. In this case, it would be found at *http:// localhost/movies_service/invoke*.

The third line actually does the work of attaching an API model class to our service. You can segment your API into as many logical chunks as you want and attach them all to the service one by one here.

With this much in place, you can now go check out the WSDL file that is automatically generated by Rails for SOAP clients. It's also good documentation for clients using XML-RPC. The WSDL is located at *http://localhost/movies_service/wsdl*.

We're also ready to write our first functional test to check that our API method, get_movie, works as expected. Example 15-10 shows how to write a functional test for a service method. Note that to make a service call, you use *invoke_direct*, *invoke_layered*, or *invoke_delegated*. We also need to require *test_invoke.rb*, which contains the unit test definitions for these methods.

Example 15-10. Functional test for an ActionWebService service method

```ruby
require File.dirname(__FILE__) + '/../test_helper'
require 'movies_service_controller'
require 'action_web_service/test_invoke'

class MoviesServiceController; def rescue_action(e) raise e end;
end

class MovieTestCase < Test::Unit::TestCase

  def setup
    @controller = MoviesServiceController.new
    @request = ActionController::TestRequest.new
    @response = ActionController::TestResponse.new
  end

  def test_movie_get
    p = Physical::Movie.create!(
      :name => 'When Harry Met Sally',
      :length_minutes => 120,
      :rating => Physical::Rating::PG13)
    l = invoke_layered :movies, :get_movie, p.id

    assert l.name == p.name
    assert l.length_minutes == p.length_minutes
    assert l.rating_id == p.rating.id
    assert l.rating_description == p.rating.description
  end

end
```

We run our test like any other. Here is the output of our test passing:

```
chak$ ruby test/functional/movies_api_test_case.rb
Loaded suite test/functional/movies_api_test_case
Started
.
Finished in 0.072195 seconds.

1 tests, 4 assertions, 0 failures, 0 errors
```

More Testing

Aside from Rails functional testing, we can test our service application in other ways as well. The first and easiest is to use ActionWebService scaffolding. This is helpful when we want to see what service request results look like on the fly. Recall in Example 15-9 we declared a scaffold at **invoke** using the *web_service_scaffold* method. This defined a set of test web pages accessible at *http://localhost/movies_service/invoke*. Figure 15-5 shows the sequence of selecting a service method to invoke, setting up parameters for invocation, and receiving the response.

Note that if our service is facing the public Internet, we may want to turn this scaffolding off for production use. If that is the case, we can also test the service via a desktop client. On the Mac, a free XML-RPC client is available at *http://ditchnet.org/xmlrpc/*. To test a service, we define the endpoint URL, the method name, and the parameters. Figure 15-6 shows the sequence of using the desktop client to test a layered service.

Regardless of how we test, the XML generated for requests and responses is the same. The beauty of XML-RPC is that we don't need to worry about what this looks like. However, for reference, a sample request is shown in Example 15-11 and a sample response in Example 15-12.

Example 15-11. The XML of an XML-RPC request

```
<?xml version="1.0" ?>
<methodCall>
 <methodName>movies.GetMovie</methodName>
 <params>
  <param><value><i4>1</i4></value></param>
 </params>
</methodCall>
```

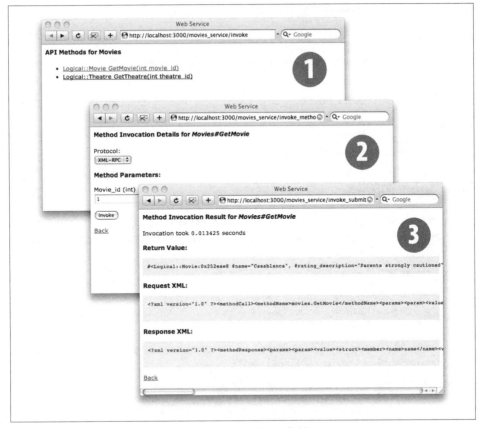

Figure 15-5. Testing an ActionWebService service with scaffolding

Example 15-12. The XML of an XML-RPC response

```xml
<?xml version="1.0" ?>
<methodResponse>
 <params>
  <param>
   <value>
    <struct>
     <member>
      <name>name</name>
      <value><string>Casablanca</string></value>
     </member>
     <member>
      <name>id</name>
      <value><i4>1</i4></value>
     </member>
     <member>
      <name>length_minutes</name>
      <value><i4>120</i4></value></member>
     <member>
      <name>rating_id</name>
```

```
         <value><string>PG-13</string></value>
        </member>
        <member>
         <name>rating_description</name>
         <value><string>Parents strongly cautioned</string></value>
        </member>
       </struct>
      </value>
     </param>
    </params>
</methodResponse>
```

The Client Plugin

Accessing an XML-RPC service from another Rails application—presumably a thin
front-end—is, like all things Rails, extremely easy. If we're within a controller, such as
ApplicationController, the following line is all we need:

```
web_client_api :movies,
                :xmlrpc,
                "http://localhost:3000/movies_service/api",
                :handler_name => "movies",
                :timeout => 5
```

If we're working from a model class, we can create a client by directly instantiating an
instance of ActionWebService::Client::XmlRpc:

```
movies = ActionWebService::Client::XmlRpc.new(
        MoviesApi, "http://localhost:3000/movies_service/api",
        {:handler_name => 'movies', :timeout => TIMEOUT_SECONDS}
        )
```

In both cases, we then call methods on the local variable movies. In the first example,
the first parameter to web_client_api defines both the local variable name of the client
to be created, as well as which API file to look for, in this case, MoviesApi. In the second
example, each of these is explicit.

Hopefully this seems strange. Why does the client need access to the MoviesApi class
defined on the server? Such a constraint doesn't seem like it provides the loose coupling
we are after with a service-oriented architecture.

In reality, we don't need to share any files between the client and server, but doing so
is what allows the Rails client configuration to be so simple. In cases where we have
control over both the client and server, and we are building both with Rails, it's not
hard to share the API definition class. For non-Rails clients, the API definition class is
clearly not needed, and they can connect in their own language or framework specific
way.

In order to share code between our two applications, server and client, we'll build a
plugin that for each installs in *vendor/plugins*.

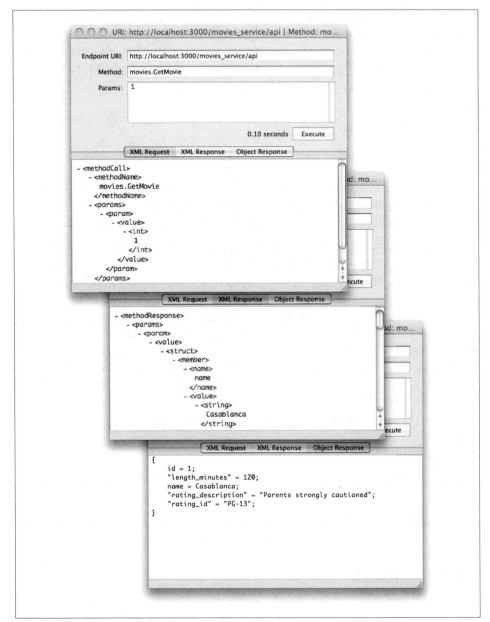

Figure 15-6. Testing an XML-RPC service with OS X Cocoa XML-RPC client

The client plugin serves a few purposes. As already noted, it allows us to easily share code between our service server and clients. If we have multiple service clients, the plugin also ensures that they have a consistent interface to the service. We'll create a wrapper around the simple client instantiation from earlier, which is described below as *the client singleton*. This wrapper, like any wrapper class, gives us the flexibility to take certain actions before, after, or around any service method invocation, on a per-method basis, or for every method. Having a shared client that we define once also lets us test the client apart from other code, and it facilitates integration testing.

As described in Chapter 3, we'll begin creating our plugin by generating plugin stub files:

```
./script/generate plugin movies_service_client
```

Shared Code

The first steps to writing the client plugin are to move the code needed on both the server and client side into the plugin and ensure the service itself still works as expected. Our unit tests will help ensure that nothing breaks as code is moved around.

Two pieces of code get moved into the plugin. First, the API declaration file *movies_api.rb* gets put in the plugin *lib* directory.

Next, the "header" file we created in Example 15-3 gets moved from the application-level *lib* directory to our plugin's *lib* directory. Armed with the identical definitions of what data is in each logical model class via this header file, the server and client are free to reopen the classes locally and add methods appropriate to their role. On the service-side, as we've already seen, the logical model classes in *app/models/logical* define, at the very least, how to build the logical objects. Those classes can contain other business logic as well. On the client-side, we can reopen the classes in the same way and add convenience methods as we see fit.

We ensure our header class gets loaded, so the following line goes in the *init.rb* of the plugin:

```
require 'movies_service'
```

We don't need to explicitly require the API definition class, as the auto-loader finds it automatically.

At this point, we should rerun our tests to ensure everything is working. Visit the scaffolding test web page again and kick the tires.

The Client Singleton

The `client singleton` is a class that automatically creates a client for our service that is accessible from anywhere within the application, controllers, and model classes alike. It also ensures that access from each type of class is consistent, as we would expect it to be. Example 15-13 shows the shell of our client plugin.

The `initialize` method instantiates an ActionWebService client and assigns it to a protected instance variable `@client`. Rather than call methods on the client object directly, callers instead invoke the service methods directly against a service client instance. We have redefined `method_missing` at the instance level to forward these requests to the `@client` object. This allows for an opportunity to modify the arguments going in or the result going out, or to perform other activities such as logging.

This class is a singleton, which ensures there is only one instance of the class in our application at any given time. Singleton class instances are normally accessed via `ClassName.instance`—in this case, it would be `MoviesServiceClient.instance`—but we've redefined `method_missing` at the class level as well to forward requests to the singleton instance.

Example 15-13. Code for a service client plugin, lib/movies_service_client.rb

```ruby
require 'singleton'
class MoviesServiceClient
  include Singleton

  def initialize
    # URL and TIMEOUT_SECONDS are defined in
    # config/initializers/movies_service_client_config.rb
    @client = ActionWebService::Client::XmlRpc.new(
      MoviesApi, ENDPOINT_URL, {:handler_name => 'movies', :timeout =>
  TIMEOUT_SECONDS}
    )
  end

  def method_missing(method, *args)
    # *args can be modified here, logging can take place, etc.
    result = @client.send(method, *args)
    # the result can be modified here, additional logging can take place, etc.
    result
  end

  # this method allows callers to avoid the dot-instance singleton access pattern
  def self.method_missing(method, *args)
    self.instance.send(method, *args)
  end
end
```

Note that we have used two constants in Example 15-13 that haven't been defined anywhere: `ENDPOINT_URL` and `TIMEOUT_SECONDS`. These are configuration parameters that could be different from one client to the next. For example, the endpoint URL could change from one environment to the next. Different clients may have different notions of what is an acceptable time to wait for a service response. In Rails 2.0, configuration such as this is placed in an *initializer*, in the *config/initializers* directory. Example 15-14 shows how to define these configuration parameters.

Example 15-14. A service client initializer, config/initializers/movies_service_client_config.rb

```ruby
class MoviesServiceClient
  ENDPOINT_URL = 'http://localhost:3000/movies_service/api'
  TIMEOUT_SECONDS = 10
end
```

Integration Testing

Integration testing is the notion of testing applications via a third-party tool, treating components like black boxes. Unlike unit testing, which has access to the application and is testing the public interfaces of the code itself, integration testing tests the public interface of an application: the service interface.

Integration testing is different from functional tests like the one in Example 15-10 (shown earlier), too. An integration test *actually* makes a remote service call to a running service to perform the test; it doesn't just simulate the request. In fact, integration tests should be run against a live setup of your entire application stack, including databases with real data in them. It should be the same environment QA uses for testing the application.

An integration test also allows us to test how multiple remote components work together. For example, if a request to one service is expected to make a request to another service, we can check in an integration test that everything that was supposed to happen did in fact happen.

Don't be intimidated by the term "third-party tool." The third-party tool can be yet another Rails application. In this case, the entire function of the application is only to run tests. To get started with our Rails integration test framework, we simply create a new rails application:

```
rails integration_test_framework
```

We ensure ActionWebService is set up correctly, as described in the first section of this chapter. Then we import our service client plugin into *vendor/plugins*, and create an appropriate initializer configuration file like the one in Example 15-14. To get started, we must also turn off the components of Rails we aren't using, so we don't have to set up, for example, our *database.yml* file. In *environment.rb*, we uncomment this line:

```
config.frameworks -= [ :active_record, :active_resource, :action_mailer ]
```

We can now proceed testing our service with the same interface a Rails client would have, as in Example 15-15.

Example 15-15. Using the service client plugin in an integration test

```
def test
  m = MoviesServiceClient.get_movie(1)
  assert m.name == 'Casablanca'
  assert m.length_minutes == 120
  assert m.rating_id == 'PG-13'
  assert m.rating_description == 'Parents strongly cautioned'
end
```

In integration testing, we can be black-box regarding the service application, and white-box regarding that service's database schema. We can connect directly to the database to insert records and ensure that the service returns them in the expected way. This sort of testing is shown in Example 15-16.

Example 15-16. An integration test for MoviesService

```
require File.dirname(__FILE__) + '/../test_helper'

class MovieServiceTestCase < Test::Unit::TestCase

  class Rating < ActiveRecord::Base
    establish_connection(
      :adapter=>"postgresql",
      :database => "movies_development",
      :host => "localhost"
    )
  end

  class Movie < ActiveRecord::Base
    establish_connection(
      :adapter=>"postgresql",
      :database => "movies_development",
      :host => "localhost"
    )
  end

  def test_movie_get
    r = Rating.find('PG-13')
    p = Movie.create!(
      :name => 'Hedwig and the Angry Inch' + rand(100).to_s,
      :length_minutes => 120,
      :rating_id => r.id)
    m = MoviesServiceClient.get_movie(p.id)
    assert m.name == p.name
    assert m.length_minutes == p.length_minutes
    assert m.rating_id == r.id
    assert m.rating_description == r.description
    p.destroy
  end

end
```

Note that in this example, we defined just enough of our schema to get the data under test into the service. We defined the database connection directly in the test, rather than via *database.yml*, because our integration testing may one day span multiple databases, one for each service under test. Since this information is repeated, and likely to change, it can and should also be moved out into an initializer.

The good news is that our test passes:

```
chakbookpro:integration_test_framework chak$
ruby test/integration/movies_service_test_case.rb
Loaded suite test/integration/movies_service_test_case
Started
.
Finished in 0.370347 seconds.

1 tests, 4 assertions, 0 failures, 0 errors
```

## CHAPTER 16

Refactoring to Services

In the previous chapter, we created a basic XML-RPC service. All it could do was return a movie object. However, even with just this simple example behind you, you should have a solid understanding of what services are for, what considerations should go into their design, and how to build a simple one. In this chapter, we'll take all of that foundation and use it to connect three applications together: two back-end services that talk to each other and our integration test framework, which in this chapter will simulate a front-end talking to those services.

Figure 16-1 shows what our architecture will look like by the end of this chapter. First, we'll build a simple orders service, which allows us to add new products to the product database and place orders. Then, we'll integrate our movies service with the new orders service. Whenever we add a showtime to the system, we'll register that showtime as a product in the orders service so that tickets can be sold. We won't actually create a front-end application, but we'll simulate doing so by building new tests in our integration test framework, which tests services the way a real client would access them.

Our main goal is to learn how to connect systems together in an efficient and natural way. While Figure 16-1 provides a picture of how these pieces link together, Figure 16-2 shows a more accurate representation of how we physically lay out such an architecture in a production environment, complete with redundancy, load balancers, and database failover.

An Orders Service

We begin with our new orders service. Previously, the tables relating to movie showtimes (movies, theatres, ratings, and the showtimes themselves) were in the same database as the tables corresponding to ordering (orders, ticket purchases, and a variety of payment processing tables). Even our simple example quickly grew to a large number of tables, and in the real world, the count would explode quickly and continuously.

Our orders tables also took on some domain knowledge of the movie-related schema. The table for order line items was called ticket_purchases because we were selling

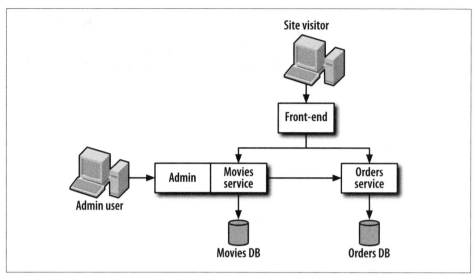

Figure 16-1. Three applications connected in a service-oriented architecture

movie tickets. But some day, we might want to use the same system for selling sodas and popcorn. Tightly coupling the movie-related tables with the order tables can block future paths or make them more difficult to implement.

If we move our orders-related tables out into their own service database, with a separate service application that knows nothing about movies, we are more likely to design a system that will be amenable to future extensions—be it selling sodas, action-hero figurines, or flight reservations. Developers who are working on the orders service can also work more adeptly in their own domain, unhindered by unrelated concerns—both tables and application code—and address their primary focus of improving or extending the orders service.

Figure 16-3 shows the tables of the orders service, extracted from our original application. There are a few changes to note. First, we have added a product table. Because we don't have access to any particular product table—in our application our product was contained within the `movie_showtimes` table—we need a place to keep track of products offered by external applications. This table allows a description to be stored, which can help debug problems. There's also a column to store a quantity of items available.

Our `purchased_tickets` table has also been renamed to make it more generic. It is now called `line_items`, which has meaning regardless of what is being sold, and particularly to developers who are working on the orders service in isolation. The foreign key pointing to the `products` table—previously the `movie_showtimes` table—has also been moved from the orders table to the `line_items` table. Whereas in our movies application it made sense to purchase tickets for one movie at a time in any given order, in a generic ordering application, it doesn't make sense to require that each type of item be placed

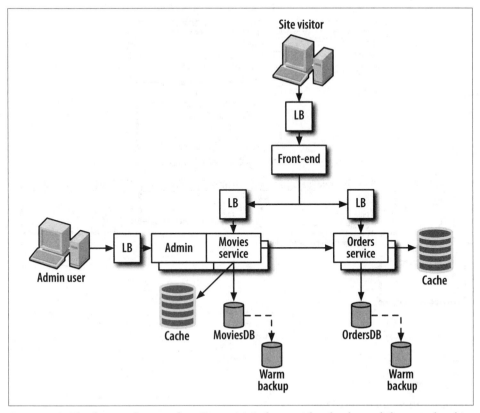

Figure 16-2. The three applications from Figure 16-1, shown with redundancy, failover, and caching servers

in its own order. Instead, an order can have line items for many types of items, and each line item can have an associated quantity.

Example 16-1 shows the Data Definition Language (DDL) for our new schema. It is much like the schema we built up in previous chapters; however, because we simplified the problem, we also simplified the solution. Now that we have a simple products table, which is domain-independent, our primary key is simply the `id` column.

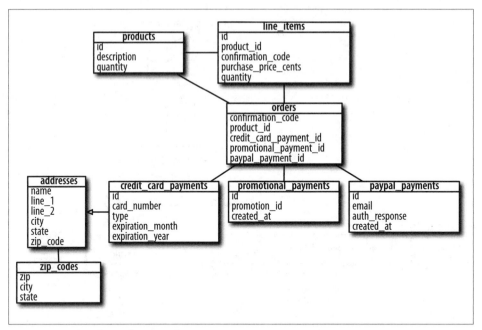

Figure 16-3. The schema for our orders service

Example 16-1. The DDL for the OrdersService schema

```
create language plpgsql;

create sequence products_id_seq;
create table products (
  id integer not null
    default nextval('products_id_seq'),
  description text,
  price_cents integer not null,
  quantity integer not null,
  created_at timestamp with time zone
);

create table zip_codes (
  zip varchar(16) not null,
  city varchar(255) not null,
  state_abbreviation varchar(2) not null,
  county varchar(255) not null,
  latitude numeric not null,
  longitude numeric not null,
  primary key(zip)
);

create table addresses (
  line_1 varchar(256) not null
    check (length(line_1) > 0),
  line_2 varchar(256),
```

```
    city varchar(128) not null
      check (length(city) > 0),
    state varchar(2) not null
      check (length(state) = 2),
    zip_code varchar(9) not null
      references zip_codes(zip)
);

-- index on zip code, a common search criteria
create index address_zip_code_idx on addresses(zip_code);

create sequence credit_card_payments_id_seq;
create table credit_card_payments (
  id integer not null
    default nextval('credit_card_payments_id_seq'),
  card_number varchar(16) not null,
  type varchar(32) not null
   check (type in ('AmericanExpress', 'Visa', 'MasterCard')),
  expiration_month integer not null
   check (expiration_month > 0 and expiration_month <= 12),
  expiration_year integer not null
   check (expiration_year > 2008),
  primary key (id)
) inherits (addresses);

create sequence promotional_payment_id_seq;
create table promotional_payments (
  id integer not null
    default nextval('promotional_payment_id_seq'),
  promotion_id varchar(32) not null,
  created_at timestamp with time zone,
  primary key (id)
);

create sequence paypal_payment_id_seq;
create table paypal_payments (
  id integer not null
    default nextval('paypal_payment_id_seq'),
  email varchar(128) not null,
  auth_response text,
  created_at timestamp with time zone,
  primary key (id)
);

create sequence orders_id_seq;
create table orders (
  confirmation_code varchar(16) not null
    check (length(confirmation_code) > 0),
  credit_card_payment_id integer
    references credit_card_payments(id),
  promotional_payment_id integer
    references promotional_payments(id),
  paypal_payment_id integer
    references paypal_payments(id),
  primary key (confirmation_code)
```

```
);

alter table orders add constraint payment_xor check(
  (case when credit_card_payment_id is not null then 1 else 0 end +
   case when paypal_payment_id       is not null then 1 else 0 end +
   case when promotional_payment_id is not null then 1 else 0 end) = 1
);

create table line_items (
  order_confirmation_code varchar(16) not null
    references orders(confirmation_code),
  product_id integer not null,
  quantity integer
    check (quanitity > 0),
  position integer not null,
  purchase_price_cents integer not null
    check (purchase_price_cents >= 0),
  primary key (order_confirmation_code, position)
);
```

In our implementation of the OrdersService tables, we have no column to store an *id* corresponding to the primary key of a showtime, our purchasable unit. Because our service is intended to be generic, it assigns its own *ids* to each product in the products table. Clients of the OrderService add new products as they need to via the remote API, and they obtain an *id* from the OrdersService as a result. They then refer to products by that *id* in future calls.

There are may benefits to having clients maintain the foreign key from the product database, among them:

- Multiple clients can add products of any type to the OrdersService and there will be no *id* collisions.
- The OrdersService can remain neutral and does not need changes if new product types or new clients are added.

Figure 16-4 shows the sequence of how we'll add products to the OrdersService, as initiated from an administrative control panel in the MoviesService application. Upon adding a new showtime, a service call is made to the OrdersService for the add_product method. The OrdersService creates a new record in the products table and returns a product_id. The MoviesService writes this value to the movie_showtimes table so that it knows how to refer to it later when communicating with the OrdersService. A page is then returned to the administrative user, just as it would have been without an OrdersService in the picture. To the system's users, nothing has changed at all.

To facilitate this interaction, we need to define an API for the OrdersService. First we need to create a plugin, orders_service_shared, as we did in the previous chapter for the movies service:

```
./script/generate plugin orders_service_shared
```

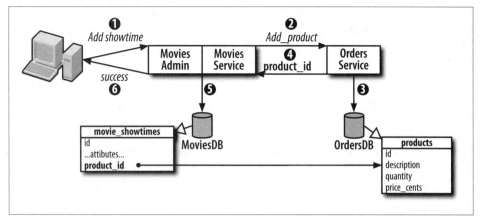

Figure 16-4. Adding a product to the OrdersService

Next we define the API. Example 16-2 shows our *orders_api.rb* file, which would be placed in the *lib/* directory of the client plugin under *vendor/plugins*. Although an orders service could have a large number of callable methods, we'll define two that suffice here. The first, `add_product`, is called from the movies service when a new showtime is added. It is the API method used in the example in Figure 16-4. The second method, `place_order`, is called by a front-end during a user's checkout process.

Note that in our API for placing an order, we just pass the line items. We don't need to create an explicit object for the order itself. It's implicit in the method name that what we're doing is creating an order out of our line items. This is in contrast to a REST approach, where we would be required to define a resource for an "order" so that we could access it at a particular RESTful URI and PUT or POST the order there. However, we clearly don't need the overhead of such an interface, which would complicate the processing to be done on both the client and the server. Here, we have an array of line items, each of which references a `product_id`, as returned from the `add_product` API method, and a quantity. The array itself is the order, and the return value of the method invocation is an object containing the order confirmation code and a final price.

Example 16-2. {plugin}//lib/orders_api.rb

```ruby
class OrdersApi < ActionWebService::API::Base

  api_method(:add_product,
             :expects => [{:description => :string},
                          {:quantity => :int},
                          {:price_cents => :int}],
             :returns => [:product_id => :string])

  api_method(:place_order,
             :expects => [{:items => [Logical::LineItem]},
                          {:payment => Logical::Payment}],
             :returns => [Logical::OrderPlaced])
end
```

The next step is to define the logical model for the OrdersService. Example 16-3 shows our classes: LineItem, Order, Address, CreditCard, Payment, and OrderPlaced. Interestingly, at this stage we have no need for a Product class. One might be necessary given a richer API, but at the moment, the context of our methods themselves can make some logical models unnecessary.

Note that previously our sense of quantity was implicit in the number of rows in the tickets_purchased table because each order could consist of tickets for at most one showtime. However, our generic OrdersService allows for more flexible orders made up of varying products. Therefore, we've added a quantity attribute to the LineItem class. There will be only one line item per product, but more than one of each product can be purchased and recorded in that line item record.

Note that although the line_items table contains a reference to the orders table, the relationship is reversed in our logical model. Here, the Order class contains an array of LineItem objects. It is frequently the case that relationships such as this one are reversed between the logical and physical models; the former is object-oriented and designed to be a natural representation of the world, while the latter is designed to eliminate duplicate data and maintain referential integrity.

Most of our other classes are fairly straightforward and based closely on the physical models underlying them. One exception is the OrderPlaced object, which is the result of calling place_order. It contains the confirmation number, which could be used to retrieve an order after it has been placed. We have also eliminated the subclasses of Payment and CreditCard here, opting instead to differentiate the payment and credit cards types based on class constants. The logical object model gains simplicity, while the physical model still contains the complexity necessary to actually process the payments and correctly record the data in the database.

Example 16-3. {plugin}/lib/orders_service.rb

```
module Logical

  class LineItem < ActionWebService::Struct
    member :product_id,         :integer
    member :quantity,           :integer
  end

  class Order < ActionWebService::Struct
    member :line_items,         [LineItem]
  end

  class Address < ActionWebService::Struct
    member :line_1,             :string
    member :line_2,             :string
    member :city,               :string
    member :state,              :string
    member :zip_code,           :string
  end
```

```
class CreditCard < ActionWebService::Struct
  AMERICAN_EXPRESS = 'american_express'
  MASTERCARD = 'master_card'
  VISA = 'visa'

  member :type,                 :string
  member :card_number,          :string
  member :expiration_month,     :integer
  member :expiration_year,      :integer
end

class Payment < ActionWebService::Struct
  PAYPAL = 'paypal'
  PROMOTIONAL = 'promotional'
  CREDIT_CARD = 'credit_card'

  member :address,              Address
  member :type,                 :string
  member :credit_card,          CreditCard
end

class OrderPlaced < ActionWebService::Struct
  member :confirmation,         :string
  member :price,                :int
end
end
```

With the API declared and our objects defined, we can now implement the API. Example 16-4 shows the *orders_service.rb* file, which we place in *app/controllers/services/*.

First, we declare which API declaration class we are implementing, here `OrdersApi` from Example 16-3. Next we define the `add_product` method. This method just passes parameters through to the physical model `Product` class, and returns the resulting product *id*.

The `place_order` method is interesting because the service API does not naturally match the physical layer data types. An array of line items and an object describing the payment are passed in. These must be translated into a payment subclass as returned from the `Payment` factory constructor method, and an `Order` object, consisting of `LineItem` objects that require looking up `Product` objects to determine the correct purchase price.

Example 16-4. controllers/services/orders_service.rb

```
class OrdersService < ActionWebService::Base
  web_service_api OrdersApi

  def add_product(description, quantity, price_cents)
    p = Physical::Product.create!(
      :description => description,
      :quantity => quantity,
      :price_cents => price_cents)
    return p.id
  end
```

```
  def place_order(items, payment)
    c = Physical::Payment.new_payment(payment.type, payment.credit_card.type)
    c.card_number = payment.credit_card.card_number
    c.expiration_month = payment.credit_card.expiration_month
    c.expiration_year = payment.credit_card.expiration_year
    line_items = items.collect {|li|
      p = Physical::Product.find(li.product_id)
      Physical::LineItem.new(
        :product => p,
        :quantity => 1,
        :purchase_price_cents => p.price_cents)
    }
    o = Physical::Order.create(:payment => c, :line_items => line_items)
    Logical::OrderPlaced.new(:confirmation => o.confirmation_code,
:price => o.order_total)
  end
end
```

While this may seem onerous, the translation layer is actually a boon as your site and business grow. Often, a young designer's first service API will exactly match the physical models' API. Remember that the physical models and data layer are geared toward ensuring referential integrity and data correctness, but the logical models and service API are intended to feel natural to clients. If the two are the same, either your physical models are too natural and likely to be in domain key/normal form, or the service API is too rigid, reproducing the fine-grained ActiveRecord API through to clients and pushing too much business logic up through to the client layer.

Even if your logical and physical models are initially very similar, over time they will diverge, and having a translation layer like the one shown in Example 16-4 gives you a natural place to translate one to the other. This is crucial if your data model is changing but you don't want clients to be aware of the change, or vice versa.

Next, we must define a standard Rails controller intended to pass control along to our service when a request is made to */orders_service/api*. The `OrdersServiceController`, which implements this behavior, is shown in Example 16-5. Just as in the previous chapter, we create a scaffolding for testing, available at */orders_service/invoke*.

Example 16-5. app/controllers/orders_service_controller.rb

```
class OrdersServiceController < ApplicationController
  web_service_dispatching_mode :layered
  web_service_scaffold :invoke

  web_service :orders, OrdersService.new
end
```

Also similar to our last service, we create a client class that we'll use to access the `OrdersService` from other applications. The client library is shown in Example 16-6. It requires that a configuration initializer be placed in *config/initializers*. This file would take the same form as the initializer file created in the previous chapter for

MoviesService, but it should define the location of the OrdersService API as the constant OrdersServiceClient::ENDPOINT_URL.

Example 16-6. {plugin}/lib/orders_service_client.rb

```
require 'singleton'
class OrdersServiceClient
  include Singleton

  def initialize
    # URL and TIMEOUT_SECONDS are defined in
    # config/initializers/orders_service_client_config.rb
    @client = ActionWebService::Client::XmlRpc.new(
      OrdersApi, ENDPOINT_URL,
      {:handler_name => 'orders', :timeout => TIMEOUT_SECONDS}
    )
  end

  def self.method_missing(method, *args)
    self.instance.send(method, *args)
  end

  def method_missing(method, *args)
    @client.send(method, *args)
  end
end
```

In Example 16-7, code from the previous chapter to "help" the Rails auto-loader is reproduced. This code is necessary for Rails to find our logical model classes, as well as our service implementation classes. The pertinent lines are in bold:

Example 16-7. application.rb auto-loader overrides

```
Dir["#{RAILS_ROOT}/app/models/physical/*.rb"].each { |file|
  require_dependency "physical/#{file[file.rindex('/') + 1...-3]}"
}

Dir["#{RAILS_ROOT}/app/models/logical/*.rb"].each { |file|
  require_dependency "logical/#{file[file.rindex('/') + 1...-3]}"
}

Dir["#{RAILS_ROOT}/app/controllers/service/*.rb"].each { |file|
  require_dependency "service/#{file[file.rindex('/') + 1...-3]}"
}
```

We now have all of the files necessary for our second service, OrdersService. The next step is to test the two API methods we created. Example 16-8 shows two tests, one for each method. In the first method, we simply test adding a product using the add_product API method. After adding the "My test product" product, we assert that a valid product *id* was returned.

The second method tests the process of placing an order. First, we add a product for which we will place an order and then create a line item corresponding to a purchase it. We create objects for all of the classes necessary to create a payment (an address, a credit card, and a payment object) and finally we call `place_order` with our line item repeated four times. We assert that the order succeeded and the purchase price returned is what we expected.

Example 16-8. Integration tests for OrdersService

```
require File.dirname(__FILE__) + '/../test_helper'

class OrdersServiceTestCase < Test::Unit::TestCase

  def test_add_product
    new_id = OrdersServiceClient.add_product(
      "My test product",
      50,
      1000)
    assert new_id
  end

  def test_place_order
    p = OrdersServiceClient.add_product(
      "My test product",
      50,
      1000)
    li = Logical::LineItem.new(
      :product_id => p,
      :quantity => 1
    )
    ad = Logical::Address.new(
      :line_1 => '123 Foobar Lane',
      :city => 'Cambridge',
      :state => 'MA',
      :zip_code => '02139'
    )
    cc = Logical::CreditCard.new(
      :card_number => '55555555555555',
      :expiration_month => '12',
      :expiration_year => '2015',
      :type => Logical::CreditCard::AMERICAN_EXPRESS
    )
    payment = Logical::Payment.new(
      :address => ad,
      :type => Logical::Payment::CREDIT_CARD,
      :credit_card => cc
    )
    result = OrdersServiceClient.place_order(
      [li, li, li, li], payment
    )
    assert result.confirmation
    assert result.price == 4000
  end

end
```

The results of our integration tests are shown in Example 16-9. Our tests pass.

Example 16-9. Result of running the OrdersService integration tests

```
chakbookpro: chak$ ruby test/integration/orders_service_test_case.rb
Loaded suite test/integration/orders_service_test_case
Started
..
Finished in 0.344523 seconds.

2 tests, 3 assertions, 0 failures, 0 errors
```

Integrating with the MoviesService

Because we've ripped our application in two, we need some way to link the data in the two applications back together. I've already alluded to the idea that a MovieShowtime object is the "product" of the MoviesService, and that the MoviesService needs to obtain and track product *ids* returned from the OrdersService. To accomplish this, we need to add a product_id column to the movie_showtimes table, as shown in Example 16-10. Note that the column type is text, rather than integer. Just as OrdersService strives to maintain independence from its clients, so too should clients add a layer of abstraction between themselves and the services they consume. Although the product *ids* are integers today, they might not be forever. Since there is no explicit reference to maintain within the movies database, the schema can be built to be generic enough to support today's as well as tomorrow's needs.

Example 16-10. Modifications to the movie_showtimes table to support an orders service

```
create table movie_showtimes (
  id integer not null
    default nextval('movie_showtimes_id_seq'),
  movie_id integer not null
    references movies(id),
  theatre_id integer not null
    references theatres(id),
  room varchar(64) not null,
  start_time timestamp with time zone not null,
  primary key (id),
  product_id text,
  unique(movie_id, theatre_id, room, start_time),
  foreign key (theatre_id, room)
    references auditoriums(theatre_id, room) initially deferred
);
```

We also need to instrument the registration of a product and the retrieval of a product *id* whenever a movie showtime is added. Example 16-11 shows how we hook into the ActiveRecord observer before_save to call the remote add_product method before saving a showtime, storing the returned product *id* for later use.

Example 16-11. physical/movie.rb

```ruby
module Physical
  class MovieShowtime < ActiveRecord::Base
    def before_save
      self.product_id = OrdersServiceClient.add_product(
        self.movie.name,
        self.auditorium.seats_available,
        1000)
    end
  end
end
```

Before moving on, we should test that saving a showtime does in fact register the showtime as a product and retrieve a product *id*. Normally, this would seem like a unit test, but since we must contact a running OrdersService to complete the test, we instead write it as an integration test within the MoviesService application, in the *test/integra tion* directory.

Example 16-12 shows our test. The portion of the test that creates a movie, theatre, and auditorium so that we can create a showtime is sectioned off in the setup method. Our test just creates a showtime and asserts that the saved showtime has product_id, even though none was ever explicitly set in the test.

Example 16-12. Integration test at test/integration/showtime_create_test_case.rb

```ruby
require File.dirname(__FILE__) + '/../test_helper'

module Physical
  class ShowtimeCreateTestCase < Test::Unit::TestCase

    def setup
      @m = Movie.create!(
        :name => 'Casablanca',
        :length_minutes => 120,
        :rating => Rating::PG13)
      @t = Theatre.create!(
        :name => 'Kendall Cinema',
        :phone_number => '5555555555')
      @a = Auditorium.create!(
        :theatre => @t,
        :room => '1',
        :seats_available => 100)
    end

    def test_getting_product_id
      ms = MovieShowtime.create(
        :movie_id => @m.id,
        :theatre_id => @t.id,
        :room => '1',
        :start_time => Time.new)
      assert ms.product_id
    end
```

```
    end
end
```

Other Considerations

Here we've constructed a simple interconnection between two services. Since we have split our database, it's no longer possible for the MoviesService to easily determine if a showtime is sold out. We could deal with this in a number of ways. One possibility would be to add a quantity_remaining API method to the OrdersService, which could take as a parameter an array of product *id*s and return, for each one, the number of seats left for sale. Although this solution is simple and straightforward, it also requires two chained service calls to display movie showtimes on our front-end website, which is contrary to our SOA guidelines. It also requires the call be made every time movie showtimes are requested. Figure 16-5 shows the steps involved.

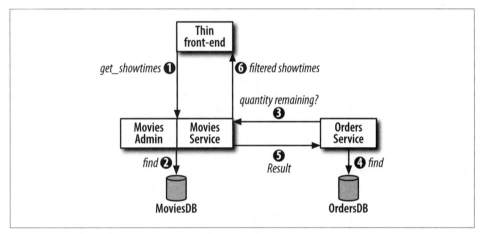

Figure 16-5. Chained requests to find available movie showtimes

Another possibility is to create a callback mechanism such that whenever a product sells out, the OrdersService will make an XML-RPC call back to the product provider, in this case the MoviesService, to notify it that a product has sold out. To facilitate this, the MoviesService would need to maintain a sold_out Boolean in the database so that it could filter out sold out showtimes when servicing requests to the front-end. The OrdersService would need to know something about the product providers so that it could make an appropriate callback. Figure 16-6 shows the entire process, with a new table, providers, containing the callback URLs product provider XML-RPC services.

This *push* rather than *poll* interface dramatically cuts down on the number of requests served over the lifetime of the app. Instead of a quantity_remaining requests for every page view (steps 3–5 in Figure 16-5), we instead have one sold_out request per sell-out event, which is rare compared to page views. In Figure 16-6, the place order process is labeled as times A through D. This is because they do not occur in sequence with the

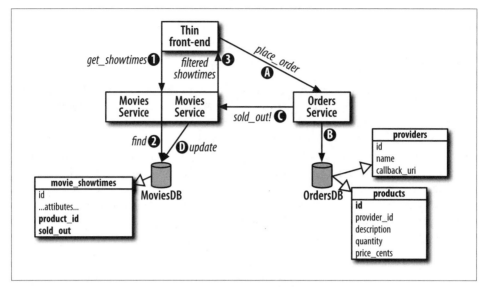

Figure 16-6. Marking showtimes as sold out via a callback

numbered steps. And further, if a product does not sell out as a result of the sale, steps C and D are skipped. For a product with a quantity of N units available, the sold_out method will only be called once if the product is sold N times.

Figure 16-7 shows a sales funnel depicting the progressively smaller and smaller numbers of users who trigger each successive event. Compared with page views, there must be fewer purchases. Compared with purchases, the number of sell-out events must also be smaller. In fact, a real sales funnel would likely be much wider, and have most steps squashed down in the bottom of the funnel. Although these sorts of metrics are highly dependent on the business, drop-off rates frequently result in one or two orders of magnitude of decline in numbers at each step. Business types use this sort of analysis to predict revenue and make business decisions. You can also use the same analysis to find the right places in the application to focus optimization efforts.

In a generic product service, where we are servicing multiple product providers, we are likely to want both mechanisms. Internally, the callback solution is the most elegant, but for external clients it is challenging to implement due to firewalls, security policies, and business goals. For the rest of this chapter, we'll assume that the callback mechanism and the showtimes returned from the MoviesService are, in fact, available.

MoviesService Object Model

We've now connected our two back-end services together. As we add showtimes to the MoviesService, we automatically add the showtimes as products in the ProductsSer

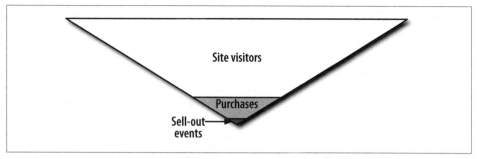

Figure 16-7. A sales funnel: progressively fewer users trigger each successive event

vice. And we have devised a mechanism for the `ProductsService` to inform the `Movie sService` when a showtime is out of seats.

The last step is to provide an API for our thin, user-facing front-end website to retrieve movies, theatres, and showtimes for display. But designing an API can be tricky. Before rushing forward, let's discuss some of the factors that will affect our design decisions.

In Chapter 15, we defined four best practices for designing an API. The first was "Send everything you need." We could interpret this literally, and simply create one service API method per page type in our application, and have the back-end construct a data structure containing all needed data, in the perfect format, for every page.

While this would certainly work, it ties the front- and back-ends together a bit too tightly. The same reasoning we discovered in the discussion of module dependencies in Chapter 5 applies here as well. If the front-end depends on the back-end services, and not vice versa, then the back-end services should be as blind to the front-end as possible. It should be possible to create another, differently behaving front-end site without resorting to creating an entirely new API on the back-end to support it.

The other extreme would be to create a finely grained API, from which it would be possible to retrieve all data from the back-end in small pieces and then put it together in the client in whatever structure we desire. This moves toward the approach taken by REST web services, where bits of data are moved from service to client, and all application logic taken place in the client. While this is flexible, it means that each client must reimplement the business logic. It also implies a large degree of overhead in making tens or hundreds of service calls rather than one.

Most good designs are a balancing act, and this one will be no different. We can compromise between the two extremes and come up with something in the middle, where the API is flexible enough so that a handful of methods can be used to generate a variety of different front-end pages but not so fine-grained that the front-end must do all of the heavy lifting. We'll seek to move obvious functionality into the service layer, so that we do not have to repeatedly implement that functionality in each front-end we might write. But we won't go so far as to move *all* logic into the back-end, leading to an ultimately thin front-end, but a rigid back-end. We'll hope that our API satisfies the

80/20 rule: 80% of future desires will be immediately implementable against our API, and the other 20% are still possible, potentially requiring tweaks to the API.

To come up with our API, we need to imagine the types of pages that will be required within our front-end. Usually, this is an easy task as the product—the website—will already have been defined by a product team. As engineers, it's our team's job to translate those functional requirements into a technical design, including the so-called *non-functional requirements*, which inform the trade-offs we will make when designing a contract between a back-end service and a front-end website. Although users of our site and members of the product team will never directly see the API contract, they may feel it as sluggish or blazing site performance, or in the product team's case, in follow-on rollouts occurring quickly or at the speed of molasses.

Let's play the part of the product team now and define the pages we'll have on our site. We'll have:

- A home page, listing the current movies, filterable by zip code.
- A page for a current movie, listing showtimes in a requested area, by theatre.
- A page for a theatre, listing the movies playing there, with showtimes.

The first page, the home page, could be created with an API called `current_movies`, which returns an array of `Movie` objects.

The second and third pages return similar data—showtimes—but in different groupings. The second page is for a single movie, grouped by theatre, whereas the third page is for a single theatre, grouped by movie. We could certainly take the easy route and lay out a separate object model for each grouping, or we could come up with a more generic object model that could satisfy both pages, and hopefully other future needs as well.

Again, we recognize that the main unit of data we are requesting is the showtime. In addition to a different grouping, our two page types showing showtimes also filter differently. So we have two challenges to overcome: first, parameterized filtering; and second, customizable grouping. Because these are two distinct challenges, we'll deal with them separately, and, as it happens, we'll solve each problem in a unique way.

The first problem, parameterized filtering, is the easier of the two. To define a forward-looking, generic API, we should provide a way to filter on any data we have: movie, theatre, or location, and let the client decide how generic or specific of a query to request. This would allow not only the two pages we have thought up so far to be created but almost any page focused around movie showtimes.

Our API declaration might look something like this:

```
api_method(:get_showtimes,
           :expects => [{:zip_code => :string},
                        {:theatre_id => [:int]},
                        {:movie_id => [:int]}],
           :returns => [:showtimes => Logical::ShowtimesResult])
```

Here we accept one zip code, an array of theatre *id*s, and an array of movie *id*s. We allow any of the parameters to be empty, in which case, that parameter does not contribute to the filter set.

Now we are left to define the `Logical::ShowtimesResult` object. How do we structure this object to be both generic enough for the two pages that we know about today, and generic enough for the pages of tomorrow that we haven't heard about yet?

We have a problem here. Not only is it challenging to create such a generic object, but we also have said time and time again that the purpose of the logical model is not to be overly generic, rather it is to be specific to the application domain, hiding highly normalized database implementations from the view of the front-end application developer. So we want a generic return type to support future needs we don't know about yet, and at the same time we want custom, nonspecific return types to ease application development. Seems like we are in quite a bind.

To solve both problems at once, we'll use a technique that may seem like out-and-out trickery. Recall that our service client plugin is a single package of code, which is available on both the back-end service side and on the front-end client side. So far, our plugin has only contained descriptions of the service—all implementation resides within the service code of the back-end application. If we want to find a place to add code that the back-end does not really know about, but which the front-end believes is a natural part of the back-end, we can add it in the plugin. In the plugin, we can add façade columns that were not in the original XML response, as long as those façade columns can be made up from data that was actually returned in the XML. We can add entirely new methods to the API, as long as those new methods are composed of existing methods. We can even create new return types that were not ever returned by the back-end service.

Since we now know customizing a generic object will be possible, we'll start by defining the generic object. Example 16-13 shows our initial additions to the `MoviesService` logical model, which will make up our generic `ShowtimesReturn` object.

First, we define our `Showtime` object. It contains a `Movie`, a `Theatre`, and `start_time` and `auditorium` fields. The first two are objects defined elsewhere in the header file, and the last two are standard datatypes.

Next, we define a "lighter" version of this object, called `ShowtimeLight`. This version returns the same data, but rather than return entire `Movie` and `Theatre` objects, it instead returns the *id*s of these objects, by which they can be retrieved in some other way.

This then leads to our ShowtimeResult object declaration. This object consists of an array of ShowtimeLight objects, and separate arrays for the Movie and Theatre objects referenced by the showtimes. In essence, we have normalized the return value. We certainly could have returned full-fledged Showtime objects, but this approach has two benefits:

- The amount of data to be serialized, sent over the network, and deserialized is much smaller, which will result in faster user-perceived performance.

- Because we have arrays of the Movie and Theatre objects in play, we don't have to process the array of Showtime objects to "discover" this information.

Thus, each movie and theatre in the result set will only be serialized to XML once, and in other places, where those objects would have appeared if full Showtime objects had been used, their *ids* will appear instead.

Example 16-13. Additional MoviesService logical model definitions

```
module Logical
  class Showtime < ActionWebService::Struct
    member :movie,              Movie
    member :theatre,            Theatre
    member :start_time,         :datetime
    member :auditorium,         :string
  end

  class ShowtimeLight < ActionWebService::Struct
    member :movie_id,           :int
    member :theatre_id,         :int
    member :start_time,         :datetime
    member :auditorium,         :string
  end

  class ShowtimesResult < ActionWebService::Struct
    member :movies,             [Movie]
    member :theatres,           [Theatre]
    member :showtimes_light,    [ShowtimeLight]
  end
end
```

With these base datatypes out of the way, we can now turn our attention to defining the custom methods that we'll layer on top of get_showtimes. Example 16-14 shows two methods we might like to have in our API, but which we can instead base on the generic get_showtimes method. Each is tailored to the pages we need to display. The first, get_movie_showtimes_by_movie_and_location, returns the showtimes results grouped by theatre. The second, get_movie_showtimes_by_theatre, returns showtimes grouped by movie. The API declarations for these methods might look something like what is shown in Example 16-15. In fact, we can add these declarations as comments, so someone reading the declarations file will know these additional methods exist as well.

Example 16-14. API wrapper methods in the MoviesService client plugin

```
class MoviesServiceClient
  def get_movie_showtimes_by_movie_and_location(movie_id, zip_code)
    result = self.get_showtimes(zip_code, [], movie_id)
    result.group_by_theatre
  end

  def get_movie_showtimes_by_theatre(theatre_id)
    result = self.get_showtimes([], theatre_id, '')
    result.group_by_movie
  end
end
```

From the code in Examples 16-14 and 16-15 it should be clear that we have additional methods to define and logical models to declare. We need to define the methods **group_by_theatre** and **group_by_movie** in the client code. Each of these will return data in a new format, as defined by the **ShowtimesByTheatre** and **ShowtimesByMovie** logical model types. We still need to declare them, pending our decision of their structure.

Example 16-15. API declarations for our new methods

```
#  commented because these methods are implemented in the client
#  api_method(:get_showtimes_for_theatre,
#             :expects => [{:theatre_id => [:int]}],
#             :returns => [:showtimes => Logical::MovieShowtimes])

#  api_method(:get_showtimes_for_movie_and_location,
#             :expects => [{:zip_code => :string},
#                          {:movie_id => [:int]}],
#             :returns => [:showtimes => Logical::TheatreShowtimes])
```

Example 16-16 shows the two new classes we define to support our two client-side API methods. The first, **MovieShowtimes**, contains a **Movie** object and an array of **ShowTime** objects. Note that the **get_showtimes_for_theatre** method returns an array of these objects. In essence, an array of these objects simulates a hash structure (although without O(1) random access). We do this because hashes do not have direct support in ActionWebService. We might have more naturally returned a hash where the keys were **Movie** objects and the values were arrays of **ShowTime** objects, but this does the trick. This supports our method **get_showtimes_for_theatre**; each instance of the array contains a **Movie** object and all of its showtimes.

The **TheatreShowtimes** class builds on this object; **TheatreShowtimes** is appropriate when we expect more than one theatre in our results. In the same way as **MovieShowtimes**, an array of these simulates a hash with **Theatre** objects as the key and an array of **Movie Showtimes** as the value. Thus, an array of objects of this type returns showtimes grouped first by theatre, then by movie. Our API method, **get_showtimes_for_movie_and_loca tion**, would return one **TheatreShowtimes** object per theatre. Each would contain the appropriate **Theatre** object and a single **MovieShowtimes** object; because the movie has already been constrained, there is only one element in the array.

Example 16-16. Logical model class definitions for client-side use

```
module Logical
  # showtimes for a movie in a single theatre
  class MovieShowtimes < ActionWebService::Struct
    member :movie,             Movie
    member :showtimes,         [Showtime]
  end

  # showtimes in a theatre, grouped by movie
  class TheatreShowtimes < ActionWebService::Struct
    member :theatre,           Movie
    member :movie_showtimes,   [MovieShowtimes]
  end
end
```

Now that we have a complete understanding of what our API looks like, including the structure of return types, we can turn to implementation. We'll start at the bottom and work our way back up to the API layer.

Example 16-17 shows a new method, get_by_zip_theatre_movie, in the logical Showtime class. This method accepts a zip code (which can be an empty string), and arrays of movie and theatre *ids*, each of which can be empty. If the parameters are not empty, they are added to the conditions of the *find* SQL we will execute. Note that we take care to separate the text of our SQL from the values to be inserted as bind variables. The helper method bind_for_array helps us accomplish this.

After retrieving the records from the CurrentMovieShowtimes view-backed model class, we reformat the ActiveRecord data into the structure of our return type, a Showtimes Result object.

Example 16-17. Logical model method to return a list of current showtimes, by zip, theatre, or movie combination; all parameters can be empty

```
module Logical
  class Showtime < ActionWebService::Struct
    def self.get_by_zip_theatre_movie(zip_code, theatre_ids, movie_ids)
      conditions_sql = Array.new
      conditions_vars = Array.new
      if !zip_code.empty?
        conditions_sql << "miles_between_lat_long(
          (select latitude from zip_codes where zip = ?),
          (select longitude from zip_codes where zip = ?),
          latitude, longitude) < 15"
        conditions_vars.concat [zip_code]*2
      end
      if !theatre_ids.empty?
        conditions_sql << "theatre_id in (#{bind_for_array(theatre_ids)})"
        conditions_vars.concat theatre_ids
      end
      if !movie_ids.empty?
        conditions_sql << "movie_id in (#{bind_for_array(movie_ids)})"
        conditions_vars.concat movie_ids
      end
```

```
      conditions_sql << "current is true and sold_out is false"
      psts = Physical::MovieShowtimeWithCurrentAndSoldOut.find(:all,
        :select => [:id, :movie_id, :theatre_id, :latitude, :longtitude],
        :include => [:movie, :theatre],
        :conditions => [conditions_sql.join(" and "), *conditions_vars])

      m_hash = Hash.new
      t_hash = Hash.new
      st_array = Array.new
      for pst in psts do
        m_hash[pst.movie_id] ||= Movie.get(pst.movie_id)
        t_hash[pst.theatre_id] ||= Theatre.get(pst.theatre_id)
        st_array << ShowtimeLight.new(
          :movie_id => pst.movie_id,
          :theatre_id => pst.theatre_id,
          :start_time => pst.start_time,
          :auditorium => pst.room

        )
      end
      ShowtimesResult.new(
        :movies => m_hash.values,
        :theatres => t_hash.values,
        :showtimes_light => st_array
      )
    end

    def self.bind_for_array(array)
      (['?']*array.size).join(",")
    end

  end
end
```

In the service implementation class shown in Example 16-18, we define the `get_show times` method that is part of our external API. This method simply calls the method we defined in Example 16-17 within the `Showtime` class. Continuing with the idea of "skinny controllers, fat models," we keep the implementation details within the logical model class rather than the API implementation class, which is really nothing more than a controller.

Example 16-18. The implementation of get_showtimes

```
class MoviesService < ActionWebService::Base
  web_service_api MoviesApi

  def get_showtimes(zip_code, theatre_id, movie_id)
    Logical::Showtime.get_by_zip_theatre_movie(zip_code, theatre_id, movie_id)
  end
end
```

With this much code in place, now we are able to call the **get_showtimes** API method. Example 16-19 shows our integration test, written in the integration test framework application. For this test, we again assume the presence of some test data in our running service's database. Therefore, we simply call the method, then verify the structure of the result. A more rigorous test would first insert the data into the database to ensure we get back exactly what we put in.

Example 16-19. Integration test for the get_showtimes API method

```
require File.dirname(__FILE__) + '/../test_helper'
class MovieServiceGetShowtimesTestCase < Test::Unit::TestCase
  def test_get_showtimes
    result = MoviesServiceClient.get_showtimes('02139', [7,12], [17,20,64])
    assert result.class == Logical::ShowtimesResult
    assert result.movies.class == Array
    assert result.theatres.class == Array
    assert result.showtimes_light.class == Array
    assert result.movies.size > 0
    assert result.theatres.size > 0
    assert result.showtimes_light.size > 0
    for movie in result.movies do
      assert movie.class == Logical::Movie
    end
    for theatre in result.theatres do
      assert theatre.class == Logical::Theatre
    end
    for showtime in result.showtimes_light do
      assert showtime.class == Logical::ShowtimeLight
    end
  end
end
```

The test passes, as shown below. Note that the number of assertions will be different depending on the test data you have in your database. Also note that the test will fail until the service call actually returns data:

```
ChakBookPro: chak$ ruby test/integration/movies_svc_test_case.rb
Loaded suite test/integration/movies_svc_test_case
Started
.
Finished in 1.442291 seconds.

1 tests, 64 assertions, 0 failures, 0 errors
```

With this method working, we can now write our wrapper methods in the client plugin on top of it. Although **get_showtimes** is extremely generic, these wrapper methods are free to restrict the inputs—and do. While generic methods can be very powerful, they can also be confusing because the interface is often more complex than it needs to be for any given task. Our two methods, then, restrict the parameter list only to relevant data and return the output grouped in the way that makes the most sense for the inputs.

Because the procedure is the same but the code is long, we'll go through the process of creating and testing only one of our wrapper methods: get_movie_showtimes_by_thea tre. It's the fact that we can have other wrapper methods, and many more as well, that's the important takeaway. Example 16-20 shows the implementation of the wrapper method, within the MoviesServiceClient class.

The get_movie_showtimes_by_theatre method has one function and that is to restrict the parameter list to a single theatre *id*. Within the method, the parameter list is re-expanded and passed to get_movie_showtimes. The result is passed on to group_by_movie, where the bulk of our implementation takes place.

Recall that the purpose of this method is to retrieve movies for a single theatre, so we group showtimes within the scope of that theatre by movie. The structure of this method is analogous to that of the get_by_zip_theatre_movie method within the logical Showtime class. There, an array of ActiveRecord objects was transformed into a different logical model structure appropriate for the get_showtimes method. Here, we transform that result into one more suitable for our new wrapper API method.

Example 16-20. Client plugin wrappers for get_showtimes

```
class MoviesServiceClient
  def get_movie_showtimes_by_theatre(theatre_id)
    result = self.get_showtimes('', [theatre_id], [])
    group_by_movie(result)
  end

  protected

  # assumes only one theatre, if multiple, not
  # organized by theatre in any way
  def group_by_movie(showtimes_result)
    movies_hash = Hash.new
    theatres_hash = Hash.new
    showtimes_hash = Hash.new
    for movie in showtimes_result.movies do
      movies_hash[movie.id] = movie
    end
    for theatre in showtimes_result.theatres do
      theatres_hash[theatre.id] = theatre
    end
    result = Array.new
    for showtime in showtimes_result.showtimes_light do
      showtimes_hash[showtime.movie_id] ||= Array.new
      showtimes_hash[showtime.movie_id] << Logical::Showtime.new(
        :movie => movies_hash[showtime.movie_id],
        :theatre => theatres_hash[showtime.theatre_id],
        :start_time => showtime.start_time,
        :auditorium => showtime.auditorium
      )
    end
    showtimes_hash.collect{|movie_id, showtimes|
      Logical::MovieShowtimes.new(
```

```
        :movie => movies_hash[movie_id],
        :showtimes => showtimes
    )
  }
  end
end
```

You should be able to trace this code to see how we transform one structure to another. Figure 16-8 illustrates the resulting structure. It's important to note that even though we appear to be repeating theatre and movie information frequently within our resulting data structure, in fact, we are not. Rather than duplicating that data, we are duplicating references to single locations of our data. Over time, we may decide to move wrapper API methods from the client into the server. However, in doing so, we lose the ability to duplicate references instead of data. While the benefit of having the method defined on the server is that non-Rails clients can have access to the same logic through a single API method name, the trade-off is that the amount of data to be serialized, transferred, and deserialized increases for all client types.

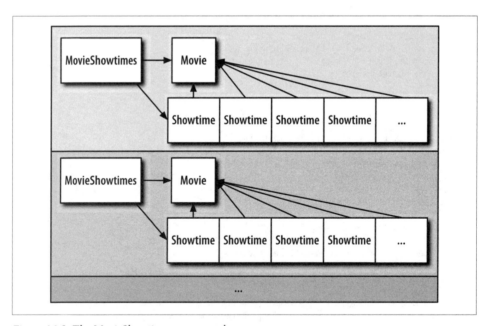

Figure 16-8. The MovieShowtimes array result structure

We can now write a test for our wrapper method, which we'll place in the integration test framework's test suite. Example 16-21 shows our unit test. For this test, we again assume the presence of some test data in our running service's database, and we only verify the structure of the result.

Example 16-21. Integration test for the get_movie_showtimes_by_theatre wrapper method

```
require File.dirname(__FILE__) + '/../test_helper'
class MovieServiceGetShowtimesByTheatreTestCase < Test::Unit::TestCase
  def test_get_showtimes
    result = MoviesServiceClient.get_movie_showtimes_by_theatre(7)
    assert result.class == Array, "Result is not an array"
    assert result.size > 0, "Result is empty"
    for by_movie in result
      assert by_movie.class == Logical::MovieShowtimes,
        "Array elements are not MovieShowtimes"
      assert by_movie.movie.class == Logical::Movie, "movie was not a Movie"
      RAILS_DEFAULT_LOGGER.debug("class is: #{by_movie.showtimes.class}")
      assert by_movie.showtimes.class == Array, "showtimes was not an array"
      assert by_movie.showtimes.size > 0, "showtimes array was empty"
      for showtime in by_movie.showtimes do
        assert showtime.class == Logical::Showtime, "Showtime was not a Showtime"
      end
    end
  end
end
```

The tests pass:

```
ChakBookPro:integration_test_framework chak$ ruby
test/integration/movies_service_get_showtimes_by_theatre_test_case.rb
Loaded suite test/integration/movies_service_get_showtimes_by_theatre_test_case
Started
.
Finished in 0.19624 seconds.

1 tests, 15 assertions, 0 failures, 0 errors
```

Putting It All Together

In this chapter, we created an orders service, in which products could be registered for purchase, and then subsequently purchased. We also connected a physical model in the movies service to our new service, so that new showtimes were automatically registered as purchasable products. We also expanded the API of our movies service API to support requests that would lead logically to the assembly of pages on a front-end website. Using our integration test framework, we tested all of these connections.

At this point, everything we need to write a front-end application that can consume multiple back-end services is in our hands. In fact, our integration test framework *is* just such an application.

## CHAPTER 17

REST Primer

REST, which stands for Representational State Transfer, is not a protocol. Born out of a chapter of the Ph.D. dissertation of Roy Fielding, one of the original architects of the Web, it is more of a description of how the HTTP protocol was meant to be used. REST has been given a lot of attention recently, especially in the Rails community, which has thrown its support behind REST with ActiveResource. Rails developers can be expected to, by and large, use ActiveResource, since it is there. But there are a number of issues that application developers should be aware of before jumping on the bandwagon.

In this chapter, I'll introduce "textbook" REST. We'll then contrast this style of REST with what most people mean when they say REST or RESTful. Then, we'll go over some of the issues you should be aware of when choosing to create REST interfaces. The first concern is with the way ActiveResource encourages you to create services based off of database tables; this problem is avoidable but becoming endemic. The next concern is with integration; because REST is a convention—and one no one agrees upon yet—integration with external parties can be a challenge compared with the relative ease of XML-RPC services.

REST Basics

To understand the problems REST faces, and the problems you may face if you adopt REST for your service architecture, first we must go back to the theory of REST and its original goals. Only then can we understand the challenges faced in creating REST services today and come up with the creative solutions to meet those challenges.

Resources and Verbs

Unlike XML-RPC, in which the basic unit is a procedure that acts on data maintained on the server, REST is about *resources*. In REST, a resource might be a web page with the universal resource locator (URL) like *http://foo.com/doc.html*. With the resource in place, the next aspect of REST is *verbs* that act upon the resources. The HTTP specification defines four verbs that can be performed on a URL. They are depicted in

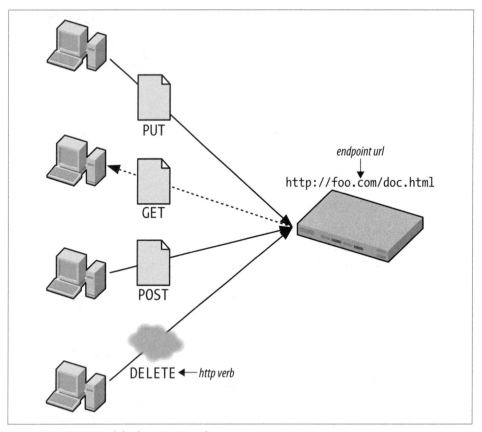

Figure 17-1. REST and the four HTTP verbs

Figure 17-1. The first is PUT, which allows the caller to store a web page at the location specified by the URL. The second is GET, which allows the web page, or resource, to be retrieved later. The third is POST, which is somewhat open-ended, but in general allows the resource to be updated in some way, perhaps with a new version. The fourth and final HTTP verb, DELETE, instructs the server to discard the web page.

In REST, the universe of resources is limitless. The universe of verbs, on the other hand, is fixed. The REST principles require you to think of your problems in terms of data elements, and how you might transition the state of each element one by one in order to accomplish some task. A by-product of the restrictive verb set is that actions must take place somewhere other than on the server. In general, the actions take place on the client. To increment a counter stored on a server, you first GET the counter value. Then you locally increment its value. Finally, you POST back the new value to the server at the counter's resource URL.

Why is this a good thing? In part, the verb set and its anticipated uses are a historical matter. When the Web was born, it was not about commerce, nor were there many complex procedural transactions. The Web was largely used for exchanging information between different government and academic bodies. When commerce applications began to appear, those applications weren't like the ones seen today, such as eBay, Orbitz, or even Google's advertising market. Rather, the commerce available in the early days of the Web was often nothing more than a web page, possibly with a few images, and a phone number to call to make an actual transaction with a human. The Web was a collection of content embodied in HTML documents.

Mosaic, the world's first web browser, adhered to the set of four HTTP verbs. When you browsed a web page, you could actually edit the text of the page directly in your browser. If you had the appropriate permissions, you could "save" the page, generating a POST, which stored the newly edited web page on the server. If you think of the Web as a participatory marketplace of ideas, as it was certainly in the eyes of its creators, this interface, plus some basic permissioning, was all that's needed. No complicated HTML forms were necessary for editing or uploading new content. Talk about a content management system!

Sadly, the "REST-ness" of browsers was soon lost as the Web became, for a long time, more of a spectator sport, where websites were "published" and browsers "watched." As a result, today's breed of browsers support only half of the original HTTP specification's set of verbs: POST and GET. By convention, we now use GET when no server-side state change is expected (like viewing information about a movie), and POST when new information is to be recorded somewhere (like when placing an order) or information is to change in some other way.

Hardware Is Part of the Application

Because there is nothing more to using REST than using the HTTP specification itself, hardware that understands HTTP can participate in the server architecture transparently. For example, a caching proxy that understands the HTTP "Expires" header can distribute a web page to clients for as long as that page is still considered fresh, reducing load on the back-end server. Figure 17-2 illustrates this behavior. A document must first be generated by the server and sent through the caching proxy, but then the same document can be sent directly from the caching proxy for each subsequent request.

It's REST's property of many endpoint URLs, one per resource, that facilitates caching via an intermediary piece of hardware because each URL represents only a single piece of data. Contrast that with an XML-RPC interface, where a single endpoint URL defines the entire service, and the methods and arguments—such as getMovie(5)—are passed along as parameters of a POST request. In the case of XML-RPC, you can't use a dumb piece of hardware like a caching proxy to speed up your application. On the other hand, do you really want to?

The "free" caching behavior of REST is great if you're serving up lots of static content but not so good if your data or its availability changes over time. The trade-off here is that the server has no way of expiring the document before the originally set expiry.

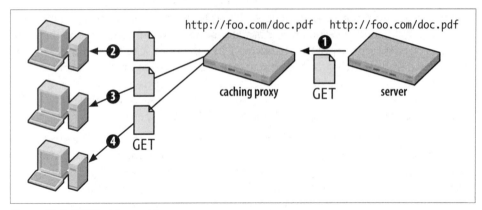

Figure 17-2. REST with a caching proxy

Even if the document becomes invalid, the caching proxy continues to serve it until the natural expiration time passes. In the traditional SOA world, a server-side cache would be shared among a number of application servers (just like Memcache) and the application can flush items from the cache whenever it makes sense to do so. This type of scheme is described in Chapter 19.

Mapping REST to SOA

With a basic understanding of the underpinnings of REST, we are now ready to discuss REST in the context of a service-oriented architecture. A good place to start is with a cautionary note from Roy Fielding himself, who wrote the following in his dissertation:

> The REST interface is designed to be efficient for large-grain hypermedia data transfer, optimizing for the common case of the Web, but resulting in an interface that is not optimal for other forms of architectural interaction.

REST is great for the types of large-grained content users are accustomed to seeing on the Web: HTML web pages, PDF documents, images, etc. In fact, you can't help but use REST when you request these documents; users of the Web do use REST every day, whenever they request web pages. What REST isn't great for is the context for which it has recently gotten so much attention, namely, mapping REST to database rows. Indeed, this is how ActiveResource, the Ruby on Rails implementation of REST, is being marketed: as an easy way to add a web-service interface atop ActiveRecord CRUD.

Mapping to CRUD

Although it is not generally desirable to do so, the four main HTTP verbs can be mapped to CRUD, as shown in Table 17-1. A create maps to an HTTP PUT, which translates to an SQL insert command. A read maps to an HTTP GET, which translates to an SQL select command. An update maps to an HTTP POST, which translates to an SQL update command. Finally, a delete maps to an HTTP DELETE, which translates to a SQL delete statement.

Table 17-1. Mapping CRUD to REST and SQL

CRUD	REST	SQL
Create	PUT	insert
Read	GET	select
Update	POST	update
Delete	DELETE	delete

It's tempting to directly map a REST interface atop each database table, moreso since Rails provides generators to automatically create code that does just that. What's missing from REST is the ability to modify more than one record at a time. Although sometimes you may be working with only a single row in a database, more often you need to update a number of rows. For example, when placing an order for movie tickets, you may need to insert a row for the order, plus individual rows for each ticket line item in the order. It is still possible to do accomplish this with CRUD-mapped REST. In order to do so, treat each row in each table as its own resource. The trade-off is performance. For an order of *n* tickets, you need to make *n* + 1 requests to your REST-based service for all the inserts. More caution from Fielding:

> The disadvantage is that [REST] may decrease network performance by increasing the repetitive data (per-interaction overhead) sent in a series of requests, since that data cannot be left on the server in a shared context. In addition, placing the application state on the client side reduces the server's control over consistent application behavior, since the application becomes dependent on the correct implementation of semantics across multiple client versions.

Worse, you have no transaction support. If an insert or update fails, there is no easy way to roll back the SQL statements that were already committed one by one in earlier REST actions. With pure REST, application logic that belongs in the back-end—where a relational database provides a great many benefits for data integrity—is suddenly moved to the client. A multistep business process that sensibly can be abstracted with a single method must be implemented step by step on the client. In these cases, a resource-based approach can become extremely fragile. Fielding talked about this, too:

> ...information needs to be moved from the location where it is stored to the location where it will be used by, in most cases, a human reader. This is unlike many other distributed processing paradigms, where it is possible, and usually more efficient, to move the "processing agent" (e.g., mobile code, stored procedure, search expression, etc.) to the data rather than move the data to the processor.

As with our XML-RPC services, we need to repeat the epiphany that ActiveRecord classes are database configuration files, and they generally do not map to the structure or size of objects we would want to work with within our application. Once we make this leap, then the criticisms just mentioned disappear. Placing an order in our

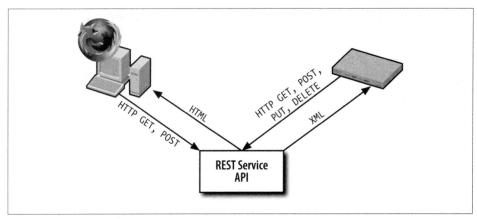

Figure 17-3. Common clients have differing levels of support for REST verbs

XML-RPC service required creating a number of records on the service side. But it only required a single XML-RPC request. This allowed all of the SQL insert statements to be wrapped in a transaction. The same would be true of a RESTful interface if the grain of the objects was large enough. In fact, it should be the same grain as the `Logical::Order` class we defined in Chapter 16.

Essentially, this reduces the differences between REST and XML-RPC greatly. The ActiveRecord models are the same. The logical models are the same. The difference is whether the object you're operating on and what operation you want to perform on that object are encoded in a single token—a method name such as `get_movie` or `place_order`, or split between the method identifier—the URL—and the HTTP verb. Viewed at this level, it becomes a question of syntax. Even the controllers (ActionController for RESTful services, and service models for XML-RPC services) could be essentially identical.

Different Clients, One Interface

The second benefit of REST's single URL per resource approach is that machine clients, as well as human clients via web browser, can access a REST service. Although there are JavaScript XML-RPC implementations, you need to write a JavaScript application that consumes the service before you can use it directly in your web browser. With REST, you can point your web browser directly at a resource URL to access it. This is facilitated by the `Accept` header. A machine client may specify that it accepts XML responses only, while a browser client would specify it accepts XHTML.

Unfortunately, REST contends with two problems here. The first is that different clients have varying levels of support for REST (Figure 17-3). As already noted, browsers support only `POST` and `GET`. So a REST service intended to serve different types of clients must "dumb it down" for the lowest common denominator, the browser. This is ActiveRecord's approach.

Second, there is no single convention for how clients specify a return type, either. While the `Accept` header is how return formats should be specified, ActiveRecord has taken a different tack. In Rails, you specify which return type you want by appending an extension on the URL. A browser client requests a resource with *.html* appended, while a machine client appends *.xml*.

The REST ideal is to have a single, uniform interface for browser and machine clients, but it pays to be pragmatic as the designer of a service-oriented architecture or public-facing web service. There is not really a benefit to tightly coupling the HTML web pages associated with a user interface and its human-oriented workflow with an API intended for consumption by programmers utilizing your service. One interface is for manipulating the resources that underlie your application; the other is for creating a user *experience*.

Although in your first iteration of your website and service design, you may be able to construct an API that satisfies both sets of customers—and hopefully without much sacrifice to either—in your second iteration, you may not be so lucky. When your company's product team comes up with a completely new perspective on how information should be delivered to visitors to your site, what do you do with the machine side of the API that thousands of people have come to depend on? Do you force those clients, whose applications were operating perfectly well based on the old machine API, and independent of your user interface, to conform to a new API simply because your user interface has changed? Or do you start supporting what essentially amounts to two API sets anyway, one for humans and their browsers and one for machine clients?

Rather than whittle at an API until it works for both humans and machines, it is often sensible to write for each separately from the beginning. When you design this way, you don't have to worry about breaking backward compatibility for your machine clients when you change your user interface. Also, if you forego pursuing the purist ideal of one interface for multiple client types, you can be truer to the original ideas of REST where they are attainable. You can design a machine API that uses all four HTTP verbs where they are appropriate, and your browser-based "API"—a.k.a. website—can evolve as necessary to suit your ever-changing application and user needs. Remember that when you write an HTTP interface, you *are* writing a REST service, even if that service is not well-suited for machine clients.

One notable exception is a JavaScript client. JavaScript clients operate within your web browser, and they can make Ajax requests back to your web service. The standard way that Rails interfaces with Ajax requests is with *.rjs* templates that render chunks of HTML to be placed in an existing page—either prepended to, appended to, or replacing an existing element. Even though this seems RESTful because small pieces of data are being requested rather than entire web pages, it really is not. The application server is still very tightly coupled with the HTML user experience and is unlikely to be useful as a generic interface for other machine clients.

HTTP+POX

In much of this chapter, I've talked about the numerous challenges REST faces in gaining adoption in the enterprise world for service-oriented architecture applications. These challenges begin with the strictness of the four verbs and the requirement that resources be transferred to the client for piecemeal processing. Further challenges ensue with purist REST due to the lack of support for the four-verb set in browsers. Finally, the lack of established convention for resource URLs and how one specifies content types (ActiveRecord does not comply) can make REST appear somewhat unpalatable.

However, outside of the Rails world, a variation on strict REST is gaining traction. This variation doesn't discount the real need to deal with process-oriented applications simply because they don't map to GET, POST, PUT, and DELETE. In fact, with this variation, you can accomplish anything you could with XML-RPC, but you can forego the added layer of indirection inherent in XML-RPC layered over HTTP. This variation is known as REST+POX, where POX stands for plain old XML.

In HTTP+POX, the REST convention I've spoken about throughout this chapter is used where a resource-based approach makes sense. Notably, everything possible with ActiveResource is in this category. But for other problems, where a process-oriented approach is required—whether to ensure the server can wrap a procedure within a database transaction or to accomplish a task without first moving all of the data to the client for processing—the POX side of the convention takes control.

What is POX in this context? It is simply a method, accessible via a URL, which takes parameters, and returns a result in XML format. It's like the page defined in the action parameter of a web form, but in this context, the parameters passed in can be complete data structures encoded in XML. In short, it is the same sort of server-side actions we've been developing for years, with the addition of complex data as parameters. The "plain old XML" part of HTTP+POX is a way of bringing the procedural actions hidden behind an endpoint URI in XML-RPC back down to the lower-level HTTP layer.

Usually, when people say RESTful, this is what they mean.

Defining a Service Contract

Although Fielding described REST many years ago, REST is still in its infancy as a practical means for building web services. How to best implement a RESTful service is something that REST proponents still do not agree on.

The popularity of SOAP and XML-RPC were propelled by a rich toolset in a variety of development environments; the tools made it easy to create and consume web services. ActionWebService is a great example; it makes child's play of developing service APIs that can be shared as a bridge between applications.

Many see REST as a reaction to SOAP. But there has been a tendency to throw away the baby with the bathwater. In this case, the bathwater is the protocol translation layer that sits atop HTTP. That's fine, as it doesn't provide a large benefit to the end user, but consumes resources to marshal and unmarshal data. The baby is a rich set of tools for creating and consuming RESTful services.

Tools all center around the contract that you, as a provider of a service, are expected to live up to. With SOAP, this contract is the WSDL file, which describes what methods are available in the web service, what the parameters to those methods are, and what the return values are.

The contract can be a great thing. It can be used to generate documentation. It can be read by a human to see what a service is all about. It can be used to generate complete client code. It can also be used to generate a skeleton of a service implementation.

The problem with a *contract* is that, like its legal equivalent, it implies some degree of commitment from the provider. Once you've published your service contract, you can't change it willy-nilly. That's good for consumers of the service but can seem restrictive to the service provider. On the other hand, one of the goals of publishing a service is to have people use it, so making it easy for clients to use your service by guaranteeing the APIs won't change underneath them is in your own best interest, too.

To encourage static APIs, it is a good practice to develop the contract first, then figure out how you are going to implement it. For SOAP, that means handcoding the WSDL file. The handwritten file would then be used as input to a program that would generate stub service code. These stubs contain declarations for each method of the API into which you insert your own code.

This process makes it a challenge to change the API because you can't easily regenerate your stubs once you've already filled them in. This discourages frequent API changes; only a change that is absolutely essential—such as for a critical bug fix—would warrant the effort of hand-editing generated code. For what otherwise amounts to enhancements and new functionality, the WSDL-first process encourages adding a whole new API version with a separate WSDL and a separate set of generated methods, leaving the old version in place, with continued support for existing clients.

But writing WSDL by hand is a terrible chore. It can seem like yet another language to master. You already know how to declare methods in the language you are using. Why should you need to declare them yet again in an XML file? Indeed, if the interpreter or compiler of your application can understand your declarations, can't those declarations also be translated automatically into a WSDL XML file for other machines to process?

The answer is, of course, yes. This is how most of the tools for working with WSDL work these days, including ActionWebService.* In fact, in ActionWebService, the WSDL "file" itself is completely ephemeral; it never is written to disk but instead is served up fresh with each request for it, based on the current definitions of methods. While this is great for development iterations, it's not so great once you are trying to lock down and stick to a published API.

But whether you prefer WSDL first or last, the point is that there are a variety of tools available to help you get your SOAP or XML-RPC service out the door. So what about REST? What is the equivalent?

Here we find another problem in the REST community. There are some—mostly those who tend toward the strict REST, not RESTful, paradigm—who believe there is no need for SOAP-like tools for communicating to clients how a service works. Since strict REST is about applying four HTTP verbs on resources, and resources contain links to other resources, you need only a URL or two defining lists of resources to discover the entire service.

Strictly speaking, this argument is correct, but it's overly restrictive. Hopefully, you've already been convinced that it's not *always* appropriate to deal in terms of resources and that the occasional verb-based URL is OK. If you are in this group, then suddenly you need a way to express to others what verbs are available, what the parameters you need to pass to those verbs are, and what the resulting return values will be. Suddenly you need something very much like a WSDL file. Even many in the RESTful—i.e., "it's not SOAP"—camp cringe at WSDL-like solutions. Therefore a standard way to describe RESTful web services has not yet been adopted, and there are also no widely adopted tools.

There have been a number of efforts toward tool standardization, though, and for REST to really become an enterprise option, as SOAP and XML-RPC are today, some kind of description language and toolset will certainly have to be adopted soon.

REST Clients in Ruby

At the moment, ActiveResource is the de facto REST client and server in Rails—so much so that it has pushed ActionWebService completely out of the core Rails distribution. This is unfortunate because ActiveResource's style, which differs in some important ways from Fielding's REST, is very far from being de facto in the REST world, much less the SOA or web-services worlds. Yet the choice by the maintainers of Rails to displace alternatives sends a message to new developers that they should use

---

* Actually, the WSDL is generated from the API declaration files we placed in the client plugin, not from the actual controller files that implemented the methods. This is because WSDL has type declarations for strongly typed languages such as Java. But, in addition to the WSDL file itself, stub controller files could easily be generated from the API declarations.

ActiveResource as their first—and apparently only—stop for implementing a remote service.

Of course, there are benefits to using ActiveResource, too. Like many other aspects of Rails, ActiveResource is a snap to set up and get running with quickly. Because it relies so heavily on convention, it is trivial to extrude an ActiveRecord model into an Active-Resource one with its own network API. Similarly, there is next to no configuration to be done on the client side, either.

ActiveResource can feel much like the original Rails screencast where David Heinemeier Hansson creates a blogging website in 10 minutes. The screencast was an inspiration to a number of developers sick of clunky development environments, including myself. On the other hand, writing a website using scaffolding is, in almost every way, a bad idea. By design, scaffolding is inflexible; although it's quick, it's not very pretty. But it is great as marketing material.

Indeed, because ActiveResource relies so heavily on convention, it does not automatically create a description of the service for clients, like ActionWebService does with WSDL. Rails clients know how to use the API for free, and for screencasts that is enough. But when you're writing web services and back-end SOA services, you can't depend on convention if your clients are not using Rails. There are description languages that can handle REST services—WADL appears to be the best contender for a standard—but Rails does not yet generate WADL files automatically.

When you're not consuming ActiveResource services, you can consume REST services just as easily in Rails if that service does provide a WADL file. Sam Ruby and Leonard Richardson have written a Ruby client that parses WADL files and creates a client library, allowing you to create Ruby interfaces to use a custom-written library or to compose and parse results by hand. Their client, *wadl.rb*, can be obtained at *http://www.crummy.com/software/wadl.rb/*.

The Way the Web Was Meant to Be Used

REST proponents argue that XML-RPC is an "unnatural" way to use HTTP because XML-RPC treats HTTP only as a transport protocol. All requests are POST transactions, and the remainder of the HTTP protocol goes unused. XML-RPC layers its own logic atop HTTP, delivering everything needed to process the request at the endpoint in the XML-PRC payload itself. On the other hand, Fielding himself provides us with all the arguments we need to dissuade ourselves from using REST for an extremely fine-grained service-oriented architecture. Inasmuch as this chapter may appear to throw FUD (fear, uncertainty, and doubt) in the direction of REST, so too do REST proponents direct FUD at XML-RPC.

As unnatural as it may seem to layer atop HTTP, in reality, XML-RPC has been serving enterprise architects well for quite some time. If XML-RPC wasn't what the architects of HTTP had in mind, certainly they may be pleased by how far it has come, driven in large part by the flexibility of HTTP itself, which performs extraordinarily well as a transport protocol for any type of packaged data. Indeed, Fielding will no doubt be pleased if some version of REST is one day heralded as the de facto mechanism for implementing SOA, even though that was not *his* original intent, either.

In the end, the decision is yours to make. If your company has something to gain from being Web 2.0 buzzword-compliant, then choosing REST may be sensible just for the press. If your goal is achieving a service architecture behind the firewall, where no external inspection is taking place, then you're likely to get more mileage, with less hassle, out of XML-RPC. In the following chapters, we'll see how to build both types of services. We'll build an XML-RPC back-end service architecture for our movies application and a HTTP+POX interface for the public-facing Internet.

For reference, Table 17-2 provides a list of the main remote service protocols and conventions, and the various considerations discussed in this and the previous chapter. In the next chapter, we'll start building our first Rails service using XML-RPC.

Table 17-2. Comparison of REST, XML-RPC, and SOAP

	Pure REST	HTTP+POX	XML-RPC	SOAP
API Discovery	WADL, ActiveResource	WADL	WSDL	WSDL
Endpoint URLs	Many	Many	1	1
Messaging Overhead	Lowest	Low	Low	High
Rails support	Partial	Full, with *wadl.rb*	Yes	Partial
Representations	Many	Many	XML	XML
Client types	Web browser, applications	Web browser, applications	Apps	Apps
Supports process-oriented methods	No	Yes	Yes	Yes

## CHAPTER 18

A RESTful Web Service

In this chapter, we'll build a RESTful web service on top of the `MoviesService` and `OrdersService` applications. Much like our user-facing public website, this application glues together the functionality provided by each service into one unified whole. We broke our monolithic application up into a service-oriented architecture (SOA) to achieve a number of benefits—scalability, reusability, and understandability of any given piece—but the collection of services are not on their own useful. They need to be composed in a meaningful way. In the case of our web service, we'd be providing a complete, machine-friendly interface for third-party affiliates who might be selling movie tickets on our behalf.

Scoping the Problem

In defining our problem, we are also implicitly defining what problem *isn't*. Specifically, we are not trying to provide a single interface that can be used by a machine as well as humans (other than for debugging purposes); our clients are defined to be other computer programs. Using the APIs we designed in Chapters 15 and 16 (or more likely, a more complete set), we can assume that a coherent website that composes both of our services and consumes much if not all of our API could and would be built. This concern —satisfying the need for an accessible machine-friendly API—is handled as a separate application.

While this may seem counter to what many are led to believe is the great benefit of RESTful applications—that the same interface can be used by both human and machine clients—the separation is actually preferable for many reasons. The first reason has been noted previously: browsers support a reduced set of HTTP verbs, `GET` and `POST`, but not `PUT` and `DELETE`. Freeing ourselves of the constraint that the same URLs must be able to service clients of varying degrees of support for HTTP verbs means your RESTful application can actually be more RESTful.

The next reason is trust. In our SOA, within the firewall, applications were within the "trusted zone." Having access to the API implied being trusted to use the service APIs without restriction. On one end, our web service is a trusted client of our back-end

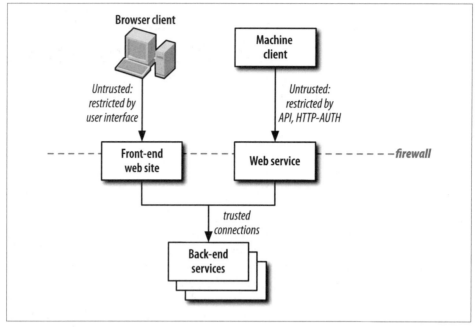

Figure 18-1. Machine and browser clients have different interfaces

services and is able to access the APIs at will. However, on the public-facing side, you may not want to allow full, open access to the world at large. You may want to limit access to a select group of third parties with whom you have business arrangements, or you may want to require that users first sign up for an account that gives them a unique, albeit free, authentication key. Doing so will allow you to monitor for abuse and lock out problematic clients one by one. Figure 18-1 shows a configuration that allows machine and browser clients to have completely separate interfaces.

But doesn't the public HTML-based website give free and open access to anyone? Would authentication restrictions be burdensome and encourage users to jettison the REST API in favor of parsing the information they need out of the HTML pages that are likely to be just a subdomain away? While this is a valid concern, most "free" websites have placed CAPTCHA (Completely Automated Public Turing Test to Tell Computers and Humans Apart), or other schemes to validate users, to ward off automated crawling or spammers (Figure 18-2).

On a site with CAPTCHA, or one that may one day need some kind of spam-proofing, sharing the same URLs and back-end controllers for human and machine clients can be quite a challenge. It's almost a nonsense exercise to devise a mechanism to disallow machine clients in the same infrastructure that tries to make machine access easy. Because the needs are different, and probably the logic, too, it makes sense to keep these as separate sites rather than repeat cumbersome conditional logic based on which representation is requested—HTML or XML—throughout an application.

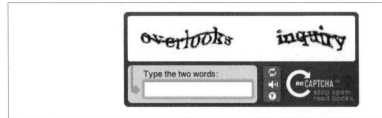

Figure 18-2. A CAPTCHA test designed to distinguish human clients from machines

Tools

In this chapter, we'll look at a RESTful web-service in two ways. First, we'll write a client and server using only basic tools for manipulating XML and using HTTP, ROXML, and Net::HTTP, respectively. Then we'll create a description of our service with Web Application Description Language (WADL)—the description language likely to become the standard for describing RESTful services—and generate a client for our service automatically using that file.

ROXML

ROXML (the Ruby Object to XML Mapping Library) does exactly what its name suggests. Given a class that has been annotated with ROXML, instances of the class can be marshaled and unmarshaled to and from XML.

To get started with ROXML, first install the gem:

```
sudo gem install roxml
```

Then, load the library in *config/environment.rb*.

```
require 'roxml'
```

In a class, include the ROXML mixin, as shown in Example 18-1. After doing so, three new class methods are available to annotate the class: xml_attribute, xml_text, and xml_object.

Example 18-1. A Movie class with ROXML annotation

```
class Movie
  include ROXML

  xml_attribute :id
  xml_text :name
  xml_text :rating
  xml_text :rating_description
  xml_text :length_minutes
end
```

Example 18-2 shows the ROXML class being manipulated. Each attribute behaves identically as if it had been defined with attr_accessor. In fact, the three xml_ annotation methods do set up instance variable accessors that manipulate instances variables, e.g., @rating.

Example 18-2. Working with the ROXML-annotated class from Example 18-1

```
m = Movie.new
m.id = 1
m.name = Casablanca
m.rating = 'PG-13'
m.rating_description = 'Parents strongly cautioned'
m.length_minutes = 120
puts m.to_xml
```

At the end of Example 18-2, the unmarshaled version is printed using to_xml. The output is shown in Example 18-3. Notice how **attribute** variables are displayed, embedded within the opening object tag, versus how **text** variables are displayed.

Example 18-3. XML output from Example 18-2

```
<movie id="1">
  <name>Casablanca</name>
  <rating>PG-13</rating>
  <rating_description>Parents strongly cautioned</rating_description>
  <length_minutes>120</length_minutes>
</movie>
```

You can also embed arrays of objects in another object with the xml_object declarator. Assuming we have created ROXML classes for **Theatre** and **ShowtimeLight**—like our ActionWebService struct classes from Chapter 16—Example 18-4 is then the corollary to the **ShowtimesResult** class of our XML-RPC API. The arrays can be accessed like regular attributes, e.g. **showtime_result.movies**, and manipulated like regular arrays with the chevron (<<) operator.

Example 18-4. A ROXML-annotated class with embedded object arrays

```
class ShowtimesResult
  include ROXML

  xml_object :movies, Movie, ROXML::TAG_ARRAY, "movies"
  xml_object :theatres, Theatre, ROXML::TAG_ARRAY, "theatre"
  xml_object :showtimes, ShowtimeLight, ROXML::TAG_ARRAY, "showtimes"
end
```

As an example, the code in Example 18-5 would produce the result in Example 18-6. Note that no theatres or showtimes were added, but sections for each are still present to denote empty arrays.

Example 18-5. Embedding objects within other objects

```
m1 = Movie.new
m1.id = 1
m1.name = 'Casablanca'
m1.length_minutes = 120
```

```
m1.rating = 'PG-13'
m1.rating_description = 'Parents strongly cautioned'

m2 = Movie.new
m2.id = 2
m2.name = 'Maltese Falcon'
m2.length_minutes = 120
m2.rating = 'PG-13'
m2.rating_description = 'Parents strongly cautioned'

sr = ShowtimesResult.new
sr.movies << m1
sr.movies << m2

puts sr.to_xml
```

Example 18-6. Resulting XML from Example 18-5

```
<showtimesresult>
  <movies>
    <movie id="1">
      <name>Casablanca</name>
      <rating>PG-13</rating>
      <rating_description>Parents strongly cautioned</rating_description>
      <length_minutes>120</length_minutes>
    </movie>
    <movie id="2">
      <name>Maltese Falcon</name>
      <rating>PG-13</rating>
      <rating_description>Parents strongly cautioned</rating_description>
      <length_minutes>120</length_minutes>
    </movie>
  </movies>
  <theatre/>
  <showtimes/>
</showtimesresult>
```

To marshal XML back into a Ruby object, we use the parse class method:

```
MovieShowtime.parse(xml_text)
```

Complete ROXML documentation is available at *http://roxml.rubyforge.org*.

Net::HTTP

With ROXML, we have a way to move data between Ruby objects and XML representations. Now we need a mechanism to transfer those XML representations from one application to another. For XML-RPC or SOAP, this was taken care of for us under the covers by ActionWebService. If we were using ActiveResource, we also wouldn't see the plumbing of how XML is passed back and forth, but we wouldn't be able to create as flexible a web service as we'd like. Therefore, we'll have to create and parse the HTTP messages ourselves for now. We'll do this using the built in Ruby library Net::HTTP.

The Net::HTTP library has methods for get, post, put, and delete, as well as additional convenience methods for GET and POST requests, since they are so common. We'll see parts of this library in action in the rest of this chapter. Complete documentation for the Net::HTTP library is available at *http://www.ruby-doc.org/stdlib/libdoc/net/http/rdoc/index.html*.

MoviesWebService

In our web service we will create an interface that is very similar to the back-end service interface we created in previous chapters. In part, this is to show that mechanisms for passing messages back and forth are largely interchangeable, and also to show that a RESTful interface does not need to represent a total paradigm shift if you don't want it to.

In fact, if we wanted to provide a RESTful interface in addition to our XML-RPC interface in our back-end service, we could do so using the same ActionWebService::Struct classes. Example 18-7 shows our Movie class from the XML-RPC service, now marked up with ROXML. Using the techniques in the rest of this chapter, we could have provided an identical interface as our XML-RPC API, using RESTful techniques. In fact, it's even possible that the RESTful interface could be generated from the same style of API definition as the XML-RPC API files. Of course, this is not currently supported, but it is a possible future direction and would certainly ease transition to REST, should your organization wish to do so.

Example 18-7. An ActionWebService class annotated with ROXML

```
module Logical
  class Movie < ActionWebService::Struct
    include ROXML

    xml_attribute :id
    xml_text :name
    xml_text :rating_id
    xml_text :rating_description
    xml_text :length_minutes

    member :id,                  :integer
    member :name,                :string
    member :length_minutes,      :integer
    member :rating_id,           :string
    member :rating_description,  :string
  end
end
```

Resources Server Implementation

In Example 18-1, we created a new class to serve as an XML proxy. Our web service is also a sort of proxy for our back-end service. In this section, I will just show how to return the data that our XML-RPC service returned, but in a RESTful way.

However, as we have noted, we are not intending this web service to be consumed by humans sitting in front of browsers. In fact, for resources—such as movies, theatres, and showtimes—we could actually have a much truer to REST interface, utilizing all four HTTP verbs where we need them.

Because ActiveResource takes the other approach—that a web service can be layered atop the web pages and interface designed for a user—it limits itself to the GET and POST HTTP verbs. Therefore, for our purposes, the routing available in Rails is not complete. In addition to routing based on the URL itself, we also would like to route based on the HTTP verb.

Examples 18-8 and 18-9 let us accomplish this. First, in Example 18-8, an abstract controller is created, which inherits from ApplicationController. This controller, AbstractResourceController, "fixes" Rails for properly dealing with all four HTTP verbs applied to a single resource URL.

Example 18-8. An extension to Rails' routing to take the HTTP verb into account

```
class AbstractResourceController < ApplicationController
  protect_from_forgery :only => []

  def http_method_dispatch
    send request.env['REQUEST_METHOD'].downcase
  end

  [:get, :post, :put, :delete].each do |http_method|
    define_method(http_method) {
      # redefine in child classes
      render :text => "Forbidden", :status => "405 Not Allowed"
    end
  end
end
```

First, we disable Rails 2.0's forgery protection. This feature requires that any non-GET request contain an authentication token, which would have been provided in some form the user retrieved before making their non-GET request. While this is great for preventing browser-based cross-site attacks, in this case forgery would also mean a machine trying to access your pages without first requesting a web page intended for humans. But isn't this the entire purpose of a web service? Therefore, the first thing we do is shut this feature off completely for our RESTful resource controllers.

The next method, http_method_dispatch, provides the magic. When a request for a resource is made, we'll send that request in to this method. The Rails built-in routing does not take care of distinguishing between GET, POST, PUT, or DELETE requests, so we'll do that here. We extract the HTTP method from the request object's env hash, and downcase it, so that GET becomes get and DELETE becomes delete. Then, using the send method, we call this method within the controller. In effect, we have reserved the method names get, put, delete, and post for each resource controllers. Note, of course, that this assumes that each controller descending from AbstractResourceController is responsible for one and only one resource.

It's now up to controllers inheriting from this abstract controller to implement those methods. For those that don't implement the complete set, we provide a default method, which returns a 405 "Method Not Allowed" when the HTTP method is called on the given resource. Four such methods are created in the loop at the bottom of our abstract controller, one for each of the HTTP methods.

Next we need to add routes that will pass control to http_method_dispatch to complete the cycle. The first two routes in Example 18-9 do what we need. Let's look at the first route. In this case, the :controller symbol names the resource, e.g., *movies*. The :id symbol names the *id* of the resource, e.g., *movies/3*. We then pass all requests to *movies/3* to the http_method_dispatch method of the MoviesController class, which should be a subclass of AbstractResourcesController. That method then further routes the request to the actions named get, put, post, or delete, depending on the HTTP method of the request.

The second route is the same, but it allows a format specifier to be passed in the URL. Normally, in a RESTful interface, the format in which the client wants to receive the response is specified via the Accept HTTP header. However, when testing from a browser, which is how many people test their REST interfaces, you often can't easily change the header your browser passes. Therefore, Rails will interpret standard extensions that fall on the :format symbol in the same way as mime types passed via the Accept header.

Example 18-9. Routes to support our HTTP verb dispatch

```
map.connect ':controller/:id', :action => 'http_method_dispatch'
map.connect ':controller/:id.:format', :action => 'http_method_dispatch'
map.connect ':controller/:id/:action'
map.connect ':controller/:id.:format/:action'
```

The next two routes in Example 18-9 are also an identical pair, one accounting for a format specifier on the URL. These routes, rather than pass control to http_method_dispatch, follow the lead of the URL. For example, use *movies/3/edit* to retrieve a form to edit the movie.

Example 18-10 shows our MoviesController class, which inherits from AbstractResourcesController. Because we can only expose methods that are exposed by our back-end service, we define just one method, get. Our method requests from the back-end service the movie passed in via the :id parameter. If no movie is returned from the back-end, a 404 is returned. Otherwise, if the client can accept XML (as specified either via the Accept header or by a passed in extension), we return an XML representation of the movie, as defined by our ROXML Movie class.

Example 18-10. A subclass of the AbstractResourcesController for Movies

```
class MoviesController < AbstractResourceController
  def get
    m = MoviesServiceClient.get_movie(params[:id])
    if !m
      render :file => "#{RAILS_ROOT}/public/404.html", :status => "404 Not Found"
      return
    end
    respond_to do |format|
      format.xml {
        m_xml = Movie.new
        m_xml.id = m.id
        m_xml.name = m.name
        m_xml.rating = m.rating_id
        m_xml.rating_description = m.rating_description
        m_xml.length_minutes = m.length_minutes
        render :xml => m_xml.to_xml
      }
    end
  end
end
```

Example 18-11 shows a series of requests for the movie with an *id* of 3. The first request is a GET request. The result has status 200 OK, and the XML describing this movie follows. The next request is for the HTML version of the file, using the extension *.html* to suggest the return type. Because we haven't defined format.html block in our get method, the response is 406 Not Acceptable. The next example is the same, but the representation is requested by passing text/html via the Accept header explicitly. In the final example, the HTTP DELETE method is called on our resource URL. Because we haven't defined this method in our controller, the default from the AbstractResourceController is called, which returns a 405.

Example 18-11. How our AbstractResourceController subclass handles a variety of requests for differing HTTP methods

```
chak$ curl -D - -X GET http://localhost/movies/3
HTTP/1.1 200 OK

<movie id='3'><name>Casablanca</name><rating>PG-13<
/rating><rating_description>Parents strongly
cautioned</rating_description><length_minutes>120</length_minutes></movie>

chak$ curl -D - -X GET http://localhost/movies/3.html
HTTP/1.1 406 Not Acceptable

chak$ curl -D - -X GET -H "Accept: text/html" http://localhost/movies/3
HTTP/1.1 406 Not Acceptable

chak$ curl -D - -X DELETE http://localhost/movies/3
HTTP/1.1 405 Method Not Allowed
```

Actions Server Implementation

Rather than repeat the above for theatres and showtimes, we'll leave those steps as an exercise. Instead, we'll move on creating the action for placing an order. However, in this case, we'll take a RESTful approach rather than a strictly REST approach. Of course, orders can easily be modeled as resources. It would be hard to argue against an API in which you post an order, and are returned that same order for future modification could make sense.

However, to stay flexible, let's assume that our orders, once placed, are not so easily modifiable. Instead of returning an object representing the order, we'll instead return an object representing an order confirmation, as shown in Example 18-12. This corresponds to the `OrderPlaced` ActionWebService class from Chapter 16. This is not strictly REST because we will post an order—essentially no differently than a plain old HTTP form posting to a URL—but we will return as XML a confirmation object. However, this does fit our definition of RESTful.

Example 18-12. A class ROXML class to describe an order confirmation

```
class Confirmation
  include ROXML

  xml_text :confirmation_code
  xml_text :price
end
```

Example 18-13 shows our action for creating a new order. First, we ensure that the request is a `POST`, and we disallow all other HTTP methods. Then, much as we did in our integration test for the order service, we build up the parameters needed for the `OrdersService place_order` method. We call this method, which returns a `Logical::OrderPlaced` object. We convert this into a `Confirmation` object, described in Example 18-12, which can be serialized to XML. We check that the caller is requesting XML, and if so, we marshal the confirmation object and return it; otherwise, a 405 error will be returned.

Example 18-13. A RESTful action for placing an order

```
class OrdersController < ActionController::Base
  def create
    if request.env['REQUEST_METHOD'] != 'POST'
      return render :text => "Method not allowed",
                    :status => "405 Method Not Allowed"
    end
    li = Logical::LineItem.new(
      :product_id => params[:showtime_product_id],
      :quantity => params[:num_tickets]
    )
    ad = Logical::Address.new(
      :line_1 => params[:billing_line_1],
      :line_2 => params[:billing_line_2],
      :city => params[:billing_city],
```

```
      :state => params[:billing_state],
      :zip_code => params[:billing_zip]
    )
    cc = Logical::CreditCard.new(
      :card_number => params[:credit_card_number],
      :expiration_month => params[:credit_card_exp_month],
      :expiration_year => params[:credit_card_exp_year],
      :type => params[:credit_card_type]
    )
    payment = Logical::Payment.new(
      :address => ad,
      :type => Logical::Payment::CREDIT_CARD,
      :credit_card => cc
    )
    result = OrdersServiceClient.place_order(
      [li], payment
    )

    respond_to do |format|
      format.xml {
        conf = Confirmation.new
        conf.confirmation_code = result.confirmation
        conf.price = result.price
        render :xml => conf.to_xml
      }
    end
  end
end
```

To make this action work at the URL *orders/create*, we add the following to *routes.rb*:

```
map.connect 'orders/:action', :controller => 'orders'
```

A Client Implementation

We now have a set of server-side methods that can be called: one for retrieving movie information and another for placing an order with the orders service. It's now time to move on to the client implementation. Because RESTful services are still relatively new, there isn't one set way to consume them. Although there are clients such as ActiveResource, because it makes many assumptions about the service itself, so often people still write custom clients for non-Rails REST services that they wish to consume.

In this chapter, we'll look at two different ways to consume a REST service. The first method is highly manual. We'll actually build URLs and make HTTP requests, and parse the resulting XML. Then we'll take a different tack. We'll create a very simple WADL file describing the GET method for our Movie resource and automatically generate a client for our service with the wadl.rb library. For both methods, we'll add the code to our integration test application.

For the first method, we create an initializer, shown in Example 18-14, to set up configuration constants that could be useful in our implementation. Here, we just set up the base URL of the web service. We could also use this class to set up constants for a connection timeout, authentication information, or anything else we might need later.

Example 18-14. Basic initializer for a RESTful web service

```
class MoviesWebServiceClient
  HOST = 'http://localhost'
end
```

Example 18-15 shows our manual tests of the RESTful order placement method. First, we create a `setup` method, which adds a product in the `Orders` service. This product represents a movie showtime. In the actual test method, we'll place an order for this showtime.

In the `test_order_post` method, we use the `HOST` constant set up in the initializer to construct the URL of our order method. This URL is passed to `URI.parse`, which will create a URI object from the URL, suitable for passing to Net::HTTP methods. We then create a hash containing all of the arguments expected by the order creation web service method. Then we call `Net::HTTP.post_form`, passing in the URI object and the parameters hash. This method takes care of the mechanics of building the HTTP post and returns an `Net::HTTPResponse` object and the data returned by the post itself. We use the XmlSimple library to parse the returned XML. Given an XML data structure contained in a string, XmlSimple will convert that data structure into a Ruby hash object, which can then be manipulated directly with Ruby hash syntax. Example 18-16 shows what the returned XML from our web service call looks like after being parsed by XmlSimple. Once we have our resulting hash, we assert that the two expected fields are present in the XML data.

Example 18-15. An integration test to test placing an order through our web service

```
require File.dirname(__FILE__) + '/../test_helper'
class OrdersServiceTestCase < Test::Unit::TestCase
  def setup
    @new_id = OrdersServiceClient.add_product(
      "Casablanca 10:00pm",
      50,
      1000)
    assert @new_id
  end

  def test_order_post
    uri = URI.parse("#{MoviesWebServiceClient::HOST}/orders/create")
    post_args = {
      :showtime_product_id => @new_id,
      :num_tickets => 4,
      :billing_line_1 => '123 Testahoma Lane',
      :billing_city => 'Cambridge',
      :billing_state => 'MA',
      :billing_zip => '01239',
      :credit_card_number => '55555555555555',
      :credit_card_exp_month => '12',
```

```
      :credit_card_exp_year => '2015',
      :credit_card_type => 'american_express'
    }

    resp, data = Net::HTTP.post_form(uri, post_args)
    doc = XmlSimple.xml_in(data)
    assert doc['confirmation_code']
    assert doc['price']
  end

  def test_order_get_fails
    get_args = {
      :showtime_product_id => @new_id,
      :num_tickets => 4,
      :billing_line_1 => '123 Testahoma Lane',
      :billing_city => 'Cambridge',
      :billing_state => 'MA',
      :billing_zip => '01239',
      :credit_card_number => '55555555555555',
      :credit_card_exp_month => '12',
      :credit_card_exp_year => '2015',
      :credit_card_type => 'american_express'
    }.collect{|k,v| "#{k}=#{CGI.escape(v.to_s)}"}.join("&")
    uri = URI.parse("#{MoviesWebServiceClient::HOST}/orders/create?#{get_args}")

    resp = Net::HTTP.get_response(uri)
    assert resp.kind_of? Net::HTTPMethodNotAllowed
  end
end
```

The second test in Example 18-15, `test_order_get_fails`, starts out the same way as
the previous test. However, rather than post the form, which translates to using the
HTTP POST verb, in this test we make a GET request with the `get_response` method.
Because the order method makes changes on the server, it should only respond to
POST requests. Therefore, we test that the request is denied and that the response re-
turned is a `Net::HTTPMethodNotAllowed` object.

Example 18-16. Result of parsing XML with XMLSimple

```
{"confirmation_code"=>["COB7AgkA8MaIA"], "price"=>["1000"]}
```

wadl.rb

In the previous examples, we had to handcraft the URLs required for placing an order.
As we saw, the mechanism for passing arguments for a GET request is different than the
one that passes in a POST request. When you are consuming a web service, the mechanics
of how to actually make your service requests are not interesting. Generally speaking,
you want to make requests, get results, and use them.

These days, having a REST web service and being RESTful in general is still somewhat
of a chic thing to do, but it's not necessarily practical for clients. REST proponents
claim that because REST (strict REST, that is) provides a uniform interface to resources,

there is no need for special clients to be written. Of course, in the real world, the result is that for every worthwhile REST service out there, for every language where someone has an interest in that service, a custom, one-off client has been written. Although the REST paradigm has many elegant aspects, it turns out that it's just no fun to handcraft HTTP requests.

This is where description languages such as WADL come in. For any given REST web service, a WADL file describes each resource and the methods that can be applied to it. WADL also supports describing actions that are not resource-based URLs but are instead URLs representing some action, like our order creation method. A WADL parser can take that description and create an application language-specific client from it that abstracts away, for the caller, the mechanics of hand-building HTTP calls of four varieties. Action or resource-based URLs simply become methods in the client, and parameters are parameters, whether the underlying HTTP method is a GET, POST, PUT, or DELETE.

A key observation when discussing service description languages for REST services is that using one doesn't imply that any change will be made to your service or the way you write it. A REST service with or without a WADL description file functions exactly the same way for those who don't wish to make use of the WADL file. The difference is that for those who do, utilizing the service becomes much simpler.

The worry that many people have about service descriptions, whether WSDL or WADL, has to do with code generation. Code generation itself is actually fairly benign. In fact, the Rails generators, which generate stub files and methods for your ActiveRecord models and controllers, do about the same level of code generation as would be expected from WADL-based code-generation. The real fear is that REST advocates do not want to see REST development begin to resemble SOAP development, as the latter is, to the REST advocate, anathema. But aside from that politically motivated concern, there are really no adverse affects to using a WADL file to describe your service, or even to generate your initial implementation stub code from that WADL, if you write it first. In fact, contract-first design is a great way to ensure that changes made carelessly do not have a negative impact on clients of your service.

Example 18-17 shows a very simple WADL file that describes applying the GET HTTP verb to our movie resource from Example 18-10.

Example 18-17. A simple WADL file describing the GET HTTP verb for the movie resource

```
<?xml version="1.0" encoding="utf-8"?>
<application xmlns:xsi="http://www.w3.org/2001/XMLSchema-instance"
             xmlns:xsd="http://www.w3.org/2001/XMLSchema"
             xsi:schemaLocation="http://research.sun.com/wadl/2006/10 wadl.xsd"
             xmlns="http://research.sun.com/wadl/2006/10">
  <resources base="http://localhost/">
    <resource path="movies">
      <method name="GET" id="#get">
        <request>
          <param name="id" type="xsd:integer" style="query"/>
```

```
        <param name="format" type="xsd:string" style="query"
                    default="xml" fixed="xml"/>
      </request>
      <response>
        <representation mediaType="application/xml" element="movie"/>
      </response>
    </method>
  </resource>
  </resources>
</application>
```

Example 18-18 shows another test case added to our integration test framework, which uses the *wadl.rb* library and the WADL file from Example 18-17 to generate an on-the-fly web service client. The `from_wadl` method accepts a string containing WADL XML description, and returns a client object. Resources can then have their methods applied to them via method calls to the client, e.g., `movies.get`. Results from *wadl.rb*-generated clients return REXML results. To keep the examples consistent, we've converted the REXML result to an XmlSimple object by first changing the REXML result to a string, then parsing the string with XmlSimple's `xml_in` method. Armed with our XmlSimple object, we assert that all of the expected fields exist in the result object.

Example 18-18. Integration test using the wadl.rb and the WADL file from the previous example

```
require File.dirname(__FILE__) + '/../test_helper'
class OrdersServiceTestCase < Test::Unit::TestCase
  def test_get_via_wadl
    wadl = Net::HTTP.get_response(URI.parse "http://localhost/movies.wadl").body

    movies_webservice = WADL::Application.from_wadl(wadl)
    result = movies_webservice.movies.get(:query => {:id => 1})
    doc = XmlSimple.xml_in(result.representation.to_s)
    assert doc['id']
    assert doc['rating']
    assert doc['rating_description']
    assert doc['length_minutes']
  end
end
```

Example 18-19 shows the result of running the integration test from Example 18-18. The test and all assertions pass.

Example 18-19. Results of running the WADL-client integration test

```
Loaded suite test/integration/wadl_test_case
Started
.
Finished in 0.212655 seconds.

1 tests, 4 assertions, 0 failures, 0 errors
```

I won't describe the entire WADL specification or show you how to handle the infinite variety of URL actions one might wish to describe with WADL. This is a topic that

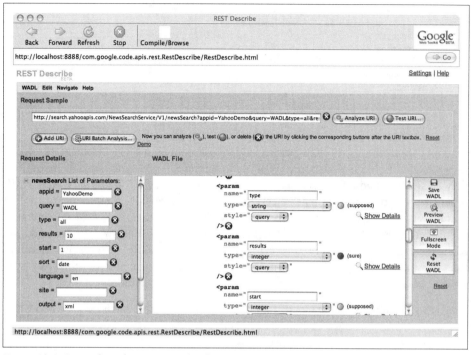

Figure 18-3. Screenshot of REST Describe, from Google Code

deserves its own book. Unfortunately, as of this writing, the WADL specification itself is the only readily available documentation for WADL, when in reality, an entire book of examples is needed. The specification for WADL, written by Marc Hadley of Sun Microsystems, can be found at *https://wadl.dev.java.net*.

REST Describe

Because WADL is not so simple to write, tools are beginning to emerge to facilitate creating these files. A Ruby tool that allows you to describe REST services similar to how XML-RPC services are described with ActionWebService seems like it would be a big win for the REST on Rails community. However, such a tool does not seem to be emerging and is likely stifled by the exuberance for ActiveRecord.

A tool that has been gaining attention lately is called REST Describe, from Google Code. This tool, shown in Figure 18-3, examines an existing web service and creates a WADL description of that service. You use REST Describe by providing a web service URL and invoking some HTTP method on a remote resource or action. Based on the parameters and the result, REST Describe attempts to create the XML description, allowing you to make modifications in places where the tool cannot definitively guess all aspects of the API—for instance types, required versus optional parameters, RUD, mapping to, and other tricky spots.

## CHAPTER 19

Caching End to End

The purpose of caching is two-fold: first, to speed up access to a specific resource that, for whatever reason, might be slower than we desire; and second, to tread lightly on that resource. These goals go hand in hand. It is a sort of Catch-22; often it is the act of saturating a resource with requests that can make it slow for future requests.

In Chapter 12, we saw an example of caching at the database layer, in our implementation of a materialized view. Indeed, we saw dramatic performance improvements, on the order of 100 to 1,000 times, with even a very small dataset and an unloaded system. The 99 or 99.9% of time that was spent idle instead of processing our requests was freed up for other requests, making them faster as well.

Caching seems like a marvelous tool that should be used anywhere and everywhere. And it should. Caching can be the difference between having a problematic bottleneck on your hands and having a site or service that hums along without a hitch.

So why do so many caution against what they describe as "premature optimization" when it comes to caching? If you take Twitter as a cautionary tale, you will agree that by the time it's obvious that you need to optimize, it's already too late. The technorati will not wait for your upgrades and performance enhancements before they declare you dead, or worse, irrelevant.

What the worrywarts are really afraid of is that caching is hard. It's also error-prone. As we saw in Chapter 12, maintaining the "correctness" of a cache can be quite an involved process. Worse, if the caching mechanism is not well devised, it can lock you into a model or convention you had not intended to marry yourself to.

But all of these cautions are actually reasons you should think about caching from the start. If you have not been thinking about caching, you could be writing something that is not easily cacheable. What does that code look like? And more importantly, what does cacheable code look like? Just as the act of writing unit tests can cause your code to look different—suddenly you must write "testable code," where each function does one and only one thing—so too would your code look different if you were writing it with caching in mind. Indeed, if you write for caching from Day One, caching itself becomes a much simpler task and far less forbidding. It is a Herculean effort to refactor a data model in situ, and so too is it terrifying to transform working code into something that can be properly cached. Caching really should be thought of from the start.

To help understand the challenges involved with caching, let's take another look at the caching we already performed with the database layer, where—as was noted in Chapter 12—caching is somewhat straightforward to implement correctly because the toolset is well established. This time, we'll treat each piece as a generic concept. Then we'll examine caching of the logical model layer and see if we can come up with a caching scheme that is just as powerful and just as correct. We'll also take a tour of other places where caching is possible and examine potential pitfalls.

Data Layer Caching, Revisited

In Chapter 12, I described view materialization as the "wax on, wax off" of caching. As complex as it may have seemed, it was easy compared to what lies ahead. But it was "correct," which is a distinction not to be taken lightly. The database—our fortress, the layer of our application built by the giants before us—has all of the mechanisms necessary to make correct caching possible. If you didn't read Chapter 12, or you didn't understand it fully, but you plan to cache at other layers, now is a good time to review that chapter again before we deconstruct it. We'll now look at each part of our implementation in turn to understand its function in the greater scheme of cache correctness.

The Snapshot

The snapshot was our original, cache-complete version of our base data, transformed into the format the client wanted. First, it was complete. If a record was not present in the cache, then we know that the record did not exist. Requests for invalid data do not result in load on the bottleneck resource we are trying to conserve. In some cases— such as when using Memcache—this is not possible. If confronted with an LRU cache, we must take the hit of having to defer to the original data store when our cache doesn't have the requested record, even if it turns out the record does not exist at all.

Second, the data is in the format that the client wants it in after joins and denormalization have been taken into account. If you are going to the trouble of caching, you should cache data *after* all of the hard work has been done, not before. We could have cached all of the base data from the tables that made up our view, but it was the process of computing the view itself that was time-consuming and challenging.

 A good caching scheme requires a way of preparing the preliminary set of data to be placed in the cache. This is often termed *cache warming*. It should also put that data in the cache in the closest possible format to what the client ultimately wants.

The Refresh Function

The element to be cached should be thought of as a new, atomic piece of data, with utility in its own right. We need a way to generate these pieces of data, which often will not correspond neatly to a database row. We need to know just how big or small this unit of data is. Our view, which was created by putting a name to a frequently requested query, defined the element for us; it was a row of the new view. Elsewhere, the process may not be so obvious, but it is the same in nature.

Although in our materialized view it was the view itself that performed the computation to produce records for the materialized view, it was in combination with the `refresh` function that the data actually made it into our cache after the initial warming produced by the snapshot.

 A complete caching scheme needs a way to recompute elements for the cache. They should be of a predefined shape and size. Elements built to replace original elements from the cache-warming process should match in structure and meaning.

Invalidation Triggers

In our materialized view implementation, we made use of database triggers to catch all moments when data underneath our cache was changing. Whether it was an `insert`, `update`, or `delete`, and whether the operation was targeted at a single item or multiple items, our triggers caught the event and called our `refresh` function. Triggers were crucial because without them, we would not have known that our cache was slowly becoming a stale collection of garbage. The benefit of the triggers' pervasive visibility cannot be understated, either; regardless of how the data came to change, the triggers caught the change.

To build our triggers, we also created a table on paper in which we tabulated, for our own peace of mind, which tables and which actions on those tables warranted some kind of action on the cache. This served two purposes. First, it ensured we were not churning the cache more than necessary, losing some of the performance benefit achieved through caching. Second, it ensured that we were aware of each and every moment where a cache invalidation was occurring. True, database triggers are infallible when it comes to detecting changes in database tables, but they do this only if you are wise enough to add the trigger in the first place.

 A correct caching scheme must be able to detect all changes that would invalidate the cache and take action at those moments. The cache designer, by extension, must be aware of all of the events that have to be monitored in order to ensure the cache does not become stale.

Indexing

In our materialized view implementation, we made short order of adding indexes to our cache using the `create index` command. Most often a cache will have some kind of key that lets you get at the data. In a database table, this would be the primary key of the table itself, and in a hash-like cache, such as Memcache, the primary key is the cache key itself.

But you don't always want a single element at a time. Although querying by the primary key is sometimes enough, often you want multiple objects at once, or you are looking for objects that satisfy some other property. Storing objects multiple times under different keys is wasteful, so where such a practice can be avoided, it should be. On the other hand, searching through the entire cache to find some element by anything other than the primary key also defeats the purpose of caching.

 A good caching scheme may need to support multiple indexes on the data being cached. That, or it must allow for loose querying against the primary index to simulate multiple indexes.

Logical Model Caching

Your logical models sit atop the physical models, often transforming them in some way before returning them as the result of a service request. Later in this chapter, we'll discuss how you can cache physical models; however, even with the majority of your physical models cached, the transformations required to turn them into logical model objects can be quite costly, too. Rather than recompute your logical model objects on each request, they too can be cached.

However, because existing tutorials do not treat logical and physical models differently, Rails websites today are not built with this principle in mind. As a consequence, there are no plugins currently available for easing logical model caching. Luckily, it's easy to accomplish even without a plugin. In this section, you'll see how to go about building a complete caching layer on your own.

To implement our caching, we'll use Memcache. If you're not already using it, download it, install it, install the `memcache-client` gem, and add the following to your *environment.rb* file:

```
CACHE = MemCache.new \
  :c_threshold => 10_000,
  :compression => false,
  :debug => false,
  :namespace => RAILS_ENV,
  :readonly => false,
  :urlencode => false

CACHE.servers = '127.0.0.1:11211'
```

To help illustrate how our caching scheme will work, we'll return to the logical model for the `Movie` class from Chapter 15, shown in Example 15-3. Just as with our materialized view from Chapter 12, we'd like our interface to cached data to be a drop-in replacement for our original data. Therefore, the first thing we do is push our original class out of the way, renaming it with the prefix `Uncached` so that the cached version can be accessible via the original name (see Example 19-1).

Example 19-1. Logical model for a movie, app/models/logical/movie.rb

```
module Logical
  class UncachedMovie < ActionWebService::Struct
    def self.get(physical_movie_id)
      return nil if !(m = Physical::Movie.find_by_id(physical_movie_id))
      Movie.new(:id => m.id,
                :name => m.name,
                :length_minutes => m.length_minutes,
                :rating_id => m.rating.id,
                :rating_description => m.rating.description)
    end
  end
end
```

Our caching wrapper classes will do most of the work, which is essentially the same for all wrapper classes we write. Therefore, we'll start by building a base class, `CachedObject`, which will define and handle the common tasks. Example 19-2 shows this class, which exists within the `Logical` module. We'll subclass `CachedObject` once for every class cache we plan.

Example 19-2. Our base class for caching wrapper classes, CachedObject

```
module Logical
  class CachedObject < ActionWebService::Struct

    def self.uncached_class
      eval("Uncached" + self.name.split('::')[-1])
    end

    def self.cache_key(*params)
      return "#{self.name}_#{self::VERSION}_#{params.join('_')}"
    end

    def self.get(*params)
      key = cache_key(params)
      CACHE[key] ||= self.uncached_class.get(params)
    end

    def self.rebuild(*params)
      key = cache_key(params)
      CACHE[key] = self.uncached_class.get(params)
    end

    def self.clear(*params)
      key = cache_key(cache_key_params)
```

```
      CACHE[key] = nil
    end

    class Sweeper < ActiveRecord::Observer
      #observe ActiveRecord::Base
    end

  end
end
```

Let's examine each piece of the `CachedObject` class, one item at a time.

The first method, `uncached_class`, defines our naming convention: all of our original classes are renamed to have a prefix `Uncached`, and the new caching wrapper classes take on the old class names. This method first peels off any modules our class might be in and then adds `Uncached` to the front of what is left. This method will be used in most of our other methods.

The next method, `cache_key`, as its name suggests, builds a key that is unique to the object being requested. It concatenates the class name of the object being cached, a version number, and any additional parameters passed in as the primary key to create a unique identifier.

Note that that idea of a version number is new. Because objects placed in the cache persist across a software upgrade, we need to be careful to invalidate cached objects if we change the structure of those objects. For example, if we added a field to the logical movie class to represent the average reviewer rating, we would need to avoid retrieving older objects out of the cache that do not have that field. Otherwise, when the new code tried to manipulate an old object, an error would occur because the field is not present in the old object retrieved from the cache.

To solve this, we add a `VERSION` constant to each class, and take care to bump this number up whenever the structure of the class changes. All of the old cache keys, which included the old version number, never get requested and slowly get purged from the cache.

To make this work, we rewrite the `Movie` class definition in our *movies_service.rb* file to look like this:

```
class Movie < CachedObject
  VERSION = 1
  member :id,                     :integer
  member :name,                   :string
  member :length_minutes,         :integer
  member :rating_id,              :string
  member :rating_description,     :string
end
```

Note also that we are now defining this class to inherit from `CachedObject` rather than directly from `ActionWebService::Struct`.

Next, we define a `get` function. This function has the same purpose as the `get` function we defined for `Movie`, but it first checks to see if the object exists in the cache. If it does, the `get` function returns that object. If the object is not found in the cache, `get` will be called on the uncached version of this class. The result is stored in the cache under the appropriate key, and it is also returned to the caller.

The `rebuild` method is very similar to the `get` method, but it reloads the uncached version of the object regardless of whether it exists in the cache or not. It then puts the newly built item in the cache, regardless of whether it was there before or not. This method would be used when we detect that an invalidation has occurred and we need to replace a stale object.

The final method in `CachedObject`, `clear`, gives us an easy way to clear an item from the cache. If passed the same parameters as passed to the `get` method, this method removes the cached item from our cache. This is useful when we detect an object has been deleted.

We also define an inner class type, `Sweeper`, based off on `ActiveRecord::Observer`. In our caching wrapper classes, we'll subclass this class to watch for events that would require an invalidation or rebuild, much like our materialized view triggers.

Because we changed the subclass of our class definition to inherit from `CachedObject` in the shared "header" file, we need to define in that shared code that `CachedObject` is simply subclass of `ActionWebService::Struct`. We do that by placing the following definition in *movies_service.rb*:

```
class CachedObject < ActionWebService::Struct ; end
```

Just as with our materialized view, we may not always want to rebuild objects as soon as they are invalidated. In N:1 relationships, this could result in a lot of rebuilding that essentially goes to waste. Therefore, we'd like a way to push off rebuilds until the end of a request. We'll give ourselves this ability by creating a cache manager class, `CacheManager`, shown in Example 19-3.

Example 19-3. The logical model cache manager

```
module Logical
  class CacheManager
    include Singleton

    def initialize
      @@objects_to_rebuild = {}
    end

    def schedule_rebuild(klass, *get_key)
      @@objects_to_rebuild[[klass, get_key]] = true
    end

    def rebuild
      keys = @@objects_to_rebuild.keys.clone
      @@objects_to_rebuild.clear
```

```
      keys.each {|k, v| k.rebuild(*v)}
    end
  end
end
```

First, note that this class is a singleton. This means that we'll access its methods via the variable CacheManager.instance. The cache manager class initializes a hash, which stores the keys and classes that have a deferred rebuild. In the event we want to rebuild an object late, rather than call rebuild on a caching wrapper class directly, we instead call schedule_rebuild on the CacheManager singleton instance. The schedule_rebuild function accepts as its parameters the caching wrapper class and the parameters that would be passed to the rebuild method. The values are added as keys of the @@objects_to_rebuild hash, rather than concatenated on an array, to ensure that each value appears only once.

The final method, rebuild, rebuilds each object defined by the cache keys of the @@objects_to_rebuild hash. It also clears the hash for the next time. Note that we clone the hash before starting the rebuild process so that we can clear it before we begin rebuilding. Why we do this will become apparent soon, as we'll see it will be possible for rebuilds to trigger other objects to get newly invalidated.

The cache manager's rebuild method needs to be called explicitly when we're ready to rebuild invalidated objects. In the materialized view implementation, this happened within the reconciler view. At the application layer, we can call this method after each request has been processed. Example 19-4 shows how to set this up with an after filter. We also do the work in a thread, so the request response can be returned immediately, and no user actually has to wait for the rebuild process to finish.

Example 19-4. CacheManager hooks added to application.rb

```
after_filter do
  Thread.new do
    Logical::CacheManager.instance.rebuild
  end
end
```

We now have enough infrastructure in place to create our first caching wrapper class. In Example 19-5, we define the Movie class again, but this time it is the class that manages caching for the UncachedMovie class. Most of the work of this class has already been taken care of within the base class. All we need to do now is define the Sweeper subclass, which will monitor the physical layer for changes.

Example 19-5. The caching wrapper for the Logical::Movie class

```
module Logical
  class Movie < CachedObject
    class MovieSweeper < Sweeper
      observe Physical::Movie, Physical::Rating

      def after_save(obj)
```

```
      if obj.kind_of?(Physical::Movie)
        CacheManager.instance.schedule_rebuild(Movie, obj.id)
      end
      if obj.kind_of?(Physical::Rating)
        Physical::Movie.find_all_by_rating_id(
          obj.id, :select => 'id'
        ).each do |movie|
          Movie.clear(movie.id)
        end
      end
    end

    def after_destroy(obj)
      if obj.kind_of?(Physical::Movie)
        Movie.clear(obj.id)
      end
    end
  end
  MovieSweeper.instance
  end
end
```

In Example 19-5, we define the `MovieSweeper` class, which observes the `Physical::Movie` class and the `Physical::Rating` class. Note that we can observe as many physical classes as we need, depending on the complexity of our logical model class.

Next, we define callback methods for `after_save` and `after_destroy`. In each, we check the type of the object being observed, as it can be either a `Physical::Movie` or `Physical::Rating`. We take different steps for each action and each type. In `after_save`, we defer a rebuild when a movie object changes, though we could have rebuilt immediately by calling `Movie.rebuild(obj.id)` directly. Instead, we call the `CacheManager` instance's `schedule_rebuild` function. If a rating object changes, many movies can be affected, so rather than rebuild them, we clear them all. They will be rebuilt piecemeal in future requests.

In the `after_destroy` method, we clear the cache of the invalid movie object right away if it is the movie object that was detected to have changed. We don't bother doing anything if a rating was destroyed or saved; our referential integrity guarantees that no movies can exist for a rating that is just now being inserted or deleted.

We can now test logical model layer caching. Example 19-6 shows these tests. We create a **setup** method that creates a new physical layer movie item. Then we clear the cache of any item that may have been left over from a previous test.

In the first test, `test_logical_caching`, we retrieve a local movie object through the `Movie` class, which now refers to our caching wrapper. We assert that the movie names are the same. After updating the physical model because we deferred rebuild, initially the movie names do not match when comparing the physical and logical models. However, after calling the cache manager's **rebuild** function, they once again match.

In the second test, `test_dependent_obj_invalidation`, we are testing that altering a physical rating object will propagate up through the caching layer of the logical objects as well. First, we retrieve the cached logical model object for the movie we created in the setup method. After changing the movie rating description, the physical and already loaded logical models do not match. However, when we request the logical model object again, it does match.

Example 19-6. A unit test for the cache manager

```
require File.dirname(__FILE__) + '/../../test_helper'

class CacheManagerTestCase < Test::Unit::TestCase
  def setup
    @p = Physical::Movie.create!(
      :name => 'When Harry Met Sally',
      :length_minutes => 120,
      :rating => Physical::Rating::PG13)

    # memcache persists between application restarts
    l = Logical::Movie.clear(@p.id)
  end

  def test_logical_caching
    # on the first get, the objects should match
    l = Logical::Movie.get(@p.id)
    assert l.name == @p.name

    # after an update to the physical model, the cached
    # value will not match
    @p.update_attribute(:name, 'new name')
    assert l.name != @p.name

    # after issuing a rebuild, the values will
    # again match
    Logical::CacheManager.instance.rebuild
    l = Logical::Movie.get(@p.id)
    assert l.name == @p.name
  end

  def test_dependent_obj_invalidation
    # initially the descriptions should match
    l = Logical::Movie.get(@p.id)
    assert l.rating_description == Physical::Rating::PG13.description

    # after updating the rating description,
    # the cached value will not match
    Physical::Rating::PG13.update_attribute(:description, 'new desc')
    assert l.rating_description != Physical::Rating::PG13.description

    # invalidation is not deferred, so logical model will pick
    # up changes immediately
    l = Logical::Movie.get(@p.id)
    assert l.rating_description == Physical::Rating::PG13.description
```

```
    end
end
```

Example 19-7 shows the results of running these two tests. They pass, as we expect.

Example 19-7. Results of running the cache manager unit test

```
2 tests, 4 assertions, 0 failures, 1 errors
ChakBookPro: chak$ ruby test/unit/logical/cache_manager_test.rb
Loaded suite test/unit/logical/cache_manager_test
Started
..
Finished in 0.033217 seconds.

2 tests, 6 assertions, 0 failures, 0 errors
```

Considerations

In a high-traffic website, clearing an object rather than rebuilding it can be much more costly than might be initially expected. For example, if you receive 10 requests for an object per second, and it takes one second to rebuild that object, then you might pay up to 10 times for a rebuild if you clear, rather than rebuild. All of the requests between the clear action and the conclusion of the first rebuild action see a cache miss, so they kick off additional, unneeded rebuilds. This is shown in Figure 19-1.

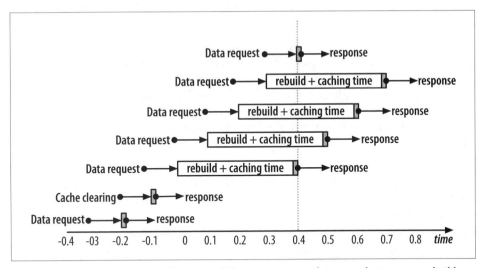

Figure 19-1. Clearing the cache after an invalidation can incur a large penalty in excess rebuilds

Previous to time –0.1, requests are processed quickly because the data requested comes out of the cache. At time –0.1, some request occurs that causes the cache to be cleared. The next request, at time 0, does not find the requested data in the cache, so the rebuild process, which takes 0.4 seconds, begins. The next three requests still do not find the

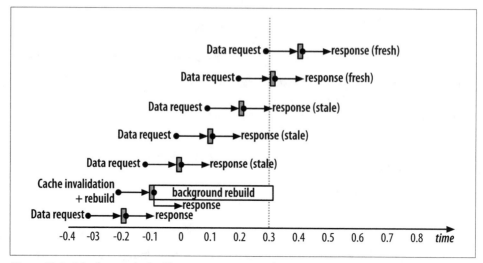

Figure 19-2. A background rebuild wastes no resources, but temporarily returns stale data

data in the cache, so each one kicks off another (unnecessary) rebuild process. Finally, at time 0.4, the first rebuild process has completed, so requests starting at this time are served from the cache. Meanwhile, three rebuild processes are still working away, sapping precious computing resources for no real purpose. In our caching mechanism, this is what would happen if `clear` is called on data that still exists, i.e., data that has not been deleted.

There are two alternatives. One, pictured in Figure 19-2, is to continue to serve the stale object while the new object is being rebuilt. This method has the benefit of not wasting any resources in rebuilding the same data multiple times. It also returns data to the caller quickly, although the data is slightly out-of-date. This is the behavior implemented in the examples above, where `schedule_rebuild` is called for data that has been detected to be invalid. While the data is being rebuilt in the background at the end of the request, subsequent requests continue to return results based on the original value stored in the cache.

A third option is a compromise between the first two, and it's depicted in Figure 19-3. If the rebuild acquires a read lock on the data, then subsequent requests wait until the rebuild is complete before returning data. This wait time is always shorter than the rebuild time itself, and the data returned from all requests will be fresh.

Unfortunately, this option is difficult to implement efficiently using Memcache, which does not provide native locking support. A lock can be simulated by adding a key to the cache that means "this data is locked," and readers would check to see if that key exists before reading. If it does, they should wait, then poll again until the lock has disappeared. Code to implement this behavior is shown in Example 19-8. However, this sort of implementation requires frequent polling to return data quickly after a

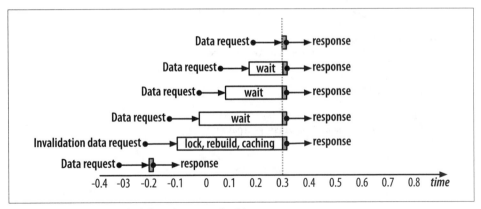

Figure 19-3. Locking cached data during a rebuild

rebuild is complete; you can save on polling by increasing the granularity of sleeps between poll attempts. However, this process adds time overhead to get back a result.

Another drawback of this approach is that each `get` request also incurs an additional round-trip penalty to ensure that the data being requested is not currently locked.

Example 19-8 shows our `CachedObject` class, modified to incorporate a locking mechanism that prevents a `get` request from completing until a simultaneous `rebuild` request has finished. Note that only the `get` and `rebuild` methods, along with new `helper` methods, are shown here, although the rest of the methods from Example 19-2 would still be part of this class. Additions are shown in bold.

Example 19-8. A locking mechanism built upon Memcache, with polling

```
module Logical
  class CachedObject

    def self.lock_key(key)
      "lock:#{key}"
    end

    def self.locked?(key, timeout_seconds = 10)
      start = CACHE[lock_key(key)]
      start ? Time.new - start < timeout_seconds : false
    end

    def self.with_lock(key, timeout_seconds = 10, &block)
      start = Time.new
      acquired_lock = false
      while (Time.new - start < timeout_seconds) && !acquired_lock
        acquired_lock = !CACHE.add(lock_key(key), Time.new).index("NOT_STORED")
        sleep 0.1 if !acquired_lock
      end
      yield
      CACHE.delete(lock_key(key))
    end
```

```
def self.get(*params)
  key = cache_key(params)
  sleep 0.1 while locked?(key)
  CACHE[key] ||= self.uncached_class.get(params)
end

def self.rebuild(*params)
  key = cache_key(params)
  with_lock(key) do
    CACHE[key] = self.uncached_class.get(params)
  end
end

  end
end
```

Since we are simulating native locking by putting a semaphore in the cache, we need a method to generate a semaphore key unique to each item we might rebuild. The lock_key method accepts the key created by the cache_key method from Example 19-2, which should be unique, and prepends lock:. This utility method will be used in our other methods.

The next method, locked?, checks the cache for the presence of the semaphore. Since it's possible that there was an error in the method doing the locking, or a power outage, or some other event beyond our control, locked? also takes an optional parameter to specify a timeout, after which it will return false even if the semaphore exists, giving the caller permission to take over the lock.

The next method, with_lock, takes a block as a parameter, and only executes that block once the lock has been acquired, or a timeout has passed. The add method of the Memcache API will only add an item if it does not already exist. When an item is successfully added, "STORED" is returned; otherwise "NOT STORED" is returned. The variable acquired_lock only becomes true when "NOT_STORED" is not found in the return string.

The get method has been modified so that it blocks while a key is locked. Again, if the default timeout, set at 10 seconds, passes, locked? will return true and the get will proceed.

Finally, the rebuild method has been modified so that the get call on the uncached class is wrapped by the new with_lock method, which ensures that calls to get on the cached class are blocked until the rebuild process is complete. Of course, this blocks simultaneous calls to rebuild as well.

Avoiding Rebuilding with Stale Data

If your logical model objects are composed of other logical model objects, rebuilding invalid items can be tricky. Take the simple example shown in Figure 19-4. Here, a

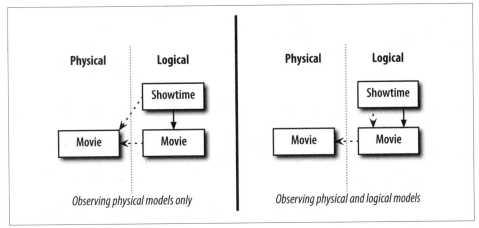

Figure 19-4. Different caching styles for the logical Showtime object

solid line indicates a composition, and a dotted line indicates an observer relationship. The logical `Movie` class observes the physical `Movie` class, and will correctly get rebuilt using the data from the physical class when the physical `movie` object changes.

However, the logical `Showtime` class gets its data from the logical `Movie` class. Yet it also must observe the physical `Movie` class to detect an invalidation because there is no easy way to observe a non-ActiveRecord type class. But there's a problem here. We have not provided a mechanism to order rebuilds. We have no way to ensure that the `Movie` object gets rebuilt before the `Showtime` object, and if the `Showtime` object *does* get rebuilt before the `Movie` object, it will be rebuilt with stale data (Figure 19-4).

Certainly, we can get around this by always relying on physical models for rebuilding logical ones, but this sacrifices a lot of flexibility, and is also very inelegant. The whole purpose of the logical models is that they more closely resemble the way we naturally think about our application's problem domain, so we'd like to use them as much as possible.

A better solution, then, is to devise a mechanism to observe logical model rebuilds as well as physical model invalidations. That way, only the logical `Movie` class need observe the physical `Movie` class, and the `Showtime` class can observe the logical `Movie` class. In general, the rule would be that you rebuild only from objects you observe.

We can accomplish this by creating a pseudoclass called `LogicalModelInvalidation` that inherits from `ActiveRecord::Base`. We'll never save records of this class, but we'll piggyback off the built-in ActiveRecord observers to simulate logical model observers.

First, we create a dummy table in the database with the attributes we want our invalidation pseudoclass to have, as shown in Example 19-9.

Example 19-9. A dummy table with the attributes for the invalidation pseudoclass

```
create table logical_model_invalidations (
  id integer,
  type text,
  object_id text
);
```

We need an `id` column because Rails expects a primary key. However, Rails does not let you easily set the value of an `id` primary key column, so we'll also add an `object_id` column to simulate the real primary key of the object being invalidated. Finally, we have a type column because we will take advantage of Rails single table inheritance. We'll subclass this class for every class that can be invalidated.

Then, within the `CachedObject` class, we define the inner class shown in Example 19-10.

Example 19-10. Inner class within the CachedObject class

```
module Logical
  class CachedObject < ActionWebService::Struct
    class LogicalModelInvalidation < ActiveRecord::Base
      def validate
        errors.add_to_base("invalid")
      end
    end
  end
end
```

This is essentially an empty ActiveRecord class, but with one special property: it cannot be saved. The `validate` method has been redefined to always fail by adding a dummy error message whenever it is run. We don't actually want to save objects of this type; we just want to gain the functionality that comes for free in ActiveRecord objects in that they can be observed by sweeper classes. Although instances of this class won't ever be saved, the `before_validation` hook can be observed.

Each caching wrapper class should subclass this class, with the name `Invalidation`. For example, in the wrapper `Movie` logical model class, inside of the class definition itself, we add the declaration shown in Example 19-11.

Example 19-11. Declaration inside the class definition

```
module Logical
  class Movie < CachedObject
    class Invalidation < LogicalModelInvalidation; end
  end
end
```

It's fine for every class to name this class with the same name because the scoping within the `Logical` model, and further within the `CachedObject` subclass gives us the context we need to take appropriate action. The `Invalidation` subclass we created in Example 19-11 is actually named `Logical::Movie::Invalidation`, and other subclasses would be similarly scoped for their logical model class type.

It's actually preferable that the name of the subclass is always the same; this lets us trigger invalidations programmatically. In Example 19-12, we make use of this when we upgrade our `rebuild` and `clear` methods to trigger an observable logical model invalidation. The additions are in bold.

Example 19-12. Upgrading the rebuild and clear methods

```
module Logical
  class CachedObject < ActionWebService::Struct
    def self.rebuild(*params)
      key = cache_key(params)
      with_lock(key) do
        CACHE[key] = self.uncached_class.get(params)
      end
      eval("#{self.name}::Invalidation").create(:object_id => params)
    end

    def self.clear(*params)
      key = cache_key(params)
      CACHE[key] = nil
      eval("#{self.name}::Invalidation").create(:object_id => params)
    end
  end
end
```

When an object is cleared or rebuilt, an instance of the corresponding `Invalidation` class is created. The `create` method tries to save the object immediately, which calls `validate`. Although `validate` adds an error and the `create` operation fails, we nonetheless have an observable event to track.

Now, other models can observe logical model invalidations. To observe the logical `Movie` class for invalidations, a sweeper would observe `Logical::Movie::Invalidation`. An example of what the logical model for the caching wrapper of the `Showtime` class might look is shown in Example 19-13.

Example 19-13. A logical model observing another logical model

```
module Logical
  class Showtime < CachedObject

    class ShowtimeSweeper < Sweeper
      observe Logical::Movie::Invalidation

      def before_validation(obj)
        Physical::MovieShowtime.find_all_by_movie_id(
          obj.object_id, :select => 'id'
        ).each do |ms|
          Logical::CacheManager.instance.schedule_rebuild(Showtime, ms.id)
        end
      end
    end
    ShowtimeSweeper.instance
```

```
    class Invalidation < LogicalModelInvalidation; end
  end
end
```

Based on Example 19-13, we now have implemented a logical model class that is composed of, and observes, another logical model object. We are no longer constrained to the left side of Figure 19-4, but can be confident that our implementation affords the cache correctness provided by the scenario on the right side of the figure.

Cache Indexes

In all of our examples of invalidation, it was necessary to go back to the database to find dependent objects. For example, when a movie was invalidated, we had to query to get the *id*s of the showtimes that were for that movie. While doing so is not the worst thing in the world—ideally, invalidations that require database access are infrequent compared to reads that do not—this does impose some additional burden on the database.

It would be ideal if the caching layer itself could maintain indexes that could be used to find associated objects without resorting to queries in the data layer. Unfortunately, Memcache does not provide any native indexing support. We could build our own and store the indexes as regular objects stored in Memcache, but it would be tedious, inefficient, and also error-prone. Modifying the index would involve acquiring a lock, which we have already seen is not Memcache's forte; it would require transferring the entire index to the client, modifying it in place, and then setting it back in Memcache. The various costs of developer and processor time are likely to outweigh the time spent in the database querying database indexes.

However, it should be noted that Memcache is not the only choice for logical model caching. SimpleDB, an Amazon web service, is even better-suited than Memcache for this task. SimpleDB, although it is a database of sorts, is not a relational database, but rather it is hash-based storage on steroids. Unlike Memcache, which provides simple key-value pair storage, SimpleDB provides key to key-value pair storage. This allows it to automatically index your data on all attributes. With SimpleDB, you can easily request all of the keys for showtimes that correspond to a particular movie.

Although SimpleDB's users will define what it can do (rare is the tool that is used only as intended), cache-complete storage atop a relational database is what SimpleDB is really for. Unlike Memcache, which is LRU only, SimpleDB's data is persistent, meaning you can create cache-complete copies of your data, and know definitively that if an item is not in the cache, it is not in the database either.

Of course, it is impractical to use SimpleDB as a cache unless your application is running on Amazon's Elastic Compute Cloud (EC2). Accessed from other places, the latency is likely to outweigh any other benefits.

A Ruby gem that provides a client interface to SimpleDB is available at *http://rightaws .rubyforge.org*.

Other Caching

There are a number of places in an application, both within as well as at the edges, for caching. Each has its own considerations and difficulties. The rest of this chapter provides an overview of these locations, and attempts to point out the most worrisome drawbacks and pitfalls, and what steps may be taken from day one to help get around them. Unfortunately, at some layers there is little recourse when the infrastructure falls short of our hopes. We will start at the bottom and work our way up.

Query Plan Caching

Whenever you execute a database query, the database first must come up with a plan for how to retrieve the data you requested. There may be many ways to go about executing your query, based on the number of tables involved in the query and the number of indexes that may be used.

For large queries, the time spent planning a query generally pales in comparison to the time spent executing the plan. However, any time spent planning queries is time not spent doing something else. And as query complexity rises, so too does the planning time. The number of possible paths to take for N tables joined in a single query is N!, even before you factor in the different ways to treat those tables due to indexes. Finding the very best plan could take an eternity. Because of this, Postgres has a cut-off point for the number of tables after which it will avoid an exhaustive search and instead do a heuristic search for the best query plan so that planning time does not blow up out of control.

For simple queries, while the plans may be quick to generate, the time spent in the query planner begins to take up a larger and larger percentage of the overall time needed to execute the query.

Luckily, these plans do not need to be created each time a query is executed. While you may execute millions of queries per day, most of them are slightly different versions of one another; the structure of the query is the same, but the values in the query change. If you can make it clear to the database that you have a certain number of "template" queries, and only the parameters are changing, then the database need only create a plan once per template. So if you execute one million queries per day, but all of these queries fall into a pattern of 100 query templates, you can eliminate 999,900 runs through the query planner by registering these templates.

You don't have to take special action to register your query templates. However, when you execute your queries, you do have to separate out the template from the parameters when passing the query to the database. These templated variables are known as *bind variables*.

Unfortunately, as of this writing, bind variables present a problem for Rails users. The Rails framework appears to support bind variables. Indeed, when you write a query, you can pass a template with question marks denote bind variables. Example 19-14 shows a snippet where we define and then pass bind variables to an ActiveRecord query, with the segments relating to bind variables in bold.

Example 19-14. Snippets of code from Example 16-17, highlighting usage of bind variables

```
...
if !zip_code.empty?
  conditions_sql << "miles_between_lat_long(
    (select latitude from zip_codes where zip = ?),
    (select longitude from zip_codes where zip = ?),
    latitude, longitude) < 15"
  conditions_vars.concat [zip_code]*2
end
...
psts = Physical::MovieShowtimeWithCurrentAndSoldOut.find(:all,
  :select => [:id, :movie_id, :theatre_id, :latitude, :longtitude],
  :include => [:movie, :theatre],
  :conditions => [conditions_sql.join(" and "), *conditions_vars])
```

However, ActiveRecord does not support passing these templates and bind variables through to the database drivers that actually communicate with your database. This means that although you are going through the motions of using bind variables, currently, with Rails, there is no benefit. Even if you have 100 templates for your one million query executions, currently with Rails, your database actually computes one million query plans.

Clearly this is a bad thing from a performance perspective, and there are other causes for concern as well. As of this writing, work is in progress for some database drivers to make ActiveRecord respect bind variables all the way through to the database. I encourage any interested readers to check the status of this work, and to lend a hand if you can.

Database Query Caching

MySQL has a feature called the *query cache*, which memorizes the results of each select query you execute. If you execute some query, and then execute the same query again, MySQL simply looks up the result from the first run and returns it.

If your application is exclusively read-based, this can give you a large performance boost when you are evaluating the same queries over and over again. However, since cache correctness is hard to maintain, as we saw in Chapter 14 in our discussion of materialized views, as well as in this chapter with logical model caching, MySQL does not attempt to maintain correctness in place within an existing query cache. Instead, to keep things as simple as possible, MySQL simply flushes the entire query cache for a table whenever that table changes in any way, be it via an `insert`, `update`, `delete`, or any DDL operation that modifies the table.

Certainly, having a query cache like MySQL's is not generally harmful. In the rare situation where your application only sees cache misses, the penalty of incurred overhead to maintain the cache is measured at 13% in the MySQL documentation.

So while the query cache can be extremely helpful in a read-only context, in practice it does not provide the boost you might expect on an active website. Because of the modest gains a query cache provides in real-world situations, this feature is not found in most databases, and even in MySQL, it should not be relied up on as your primary caching mechanism. An architecture that relies on a query cache begs the following question, which will come up again in the following discussion of the Rails query cache: Why does your application request the same data over and over again?

If you know you need the same data repeatedly, why isn't it being cached closer to the user? Not only is the database the furthest point from the original request, but it is also the likeliest to become your bottleneck. Even if the queries you execute are fast, avoiding them altogether is still faster. In this chapter, we've already seen how we can avoid most queries with logical model caching.

Rails Query Caching

In Rails 2.0, an application layer query cache was introduced, which, for the period of a single request, caches the results of each select query you execute.

This feature is actually quite puzzling. If you don't have a functional logical model cache, it makes sense that successive requests might need to access the same data anew from the database. But it is perplexing why, within a single request, you would need to request the exact same information twice, rather than store the result in a variable and reuse the data stored there throughout the request.

Rather than providing any performance gain you could not achieve through good programming practice, the Rails query cache actually encourages you to write bad code. Example 19-15 shows the same process, once without utilizing the cache, and a second time relying on it.

Example 19-15. Avoiding and using the Rails query cache

```
# avoiding cache, good style
m = Movie.find(5)
if m.rating == Rating::R
  # do something
end
if m.length_minutes > 90
  # do something else
end
```

```
# relying on cache, bad style
if Movie.find(5).rating == Rating::R
  # do something
end
if Movie.find(5).length_minutes > 90
  # do something else
end
```

Of course, this is a contrived example. The real benefit would be seen if multiple functions took a `movie_id` argument and proceeded to look the movie up in the database for each call to the function. But that, too, is bad practice; it's just harder to see it.

Instead, you can define functions that accept objects as arguments and depend on the caller to do the database lookup. Example 19-16 shows two versions of the same method, `needs_id_check?`, which returns true if the movie rating is R.

Example 19-16. Two versions of the same method, one intended to avoid the Rails query cache

```
# relies on query cache, bad style
def needes_id_check?(movie_id)
  return Movie.find(movie_id).rating == Rating::R
end

# avoid cache, good style
def needs_id_check?(movie)
  return movie.rating == Rating::R
end
```

Of course, the second method is preferable, and outperforms any query cache that can be build because the object is immediately present—it need not be looked up in a database *or* query cache.

Fragment, Action, and Page Caching

Rails has a number of built-in mechanisms for caching the result of page rendering, either the entire page by URL, an action, or a fragment of a view. These mechanisms can speed up your page rendering times dramatically, dropping them to nearly zero, but maintaining cache correctness at the granularity of an entire page is a large challenge.

If your goal is scaling, and if you have maintained cache correctness at your logical model layer, you don't need fragment, action, or page caching. While it is true that they do improve *speed* of page rendering, they do not do more for you with respect to scaling than a cache complete logical model layer would do.

Remember, the definition of *scaling* is the ability to serve a linear growth of users by adding hardware linearly. To scale, we need only to ensure that we have no bottlenecks that cannot be eliminated with additional dollars and hardware. In almost all cases, the challenge is with squeezing more and more queries through the database layer. However, if you are cache-complete, you won't execute database queries to render your pages. An increase in requests *can* be handled by adding more application servers. Rather than request data from the database, it will be requested from the cache. The best case scenario for your users would be if you maintained one server per visitor, so each user feels as if she is the only one browsing your website. Of course, this is not practical, but it is possible with a complete and shared cache. With this in mind, it should be understood that adding additional fragment, action, or page caching on top of these other caches gives you an improvement in *speed*, not an improvement in your ability to *scale*.

Index

Symbols

1:1 updates, 167
1:N updates, 167
1NF (first normal form), 73
2NF (second normal form), 73
3NF (third normal form), 51, 73–83, 85
    abstraction barriers and, 218
:=, using PL/pgSQL variables, 122
<< (chevron) operator, 282
<<-DELIM ... DELIM extension, 27

A

abstraction barriers, creating, 218–230
Accept header, 272
ACID (atomicity, consistency, isolation, and
        durability), 6
ActionWebService, 217
    Base, 227
    Client::XmlRpc, 232
    Struct class, 222
ActionWebService::Struct class, 300
ActiveRecord, 34
    Base, 39, 134, 219
    ORM (Object Relational Mapping), 44
    physical model layer and, 218
    validations, 42
acts_as method, 27
Agile Web Development with Rails (Thomas,
        Dave), 11
Ajax, 273
Amazon web services, 312
API, 203
    contract, 184, 201, 204, 256
    defining, 225–230

design best practices, 205–212
app directory, 32
app/controllers/services, 227
app/models/services, 227
application layers, 8
    object/logical, 220
    physical, 218–230
    service, 189
ApplicationController, 232
array.collect method, 139
array.compact method, 140
assertion failures, 61
association_methods method, 141
atomicity, 6
attr_accessor, 281
authorize( ) method, 189

B

base64 type (XML-RPC), 222
BDB (Berkley Database), 12
before_create method, 104
belongs_to relationships, 137
Berkley Database (BDB), 12
bind variables, 314
blocks (PL/pgSQL), 123
bool type (XML-RPC), 222
bugs, 42, 53
business logic, separating from code, 20

C

C programming language, 184
C++ programing language, 184
caches, 155, 295–317
    action, 316

We'd like to hear your suggestions for improving our indexes. Send email to *index@oreilly.com*.

duck typing, 130
durability, 7

E

EC2 (Elastic Compute Cloud), 312
EDITOR environment variable, 30
endpoint URLs, 213
enterprise, 1
Enterprise Service Bus (ESB), 16
enum.inject method, 140
environment.rb file, 38
ESB (Enterprise Service Bus), 16
exceptions (database), 58
exclusive or (XOR), 135
extension plugin template, 26
external foreign keys, 193, 194

F

factory classes, 143–144
Fagin, Ronald, 101
fail fast triggers, 123
fail safe triggers, 123
failover, 3
Fielding, Roy, 267
firewalls, 16
first normal form (1NF), 73
float type (XML-RPC), 222
foreign key constraints, 106, 109–111
foreign keys constraints, 96
fragment cache, 316
freshness of data (caching), 155
front-end application layer, 9

G

Gang of Four, 143
Gardner, Jonathan, 156
GET HTTP verb, 268
    CRUD, mapping to, 271

H

Hansson, David Heinemeier, 277
hardware, 269
Heisenberg Uncertainty Principal of Website
        Reporting, 48
helpers directory, 32
"high REST", 212
HTML, 269
HTTP

XML-RPC and, 277
HTTP verbs, 267–272
HTTP+POX, 274

I

IBM Research Laboratories, 101
id columns/keys, 95
IF-THEN-ELSE structures (PL/pgSQL), 124
include keyword, 26
indexes, 70, 112, 153, 298
    cache, 178, 312
    databases, 113, 191, 312
information technology engineer (IT), 2
inheritance, 82, 130, 131–143
    database, 78
    multiple table, 127–146
    Ruby, 79
    single table, 129, 131, 132
init.rb file, 22, 25
initialization templates
    custom extensions and, 26
    enhancing core classes, 22
initialize method, 234
inject method, 140
insert statements, 151
    anomalies, 49
InstanceMethods module, 27
int type (XML-RPC), 222
integration testing, 236
interfaces
    Java, 130
    RESTful web services and, 280
invalidation functions, 157, 161–168
    triggers, 168–174
isolation, 7
isolation of service-oriented architecture, 200
IT (information technology) engineer, 2

J

JavaScript, 42, 272
    XML-RPC libraries, 213

K

Kimball, Ralph, 49

L

left outer joins, 158
load order of classes, 38

local complexity, reducing, 197
logical and service category, organizing
    modules, 32
logical model caches, 14, 298–313
Logical::Order class, 272

M

Mac OS X, testing XML-RPC services on, 230
Mason (Perl), 42
materialized views, 155–181
    invalidation functions, 157, 174
    principles, 156
    reconciler view, 157, 174–178
    refresh function, 161
member keyword, 222
Memcache, 197, 296, 298, 306
memcache-client gem, 298
messaging systems, 16
method overrides, 108
methods, using object-oriented programming,
    184
method_missing method, 23
migrations, 42, 44–46
models directory, 31, 32
models/apis directory, 225
modules, 31–40
    logical, 32
    namespacing, 33
    physical, 32
    refactoring, 39
monolithic application design, 184
Mosaic web browser, 269
MTI (multiple table inheritance), 127–146,
    129, 131, 133
multiple table inheritance (see MTI)
MySQL, 44

N

N:1 updates, 168
namespaces, 33
natural keys, 95
    (see also composite keys)
    method overrides, 108
    spotting composite keys and, 99
    trade-offs, understanding, 111
Net::HTTP, 283
NF2 (non-first normal form), 73
*NIX servers, 44

nonfunctional requirements, 256
Normal Form for Relational Databases That is
    Based on Domains and Keys (Fagin,
    Ronald), 101
not null constraint, 61

O

O(1) time, 156, 165, 166
object model layer, 220–225
object models, 219
Object Relational Mapping (ORM), 44
object-oriented programming, 184
Object.subclasses_of method, 140
observers, 309
    before_create, 104
    before_save, 251
    logical models, 257
    physical/logical models, 298
OLAP (Online Analytical Processing), 48
OLTP (Online Transaction Processing), 48
Online Analytical Processing (OLAP), 48
Online Transaction Processing (OLTP), 48
operations, 47–49
Oracle, 43
organization, 19–30
    modules and, 31–40
ORM (Object Relational Mapping), 44

P

page caches, 316
parallelization, 209
periodic refreshes, 177
Perl, 42
persistence layers, 5, 131–143
PHP, 42
physical directories, 32
physical inheritance, 132
physical model caches, 12
physical modules, 32
PL/pgSQL, 147
    blocks, 123
    conditionals, 124
    functions, 121
    IF-THEN-ELSE structures and, 124
    triggers, 124
    variables, 122
plugins, 19–30
    deployment and, 30

writing, 21–30
polymorphic associations, 127
polymorphism, 129
POST HTTP, 271
POST HTTP verb, 268
PostgreSQL, 43
pre-built caches, 12
premature optimization when caching, 295
primary keys, 99, 102
    composite, 99
    editing, 96
    natural, 100
    single column keys, 102
private classes, 184
procedural programming, 184
PUT verb, 268
    CRUD, mapping to, 271

Q

QA (quality assurance), 2
quality assurance (QA), 2
query caches, 314
    MySQL, 314
    Rails, 315
query plan caching, 313

R

rails command, 32
    application layer and, 8
rails query caching, 315
Rails::Initializer.run, 38
RDBMS (Relational Database Management
    System), 5
    choosing, 44
    MySQL, 44
    myths of, 46
    PostgreSQL, 44
real-time caches, 12
reciprocal relationships, 35
reconciler views, 157, 174–178
redundancy, 3
refactoring, 93
    inheritance and mixins, 78
    modules, 39
    to services, 239–265
references, 152
referential integrity, 64–70
reflection_symbol method, 140

reflect_on_association method, 140, 141
refresh functions, 157, 161–168, 297
    triggers, 168–174
Relational Database Management System (see
    RDBMS)
remote procedure call (RPC), 212
    (see also XML-RPC)
replication (database), 194
reporting, 47
Representational State Transfer (see REST)
resources
    REST, 267
    shared, 187
REST, 186, 201, 267–278, 279–294
    SOA, mapping to, 270–278
    vs. XML-RPC and SOAP, 212–215
REST Describe, 294
Richardson, Leonard, 277
.rjs templates, 273
ROXML (Ruby Object to XML Mapping
    Library), 281
RPC (remote procedure call), 212
    (see also XML-RPC)
Ruby Object to XML Mapping (ROXML), 281
Ruby on Rails, slowness of, 25, 210
Ruby, Sam, 277

S

scalability of service-oriented architecture, 200
scaling, 316
script/console, 104
script/runner, 32
second normal form (2NF), 73
service level agreement (SLA), 2, 210
service requests, 189
service responses, 189
service-oriented architecture (see SOA)
services, 9
    breaking up projects into, 4
    monolithic applications and, 185
    refactoring, 239
session objects for sites, 203
set_primary_key method, 87, 103
set_primary_key plugin, 105
set_primary_keys plugin, 105
set_table_name directive, 134
shared code, writing client plugins, 234
shared databases, 188
shared resources, 187–190

SimpleDB, 312
Simple Object Access Protocol (see SOAP)
Simple Queue Service (SQS), 190
SimpleDB, 312
Simula 67, 184
single column keys, 102
single table inheritance (STI), 129, 131, 132
SLAs (service level agreements), 2, 210
Smalltalk, 184
SOA (service-oriented architecture), 183–200
    anti-pattern, 192
    considerations, 201–215
    database load and, 190–196
    local complexity, reducing, 197
    REST, mapping, 270–278
    service-oriented architectures and, 189
    shared database, 188
    shared resources and, 187–190
SOAP, 201, 278
    vs. XML-RPC and REST, 214
source control repositories, 2, 30
SQLite, 42
SQS (Simple Queue Service), 190
stale data, 308
STI (single table inheritance), 129, 131, 132
sticky sessions, 203
stored procedures, 117
strategy patterns, 89–93, 132
string type (XML-RPC), 222
strings, 122
Struts, 42
svn:externals property, 30
synchronized tables, 187

T
table-backed models, 152
target audiences for websites, 9
Third Normal Form (see 3NF)
third-party plugins, 20
third-party tools, 236
Thomas, Dave, 11
time type (XML-RPC), 222
triggers, 117–125, 157
    fail fast, 123
    fail safe, 123
    invalidation, 297
    refreshes and invalidations, 168–174

U
underscore( ) method, 140
understandability of service-oriented
    architecture, 200
uniform access of service-oriented architecture,
    200
"Uninitialized constant ActionWebService"
    error, 217
unique constraint, 61
unit tests, 54
universal resource locators (URLs), 267
update anomalies, 49, 151
update_attribute( ) method, lack of validation
    and, 63
update_attribute_with_validation_skipping( )
    method, lack of validation and, 63
URLs (universal resource locators), 267
user-level caches, 14

V
validations, 63
variables (PL/pgSQL), 122
vendor/plugins, 236
vendor/rails, 217
verbs (REST), 267
    CRUD, mapping to, 270
VERSION constant, 300
view-backed models, 147–154, 152
views, 148
    materialized, 155–181
    models, basing on, 149
    reconciler, hiding implementation with,
        174–178
virtual IPs (VIPs) = VIPs, 202

W
W*DL, 203
WADL, 292
Web Application Description Language (see
    WADL)
web frameworks, 41
web servers, 16
web services, 183
web-services layers, 10
where clause, 71
    cache indexes and, 179
WSDL, 275

X

Y

Z

About the Author

Dan Chak has varied education in real-world web architecture that gives him a unique perspective on the challenges of building rock-solid web applications. Dan has worked at Amazon.com, the world's biggest online retail store, where seemingly small technology problems become big ones due to enormous scale. Dan also directed software development at CourseAdvisor Inc., a Ruby on Rails startup company. A nearly instant success, CourseAdvisor was acquired by the Washington Post Company in October 2007.

Dan received a B.A. in computer science and engineering from MIT and an M.A. in media arts and sciences from the MIT Media Lab.

Dan is now investigating the Internet's next big challenges. Visit his blog at *http://blog .chak.org*, and go to *http://enterpriserails.chak.org* to join the discussion about this book.

Colophon

The animal on the cover of *Enterprise Rails* is a sturgeon. Although sturgeon is the common name for more than 26 species of fish in the *Acipenseridae* family, it is often used to identify the two most common generas in the family: *Acipenser* and *Huso*.

Among the most ancient of the bony fish, sturgeon first appeared in the fossil record more than 200 million years ago. They are found from the subtropic waters of North America all the way to the subarctic waters of Eurasia; their high tolerance for a wide range of temperatures and salinity (the amount of salt in the water) partially explains why the species has undergone very little morphological change since its existence was first recorded. Other reasons they have achieved the informal status of "living fossil" probably include the lack of predators that hunt them because of their size; and, as bottom-dwellers feeding in the benthic zone (the ecological region at the lowest level of water, including the sediment surface and some subsurface layers), they always have access to a wealth of prey.

Unique-looking fish, sturgeon are covered in bony plates called scutes and have four barbels—tactile organs that precede their toothless mouths. Their bodies are long, and they have a flat rostra (Latin for beak; used to describe the snout of an alligator or dolphin). Having no teeth, sturgeon use their snouts to stir up the ocean bottom and their barbels to detect the crustaceans and small fish they feed on. Larger sturgeon have been know to consume whole salmons and even baby seals.

Although sturgeon have to worry about few predators in the sea, their existence is severely threatened by water pollution and the fisherman who hunt females for their ovaries, which are prepared and sold as caviar.

The cover image is from Dover Pictorial Archive. The cover font is Adobe ITC Garamond. The text font is Linotype Birka; the heading font is Adobe Myriad Condensed; and the code font is LucasFont's TheSansMonoCondensed.